(UN)CIVIL WAR OF WORDS

(UN)CIVIL WAR OF WORDS

Media and Politics in the Arab World

Mamoun Fandy

PRAEGER SECURITY INTERNATIONAL
Westport, Connecticut • London

Library of Congress Cataloging-in-Publication Data

Fandy, Mamoun, 1961–
     (Un)Civil war of words : media and politics in the Arab world / Mamoun
     Fandy.
          p. cm.
     Includes bibliographical references and index.
     ISBN-13: 978–0–275–99393–1 (alk. paper)
     ISBN-10: 0–275–99393–0 (alk. paper)
1. War on Terrorism, 2001—Press coverage. 2. Mass media—Political
aspects—Arab countries. 3. Mass media and propaganda—Arab countries.
4. Arab countries—Politics and government—21st century. I. Title.
P96.W362A654   2007
302.230917'4927—dc22   2007003038

British Library Cataloguing in Publication Data is available.

Library of Congress Catalog Card Number: 2007003038
ISBN-13: 978–0–275–99393–1
ISBN-10: 0–275–99393–0

First published in 2007

Praeger Security International, 88 Post Road West, Westport, CT 06881
An imprint of Greenwood Publishing Group, Inc.
www.praeger.com

Printed in the United States of America

The paper used in this book complies with the
Permanent Paper Standard issued by the National
Information Standards Organization (Z39.48–1984).

10 9 8 7 5 4 3 2 1

In memory of my late mother and aunt, Daifia Yaseen and Ni'ma Mahmoud. May God rest their souls in peace.

Contents

Acknowledgments

This book is a product of a two-year fellowship at the James A. Baker III Institute for Public Policy at Rice University. Here I would like to express my gratitude and thanks to Secretary of State James A. Baker, III, the Honorary Chair, and to Ambassador Edward P. Djerejian, the Founding Director and to all the staff of Baker Institute for their help and support. I would like also to thank the staff of my current research home, the International Institute for strategic studies in London (IISS), for their help and support, especially Dr. John Chipman and Dr. Patrick Cronin. I also would like to have special thanks for Hesham Sallam for being a great assistant. I also would like to thank Professor Susan Ossman of Goldsmith College for reading and commenting on parts of the manuscript. May thanks also go to Katharine Fletcher and Gregory Gause for their very helpful comments. Although many Arab journalists provided a lot of help in allowing me to interview them, they did not want their names to be mentioned and did not want to be quoted. Their input however is extremely valuable and I owe them a great deal of thanks.

INTRODUCTION: THE POLITICS OF THE ARAB MEDIA

Since 9/11, people seeking information about Bin Laden's next target have turned to Al-Jazeera for the latest bulletin. In the summer of 2005, when I visited Tokyo, people asked me "Is Tokyo on Bin Laden's target list after Madrid and London? And what did Al-Jazeera say?" In their minds, Al-Jazeera, the Arab world, and Bin Laden were one and the same. Western officials who wanted to isolate Bin Laden and "win the hearts and minds of Muslims" turned to Al-Jazeera. Condoleezza Rice went to the Al-Jazeera offices for an interview as part of her Sunday morning media rounds.

Both governments and ordinary people in Washington and London and all over the world consider Al-Jazeera to be synonymous with the broader Arab media. Central to this premise is Al-Jazeera the station's virtually exclusive access to Bin Laden's stream of videotapes threatening attacks on Western targets. As a result of this access, a polarizing debate has emerged in the West about Al-Jazeera. At its core is the question: Is Al-Jazeera an independent source that scoops the Western media on Bin Laden's story, or is it the media arm of Al-Qaeda?

As the two camps have consolidated their positions, the debate on Arab media has become more ideological than informative. This book provides a corrective to this debate at both the factual and the theoretical level. For instance, while I discuss Al-Jazeera in depth, I also point out that it is just one actor amidst the more than 700 satellite television stations that compete for audiences in the Arab world. What is the nature of these other media and who is behind them? What characterizes their programming? These questions deserve to be addressed.

A first step is to explore how different media outlets relate to the governments of the region and their internal and external political battles. How does Al-Qaeda's message connect or intersect with the agendas of various competing governments and religious or ideological groups in the region? These questions are impossible to answer if one ignores the history of Arab media, emerging patterns of ownership and the context of conflicts between the various Arab states, as well as between individual Arab states and their oppositions—be it the Muslim Brotherhood in Egypt, Hezbollah in Lebanon, or Hamas in the occupied territories.

Reliance on contemporary Western theories of media is insufficient when building a framework for understanding Al-Jazeera, Al-Arabiya, or even Al-Manar, three distinct creatures in the world of Arab news media. For instance, the three models that Hallin and Mancini lay out in *Comparing Media Systems*[1] distinguish a commercial media dominant in North America and Britain, a corporatist model dominant in northern Europe, wherein media is a mix of commercial media and media tied to various social and political groups, and the southern European model, exemplified in Spain and Italy where political parties and the state have a strong role. Al-Jazeera, Al-Arabiya and Al-Manar do not fit well into any of these categories. This is because the state of Qatar where Al-Jazeera is based is not the United States; Qatar is not France and does not resemble Spain or Italy.

We also cannot reduce Arab media to Al-Jazeera. Arab news media are operated by states, state proxies or various ideological religious or ethnic groups. For example, Al-Arabiya, Al-Jazeera's main news competitor in the region, is owned by a proxy of the Saudi state while the Al-Manar news channel is owned and operated by Hezbollah, a movement on the U.S. State Department list of terrorist organizations. Understanding all of this might help one to delineate some of the characteristics of the Arab media, but it is not enough for developing a theory or a model of the Arab media. What I attempt to do in this book is to propose some avenues for thinking about the media in the Arab world in a manner that lends itself to liberating the debate about these media from the "East versus West" obsession that has tended to focus attention solely on Al-Jazeera. Once we consider the lateral dynamics within the region regardless of where the West may or may not fit, the scope, the depth, and the trajectory of the debate change significantly. It is by working to develop this alternative gaze that a discussion of the Arab media can inform theorizing about "global media."

These cases I present help critique, refine, or revise the way in which we theorize about the relationship of the West to the Arab world. Moving away from the East–West focus to interregional focus is a first step toward understanding the dynamics of the Arab media and global media in general. This is my contribution to the emerging debate that is aimed at de-Westernizing media studies.[2]

Thus, instead of examining where news outlets like Al-Jazeera stand relative to CNN or Fox News, or focusing on images of the West in the Arab media, I explore how Al-Jazeera and Al-Arabiya function in the tension between Saudi Arabia and Qatar (Chapter 2). I go back in history to show how Nasser's Sawt Al-Arab radio station of the 1960s shaped the Saudi–Egyptian conflict and how Al-Jazeera adopted a visual version of Sawt Al-Arab. I explain how the Lebanese Broadcasting Corporation (LBC), Future TV, and other Lebanese media function within the ethnic and religious conflict with Lebanon between Maronites and Sunnis, between Sunnis and Shia, and between pro- and anti-Syrian political forces (Chapter 3). Only by providing an analysis within the parameters of regional dynamics can we understand things like the image of America or the West on Arab TV screens. Ignoring the history of the region and the specific histories of its local politics will undoubtedly limit any analysis of the Arab media. Only through understanding this larger context can we begin to comprehend what people in the Arab world watch on TV or why they watch.

Despite certain satellite channels' claims of independence, the fact remains that it is the state and not market forces that is the main player in shaping the Arab media. In addition to state influence on programming and the general direction of a news channel, perceptions of other states are also significant. For example, many Arab states still perceive Al-Jazeera to be an arm of the state of Qatar. This is why the responses to criticism by Al-Jazeera have been in keeping with state-to-state response rather than state-to-media response. In one incident, Saudi Arabia responded to the intensification of anti-Saudi programming on Al-Jazeera by recalling its ambassador from Qatar in 2002. Jordan recalled its ambassador to Doha in response to perceived insults against the Hashemite ruling family on Al-Jazeera that same year. Anti-Egyptian government coverage on Al-Jazeera prompted Cairo to recall its ambassador from Doha in 1997. So it seems that Arab states are in no doubt that Al-Jazeera, which professes to be independent, is directed by the Qatari government. They have thus reacted to Al-Jazeera's programming using a state-to-state response, namely by severing their diplomatic ties with Doha. Even America responded to what it perceives as anti-American programming content on Al-Jazeera by launching its own satellite news television: Al-Hurra. In addition, American officials raised their complaints about Al-Jazeera in their meetings with Qatari officials—once again, a state response. But this is not the whole story.

All these incidents reflect a bigger role for the state in the Arab media than many would like to acknowledge. The Arab media are literally transnational in character. The disproportionate amount of airtime devoted to the outside world, relative to the meager content awarded to domestic issues in the host state, proves this point. Even the focus on domestic audience and domestic coverage tends to be geared toward mobilization of journalism rather than professional reporting. The programming and content of Arab media tend to serve the interests of the host state. Domestically, the function of the media is to rally support for regime policies and in many instances attribute the failures of these policies to outside powers, especially Israel and the United States. The media also target other governments who are critical of the local regime. Thus, a closer look at the role of states in the Arab media is essential if we are to move away from naïve descriptions to in-depth analysis.

The history of the relationship between the media and the state in the Arab world is different from that of its equivalent in the West. The nature of the Arab state is also different. For example, Hamad bin Jasem bin Jabr Al-Thani, the man behind Al-Jazeera, is a member of the Qatari royal family. He is also the Foreign Minister of Qatar. He is an investment banker. He has his own charitable organization. Is he part of the state or part of civil society?

Like most royal family members in the Gulf region he is part of both. He is a member of the state when he dons Western clothing and goes to conferences on behalf of Qatar and he is member of his tribe when he puts on his local headgear and traditional clothing. The point here is that the binary categories or explanatory concepts such as state and society and public and private that dominate the Western debates on media and politics do not make sense in the Arab context or at least they do not have the same analytical power. We cannot speak of the state and civil society in the same way in relation to every Arab country. When we do, we view the Arab media through the wrong lens, reducing it to Al-Jazeera or generalizing about the Arab media as a whole. Clumsy analysis is the result when we assume that the divide between public and private enterprises in the West is accurately replicated in the Arab world.

Even private media in the Arab world are not necessarily independent or professional. If one looks at the case of Kuwait or that of the United Arab Emirates (UAE) one can easily surmise that there is little relationship between professionalism, independence, and private ownership. Central to this is the larger context in which these media operate. For example, the *Al-Qabas* newspaper is privately owned by four Kuwaiti commercial families: Al-Kharafi, Al-Sager, Al-Sadoun, and Al-Nisf. Yet it rarely crosses the redline or breaks taboos because the welfare of these families depend on the largess of the ruling family of Kuwait. The same can be said of the *Al-Riyadh* newspaper in Saudi Arabia and the *Al-Khaleej* newspaper in the UAE. Both are private newspapers but they operate within a rentier economic system not a free market one. Thus, to view privately owned newspapers as independent or professional newspapers is to fail to see the larger context. One has to look at the big picture to understand that private means are dependent on rent and on the largess of those in power. Understanding the "Kafil" system that I describe toward the end of this introduction is central to comprehending this point. As we begin to analyze media systems in the Arab world, it is important to know that Egypt is vastly different from Qatar or Saudi Arabia, and that Morocco is different from Oman or Syria. We can begin to recognize these differences by examining the role of the media in interstate relations as well as within the particular local context of each country.

To provide some understanding of the complexity of the politics of the Arab media, I will describe the current state of the Arab media by grounding it in the political and historical context of the region. This should ultimately help to expand the scope of the debate on media in the Arab world. I also hope to add depth to discussions of the media by taking a closer look at several important examples: Saudi Arabia, Egypt, Qatar, and Lebanon. In these cases, media ranging from radio to print to local or national television, be it satellite or terrestrial, are addressed. Here, I use media analysis to provide another way to understand the distinctive political differences between states, ethnic groups, parties, and corporations in the Arab world.

Any informed debate on Arab media must take into account the complexity of and interrelationships within such a diverse media as this, as well as the major political differences across Arab political and economic contexts. In this spirit, this is not an Arab media project per se, rather it is an attempt to locate the Arab media within the larger sociopolitical context of the Arab world.

Such a debate should also take into account the role of journalists and broadcasters in authoritarian settings (Chapter 4). It is easy to portray these journalists either as martyrs or as corrupt culprits of regimes like that of Saddam Hussein. In reality, they are neither. Understanding their role requires a specific understanding of individual cases and their relationship to those in power and their allies as well as their enemies.

While there are Arab journalists sacrificing their lives to challenge the authoritarian system that governs the Arab media, other journalists sacrifice their principles and professional integrity to conspire with authoritarianism against journalistic freedom. Two years ago, Rida Hilal, a journalist for the Egyptian daily *Al-Ahram* disappeared at midday in Cairo. Although no one is certain what happened to him, most people in Egypt believe Hilal disappeared because of his writings against the regime of Saddam Hussein and its supporters in the Arab world. When Samir Qaseer, a prominent Lebanese journalist working for the *Al-Nahar* newspaper, was killed by a car bomb in Beirut on June 2, 2005, images of his dismembered body littered Arab papers and television screens.[3] Some accused the Syrian government of killing him because of his anti-Syrian writings,[4] while others claimed the Lebanese security apparatus, of whom Qaseer was equally critical, was responsible for the crime. Reading accounts of his assassination, one cannot help but think of Rida and of other journalists like Kamel Marwa, the Lebanese founder of *Al-Hayat* who was assassinated in his office in 1966, and Algerian journalists such as Mekhlouf Boukzer, Rachida Hammadi, and Mohamed Salah Benachour, who were killed by Islamic fundamentalists during the Algerian civil war in 1994 and 1995.

It is not uncommon for journalists to be killed in Arab countries because their writings have enraged a state, a political faction, or religious movement. At a moment in history when we see people killing others on television and when so many journalists are killed in conflict zones like Iraq, the use of assassination can be seen as an ultimate form of censorship.

In the Arab world, writing and speaking one's mind is a high stakes game. The price of writing could be the journalist's head if he is critical of those in power. In contrast, writing can bring fame and fortune if the journalist is doing the bidding of repressive regimes and intolerant political movements. Journalists in the Middle East gamble on one or another of these positions on a daily basis. These positions are complex, for "those in power" include not only the states in which one lives or of which one is a citizen. Threats or fortune do come the journalist's way from state regimes and political organizations, but they also come from transnational entities like Al-Qaeda and other Islamic groups, and other non-state actors. The Egyptian secular writer Farag Fouda, for example, was killed by Islamists in Cairo in 1992. Other journalists and writers have been killed or banished in the name of God, or in the name of national security, or both. Many writers and journalists get death threats daily for breaking away from the "Arab consensus." Ready-made fatwas (religious edicts) similar to the famous fatwa issued by Ayatollah Khomeini against the British author Salman Rushdie are daily affairs in the Arab world today.[5] Fatwas can reach the level of absurdity, as in the case of the separation of Egyptian writer Nasser Hamed Abu Zeid from his wife in 1993. Abu Zeid's writings do not threaten the stability of Egypt; they are simply what one thinks of in the West as alternative interpretations of the history of ideas in Islam. As a result of the fatwas against him and the threats they prompted, Abu Zeid had to leave Egypt for the Netherlands and has been living there ever since.[6] In 1994, the Nobel Laureate and Egyptian writer Nageeb Mahfouz was stabbed in the neck in Cairo. Punishment is a serious affair in the world of Arab media. But so is reward.

There is a world of rewards for writers who toe the line and for journalists whose main job is to hide the oppressive nature of the regimes and to make them look legitimate. The journalists who gain rewards from regimes are those who make murders such as those mentioned above look legitimate in the eyes of the public. They vilify the likes of Qaseer, Hilal, and Fouda as traitors to the Arab/Islamic cause.[7] And they reap financial and political rewards for doing this.

In the 1980s and 1990s, Saddam Hussein gave many editors of Arab newspapers Mercedes as recompense for their efforts on his behalf. Likewise, the familiar reference to "Barrelgate" in the Arab world refer to the numerous Arab journalists who received oil-barrel vouchers to be cashed from oil companies. "The names included former members of parliaments, sons of rulers and Arab journalists."[8] At the same time Islamist groups including Al-Qaeda have been known to provide protection to journalists who support their cause, sparing them the fate of Hilal and Qaseer.

To comprehend why certain journalists are targeted while others are rewarded with expensive cars requires an in-depth understanding of the Arab media system and of Arab journalists as transnational actors. It also requires a sensitive appreciation of the authoritarian political context in which these media operate.[9]

In an authoritarian setting, it is very difficult to speak or write freely about the maladies of a particular government or society. The price paid by those who violate the heavy regulations of the state and government ranges from imprisonment to kidnapping or disappearance, to in many instances death, as the cases cited before illustrate. Given this state of affairs, most journalists give their accounts of the problems of their own societies and the abuses of their own governments in fictional rather than journalistic form. For example, when the Egyptian journalist Gamal

Al-Ghitani wanted to write a critical account of the Nasser era, he did not write it for *Al-Akhbar*, the semi-government daily newspaper that he worked for. Instead, he wrote his famous novel, *Zeini Barakat*. The critical account of Nasser's rule was transposed to the period of the Mamluk-ruled Egypt (1250–1517). Although the main characters portrayed resemble the important figures in Nasser's government, the estrangement created by casting them in the remote era of the Mamluks saved Ghitani from being put on trial for defaming the Egyptian government and ridiculing the president, a charge still used to silence opponents of the regime. The latest case is that of Saad El-Din Ibrahim of the Ibn Khaldoon Center in Cairo.

The point here is that oftentimes in an authoritarian setting, newspaper reporting and fictional account trade places. While Egyptian newspapers put forth fictionalized accounts of happenings in the country, the most insightful accounts of Nasser, Sadat, and Mubarak's eras can be read in novels such as Gamal Al-Ghitani's *Zeini Barakat*, Waguih Ghali's *Beer in the Snooker Club*, Ahdaf Soueif's *In the Eye of the Sun*, and many similar works. The classic example of a critical take on Cairene society can be found in Nageeb Mahfouz's famed trilogy that is comprised of "Sugar Street," "Palace Walk," and "Midaq Alley." The interchangeable quality of fiction and journalism is very common in settings where a confrontation with power could prove costly.[10] This is always the case in the context of asymmetrical power relations between states and their subjects or masters and their slaves. James C. Scott gives the example of the slave woman bowing to power and saying "sir" in the living room and cursing her master as she talks with her daughter in the kitchen.[11] Arab journalists say "yes" on the screen and in the newspaper and curse their masters in fiction. The onstage performance of Arab media and journalism should be taken with a pinch of salt. The substance of debate and the transmission of real information almost inevitably occur offstage in private gatherings in mosques, souqs (market places) and clubs. This undoubtedly helps to explain why, despite the government's ownership of almost all means of information dissemination, we find that Islamic discourse still resonates. Although the Islamists do not have the same means, their discourse remains pervasive because communication in the Arab world depends on trust, and that trust is generally built on interpersonal situations. Mosques and sokqs provide a forum for trustworthy exchange of information (Chapter 6). These safe areas are the equivalent of the kitchen in southern US during the time of slavery America. Any violation of the boundaries between what is supposed to be said offstage and onstage could prove very costly. The writers who are killed or who disappear are the ones who violate this formula or attempt to rupture the wall that separates fiction from reality, the offstage/onstage division, as with the murders of Rida Hilal and Samir Qaseer. Those who remain faithful to their assigned position, bolstering the existing hegemony and legitimizing the practices of the ruling elite, are rewarded. Where they are not rewarded handsomely, at least their lives are spared. The fact that fiction and real reporting trade places in Arab politics is a central characteristic of Arab media that should be taken into account. Without understanding, at least, the four main characteristics of the Arab media that this book identifies, one could easily confuse the facts of the Arab media with the fiction that is spread around as part of a promotion campaign for a particular media outlet or a particular country. These characteristics are directly linked to issues of ownership, media rules and regulations, content, and habits and practices at both individual and institutional levels.

Firstly, Arab media outlets may at times give the impression that they are independent, but they are in fact still government-controlled, whether directly or indirectly. This casts doubt on the analytical usefulness of the private vs. public dichotomy, often used to assess media in Western societies, when examining the Arab media. Another characteristic of the Arab media is what I call the "anywhere but here" phenomenon. The Arab media are quick to criticize other Arab regimes, while at the same time ignoring problems with their host governments. Finally, I introduce the topic of "news receiving" as opposed to "news gathering."

False cultural cognates are at the heart of Arab media analysis. For example, many Western analysts today talk about television channels like Al-Jazeera and Al-Arabiya as if they were the Arabic-language equivalents of Cable News Network (CNN) and BBC or CNN and Fox News (FNC). Implicit in this kind of comparison is that context does not matter. If this is the case then there is no place for a whole stream in media and communication studies called comparative media systems. Despite the fact that all media studies look at the relationship between media and the societies that produce them, such established conclusions about media in other societies are usually thrown out when we talk about things Arab. There are still analysts, it seems, who are taken by the public relations lines of Al-Jazeera and Al-Arabiya, which claim that funding sources and state control are of no importance in deciding their news agenda or news reporting. In the same way the British government pays for the BBC, Qatar pays for Al-Jazeera, Al-Jazeera's public relations line tells us. The systems of governance in Britain and in Qatar are made to look alike, making no mention of the differences between the old Westminster democracy and the tiny authoritarian state of Qatar. As these analysts make this false analogy, they assume that the laws that protect press freedom and freedom of information in Britain are somehow similar to those in Qatar. This is simply not the case. Another obvious difference between the BBC and Al-Jazeera is that while the BBC is financed by taxpayers' money that is spent according to very clear rules and regulations, funding for Al-Jazeera comes from the emir of Qatar himself. If one were tempted to do a comparative ideology study of Al-Jazeera and its Islamic hue, the most similar channel in the West would be the American Christian Broadcasting Network (CBN), not the BBC, and not CNN for sure. Appearances can be quite confusing.

Secondly, it is absolutely necessary to understand that even if not all Arab media are formally state-owned, the state retains strict control over them. The electronic media of Arab countries are instruments of the regimes. Licensing regulations allow the government to decide who can own a television channel, radio station, or newspaper. One might argue that ownership drives coverage everywhere, but in discussing Arab media ownership, the distinction between private and state media, according to the models developed in Europe and the United States, is of little analytical value. This is because the owners of the media have not only close political ties to the state based on ideological positions or self-interest, but also close *family ties* and *religious affiliations* that ultimately link them to their respective governments. Thus questions of ownership encompass economic, political, and family interests. These cannot be simply reduced to "cultural context." Strategic political and economic motives structure this context. For example, in analyzing the Lebanese National Broadcasting Network (NBN), it is not enough to know that it is owned by Nabih Berri, it is also important to take into account that Berri is the head of Amal, a Lebanese Shia armed militia. He is also the head of the Lebanese parliament and a member of the transnational Shia cultural domain that includes Hezbollah and other less organized groups. Given the close connections between private media and the state and ethnic and religious communities, it is not surprising that the news media steer clear from discussing the sensitive social and political issues that affect the political position of owners, be they a state or a political group.

This leads me to the third characteristic of the Arab media. As I have said, "anywhere but here" could be the motto of Arab media reporting. Al-Jazeera reports on other Arab countries, but conceals the problems of Qatar, its owner. For example, on September 18, 2007, Al-Jazeera ran a documentary attacking senior members of the Saudi royal family, in particular the country's defense minister, Crown Prince Sultan bin Abdel-Aziz. The documentary was based on a story British newspaper the *Guardian* had published about defense company BAE Systems and its bribing of Saudis to secure defense contracts. The station trailed the story heavily the week before the documentary was aired, and continued to feature it on news bulletins throughout the subsequent week. The irony is that the *Guardian* had also run numerous stories about BAE Systems's corrupt dealings with senior officials of the state of Qatar. For example under the headline "Riddle of Sheikh's £100m Secret Fund," the paper reported that two years earlier "an official at the ANZ Grindlay Trust bank in Jersey stumbled across strange payments by British Aerospace, now known as BAE Systems, into the exotically named Havana and Yaheeb trusts."[12] The article added that "Detectives from Jersey's financial crime unit quickly discovered the ultimate beneficiary of these secretive trusts was the foreign secretary of Qatar, Sheikh Hamad bin Jasim bin Jaber Al-Thani, uncle of the emir of Qatar and a man of huge wealth and influence throughout the Gulf."[13]

So while Al-Jazeera prides itself on exposing corruption in the Arab world, it failed to report a Qatari example involving the very same company that had supposedly bribed the Saudis, reported by the same newspaper that Al-Jazeera depended on heavily to document Saudi corruption. Similarly, Al-Arabiya criticizes every country in the Arab world except Saudi Arabia. Other satellite channels that I will examine here, such as the LBC, Future Television (Future TV), and the Lebanese NBN also follow the same policy vis-à-vis the social groups behind them.

Another element of the Arab media that should not be ignored as we embark on our analysis is the phenomenon of what I refer to as "call-out," rather than "call-in," shows. I personally have participated in several talk-show programs on Al-Jazeera, Al-Arabiya, Egyptian TV, and ART TV. One evening I took part in a show on ART, hosted by the famous Hala Sirhan. The producer of the show, Mr. Amre Khafagy, had called my office at Georgetown University asking me to participate in a show about America and the Arab world. He called me in the middle of the show. I listened for a few minutes to other participants, including people I know, such as Dr. Osama Harb of *Al-Ahram*. I exchanged views with the guests for ten minutes and before I hung up Ms. Sarhan said on the air, "I would like to thank Mr. Fandy for calling in on our show from the United States." I responded, "It was you who called me. Not me who called you. I've never watched your show before." The audience broke into laughter. This example is illustrative of many shows conducted by Al-Jazeera, especially the well-known *Al-Itijah Al-Muakis* ("the opposite direction"). Many times guests from Cairo or other parts of the Arab world tell me that they are going to appear on this show, and Al-Jazeera will call me to support their side of the story.[14] It is rare for people to call in of their own accord, because international calls in the Arab world are very expensive given the meager salaries that middle-class individuals make. Thus call-out rather than call-in is the dominant mode of Arab talk-show culture.

The final characteristic of the Arab media is that of news-receiving as opposed to the Western concept of news-gathering. The obvious example is that of Al-Jazeera and the Bin Laden tapes. Al-Jazeera receives video tapes and faxes from Osama bin Laden and the Al-Qaeda organization, or those who claim to be the Al-Qaeda organization, and airs them without authentication. The last instance of such practice was the airing of the video tape of Mr. Ahmad Abu Addas, who claimed responsibility for the assassination of the Prime Minister of Lebanon, Rafiq Al-Hariri.[15] No one in Lebanon or anywhere else in the Arab world, including Abu Addas's family, believed the content of this video tape to be true. In an interview with Future TV, Abu Addas's family made it very clear that their son could not have done this. In fact, his sister said that she was very sure he did not commit the act. "Maybe he taped the video under extreme conditions, but I am certain that he was not involved in the assassination," she says. This kind of news-receiving is an extension of the daily practice of the Arab media in their relationship with their own governments. In most cases, a news item about any government function is written not by a news person, but by a bureaucrat in the Alaqat Ama (public relations) office of the president, the governor, minister or any other public official. These statements are usually published as is, even in the most respected newspapers such as Egypt's *Al-Ahram*. Given this tradition of press–government relations, it is not surprising that press–opposition relationships follow the same pattern. The Al-Jazeera–Qatar relationship resembles the Al-Jazeera–Al-Qaeda relationship. Similarly, Egyptian TV's or *Al-Ahram*'s relationship with the Egyptian government resembles these news organizations' relationship with the opposition of the regime. It's all about news-receiving rather than news-gathering. The authentication of information is not part of the tradition of the Arab press.

What we see on Arab television screens are not commercial advertisements, but political advertisements, something akin to infomercials in the United States or political ads during the U.S. presidential campaigns. Media content is directly linked to money, ownership, and political power. This is especially clear when we look at the resources that are put into the media relative to their financial returns. There is a huge gap between what mass media production costs and the money generated from commercial advertising. This makes sense only if we are aware that the Arab media are policy tools of their owners rather than money-making ventures. Across the Arab world, outrageous sums of money are spent to support media outlets that offer little, if any, financial return. For example, the annual cost of operation of all Arab media from Morocco to Oman is $17 billion, while net advertisement spending in the Gulf States barely exceeded $3 billion in 2004.[16] Who pays the difference? The figure for satellite television is especially small. Most of the $3 billion was earned by the print media sector. Even when we look at the aggregate figures for advertisement spending in the region, we can see that television advertisement spending accounts for only half of the total ad expenditure, as the chart below indicates. Moreover, these figures do not take into account the 25–30 percent commission paid to advertising agencies.

Media outlet	Amount in U.S. dollars	Percentage of total ads
TV	2,022,164,505	51
Newspapers	1,397,869,902	35
Magazines	270,503,321	7
Outside Advertising	219,073,398	6
Radio	40,374,934	1
Movies	13,134,979	0
Total	3,963,119,039	100

The Advertising Market in the Arab World[17]

Even with the projected increase in aggregate advertisement spending throughout the Arab world, the decline in the advertisement revenues of individual television stations is expected to persist given the growing number of competing satellite channels relative to the modest size of the advertisement industry. In simple terms, the gap between advertisement revenue and costs will not disappear any time soon. This raises the question of who is paying to fill this $14 billion dollar gap and for what purpose? Here it becomes imperative to investigate who owns the Arab media and how this ownership is constructed.

Politics is central to the drive to develop costly new media ventures. Arab governments' treatment of Al-Jazeera makes the point. When Al-Jazeera reported the anti-Mubarak demonstrations in Cairo led by the Kifaya (enough) movement, Egypt sent the president's foreign policy advisor Osama Al-Baz to Qatar to talk to the emir. The substance of their discussions on May 29, 2005 convinced officials in Doha that Al-Jazeera needs to be more considerate in its reporting about Egypt given the sensitive political situation at the present time. Subsequently, stories about developments in Egypt became more circumspect and limited. For example, Al-Jazeera's coverage of a demonstration in Cairo in June 2005 was very brief and simplified, while Al-Arabiya made no mention of the event at all. Convincing Al-Arabiya to tone down its coverage was much easier for Egypt because leading investors in the station are linked to Cairo by strong ties and interests. Like Egypt, almost all Arab states, including Jordan, Libya, Tunisia, and Saudi Arabia, treat Al-Jazeera as part and parcel of the Qatari state despite Qatar's claim that the station is independent. Libya and Tunisia withdrew their ambassadors from Qatar, citing Al-Jazeera's critical coverage of their regimes as the main reason. Transnational Arab media cannot be analyzed properly without being seen as part of interstate conflict or cooperation between Arab states. This book will show that Al-Jazeera and Al-Arabiya are better understood as elements in Saudi–Qatari rivalry than as independent media entities (Chapter 2). Such an approach, of course, does not ignore the fact that journalists themselves can be free agents who promote their own agendas. I look at this in detail in Chapter 4, which focuses on journalists as transnational actors. As the chapter on the Lebanese media (Chapter 3) also shows, intra-state conflict between various social groups shapes the context in which the media operate.

I come to this project both as a political scientist interested in media and politics and as a participant in the Arab and Western media. I write for two major newspapers in the Arab world, the London-based *Asharq Al-Awsat* and the Cairo-based *Al-Ahram*. Like most people who write for the Arab press, I have developed an unconscious self-censorship, having had rejections from both newspapers of a number of articles I wrote. For the past decade, I have also appeared regularly on various Arab television channels including Al-Jazeera, Al-Arabiya, ART TV, Dubai TV, Kuwait TV, and Egypt TV and more regularly on *Ala al-Hawa* a daily show hosted by the Egyptian journalist Emad Eldeen Adeeb on Orbit TV. Throughout these years I have taken notes of the various practices of each station and thus formulated a set of features that govern the Arab media of laid out in this book as a result of these observations. Over the same period I have also written occasionally for the American press and appeared on television news shows on CNN and the Public Broadcasting Service (PBS), Fox News, the BBC, and Canadian Broadcasting, to talk about Arab politics and media. Inevitably, a comparison between my experience with the Arab media and the English-language media in Britain, United States, and Canada has shaped my approach to the questions that I try to answer in this book. At the same time, what follows draws on my scholarly explorations of media and politics that I first developed in my work on transnational Islamic movements and networks. For the present study, I interviewed many Arab journalists, publishers, and producers and watched more than 400 hours of Arab TV over the past two years. I read the major Arabic newspapers and news websites daily. From within this corpus, I have focused on a series of specific events in order to examine news coverage: for instance I have compared Al-Arabiya's and Al-Jazeera's coverage of the Iraq war and the assassination of the Lebanese Prime Minister Rafiq Al-Hariri. For this last event, I watched every Lebanese satellite station—LBC TV, Future TV, NBN TV, New TV, and Al-Manar TV—to see how each of the channels covered this event. I also watched the newly launched American television station aimed at the Middle East, Al-Hurra, and listened to its sister radio network, Radio Sawa. This content analysis would not make sense without the extended interviews I had with those producing the news as well as owners of these media outlets. My own observation has also given me special insights about the day-to-day workings of these stations. The result of this research will, I hope, lead to a more in-depth understanding of the Arab media than can the de-contextualized examination of content alone or the assumption that the Arab media are different simply because of cultural factors. My main argument in this book is that politics is central to under-standing even the most lighthearted television show in the Arab world. Models of the public and of advertisers developed in America do not capture the story of the Arab media. Understanding the boundaries of the private and public, culture and politics, are central to the final portion of this study, in which I propose some policy recommendations for dealing with the Arab media. Understanding anti-Americanism and developing an effective public diplomacy initiative for the Arab world require a new approach and new thinking about the nature of the news media in that part of the world.

To understand Arab media practices, one has to look at a broader web of social and political practices that extends beyond, yet permeates, every media outlet. Only in the context of this broader picture can we begin to understand the media in the Arab world and the impossibility of simply adapting American or European models of media systems to examine how Arab media, economics, and politics mesh. The world of the Arab media has little to do with advertising revenues and Nielsen ratings, nor can it generally be compared to the European opinion press. To understand the Arab media we cannot focus merely on media institutions, as the spate of recent Al-Jazeera studies has done.[18] Approaches like that of political economy that dominate the American academy simply do not have the tools to make sense of the ways in which Arab media, societies and economies are dominated by politics. In the following chapters, I propose some key concepts that help to clarify this world in which issues of clienteles and clans overshadow questions of audience and advertising, and in which ownership of corporations, family ties, and political choices go hand-in-hand.

General media studies often focus on the political economy of media in terms of ownership. They use private vs. public as a key analytical concept, yet depending on such analytical tools would limit our analysis in the case of the Arab media. Even those who look at the Arab media from an area studies point of view, employing concepts such as patrimonial order and rent societies, fail to comprehend the subtleties of the connections between journalists, owners, repressive apparatus uses, and a very peculiar system of punishment and reward. This is why I find it useful to use key indigenous concepts that can help us navigate the complex world of the Arab media. Instead of looking at the public/private division, I introduce Wada' Al-Yad (squatting) as an instructive alternative. Instead of patrimonialism, I look at the Kafil (sponsor). Although these translations approximate the meaning of these ideas, the real practice is something else altogether. Grasping these concepts will help us to avoid the misreadings and false cultural cognates that lead us to believe that Al-Jazeera and Al-Arabiya are the CNNs or the BBCs of the Arab world.

Wada' al-Yad

In the Egyptian movie *Idhak Al-Sura titla Helwa* (Smile so the picture is beautiful), the late famous actor Ahmed Zaki plays the role of a street photographer (Sayed) on the Nile Corniche. He falls in love with a reformed petty thief who has a small kiosk selling Coke and cigarettes, played by the famous actress Laila Elwy. When another photographer comes to the area to photograph couples lounging on the corniche, Sayed sees this as an encroachment on his domain. A fight ensues between the two men. According to the laws of thieves and vendors in the area, the new photographer has no right to encroach upon areas that have already been claimed by others. The kiosk women and the rest of the street vendors give the intruder photographer a beating for violating the norms of the trade and the man vanishes from the area.

Asserting one's claim on a piece of land, on a job, or on a street sidewalk is very common in Egypt. This is the accepted way of staking a claim in a society where there is little regard for the formal and codified law. It is apparent in its various forms in the daily practices of Egyptians. Take Cairo airport's restroom where you cannot help but notice a man standing with a paper towel waiting for you with a broad smile. As you go in, he gives you the paper towel with the understanding that you have to pay him on your way out. In broad daylight and with the consent of all, this supposedly public facility that is run by the airport authority and owned by the state of Egypt is turned into a privately owned restroom through Wada' Al-Yad (which literally means "by putting his hand on it"). This is a particularly Egyptian and Arab way of asserting ownership, something akin to squatting, but with one major difference. In these cases, you cannot evict people on the basis that the land or building belongs to the state. No one in society contests this assertive private claim on public property. People accept low-paid government jobs because they know that they can turn the public facility into a private one as soon as they get their foot in the door, or as soon as they put their hands on it.

Squatting depends on a peculiar form of legitimation. First, there must be someone in power who gives you the right to be in that place, a minimal rule of power, or of some rule or regulation. It is not the law, but something approximating to it, that is getting your foot in the door. As soon as the squatter occupies the target place, a different form of law applies. It is the law of *urf* (what people in society see as acceptable). This does not apply only to the restroom at Cairo airport, it applies to all sectors of society and even to the state itself. Squatting defies the written laws. It is connected to the living beings who make the claim. Thus, squatters cannot pass on the job to their sons and daughters after they die. They have to do so while they are alive.

Wada' al-Yad is also present in the realm of inter-Arab politics. Saddam Hussein invaded Kuwait because he saw the ruling elite there as illegally squatting part of Iraq. Although the Sabah family had ruled the country for almost two hundred years and they might not be squatters in the eyes of a Kuwaiti, for Saddam they were squatters. Syria viewed the Lebanese government as squatters too, thereby justifying their occupation of Lebanon. In the same way that people accept the privatization of the bathroom at Cairo airport by squatters, the Arab states accepted Syria's rule over Lebanon for many years. In the 1960s, Nasser invaded Yemen because he thought of the Yemeni regime of Imam Yahiya as a regime of squatters. Saudi Arabia fended Nasser off and kept the "squatters" in their place. Morocco's "green march" to the Western Sahara was an extraordinary example of squatting that involved getting an entire population to extend into territories claimed by both the Cherifian kingdom and the Saharouis. The idea is that if you can occupy a space, you can rule it. It is a kind of bullying that extends from the pettiest actions of everyday life to the top levels of state. It is a system that serves the rich and the poor alike. This modus operandi permeates life at every level.

How does this apply to the media? Al-Jazeera is a space like the airport bathroom. The Qatari government built the structure known as Al-Jazeera, but within that space there are many squatters. They all pay nominal homage to the owners of Al-Jazeera and the agenda of the state of Qatar. In reality, however, the squatters use the space to achieve their own goals. Some of the aims are simple, like making money or appearing on TV, but other aims are more political. One example of this is the Muslim Brotherhood takeover of Al-Jazeera. Their head, Sheikh Yousef Al-Qaradawi, makes sure that Al-Jazeera serves the Brotherhood's agenda. For instance, he has a daily show called *Sharia and Life*. Other Muslim Brotherhood activists like Ahmed Mansour have two shows a week. Senior correspondents, include Tayseer Alouni, a Muslim Brotherhood member from Syria who is currently serving a prison sentence in Spain in connection with the Madrid bombing.

This is not only a Qatari phenomenon. We see Wada' Al-Yad at work at Al-Hurra and Radio Sawa as well. These U.S.-sponsored media outlets might be thought to be immune to this practice due to American law and professional standards. However, a quick look at the personnel and media content of both reveals that they are not. Not only is clientelism (Kafil) rifc—more than 85 percent of the people working at Al-Hurra and Radio Sawa are Lebanese—but there is also a gap between the agendas of the squatters and those of the U.S. government who owns and finances the station. On air one regularly hears expressions like "the so-called war on terror." On almost all political talk shows, hosts and guests beign by demonizing America and American policies to establish their Arab nationalist credentials. Thus, even in the United States, the squatters' agendas take hold. In the case of both the U.S. and Qatari governments, the owners do not know (and perhaps they do not care) how the squatters are using the fully furnished space given to them. There are those who say that even the established BBC Arabic suffers from the squatters syndorme.

If we understand the concept of Wada' Al-Yad, we no longer need public and private as differentiating categories for state-owned media and other media. This is because state-owned things can be privatized by Wada' Al-Yad, or squatting. This distinction is further complicated by another concept that I will explain in the following pages: the kafil (sponsor).

The Kafil (Sponsor)

"Kafil" is part of the daily lives of those who work in the Persian Gulf region. One cannot work in places like Saudi Arabia, Qatar, and Kuwait without a local Kafil (sponsor). In almost all cases the Kafil keeps the passport of the employee in his custody so that the worker cannot leave the country without his permission. Those who have researched the phenomenon of Kafil applied it only to the status of foreign workers—Pakistanis in the UAE, Philippinos in Kuwait, or Bengalis and Egyptians in Saudi Arabia. The reality is that the Kafil system also applies to the natives of the Gulf countries themselves. Also, the concept is a broad one, incorporating the notion of the muhrim (a male relative who travels with a single woman as companion). This part of the concept will become clear as we discuss gender relations within the Arab media. Every woman who works in the Arab media needs a muhrim, or male Kafil.

If one looks under the veneer of what claim to be independent media in the Arab world, the Kafil behind them can easily be detected. For example, although New TV in Lebanon is owned by Tahseen Khayat, a Lebanese businessman, the station's main Kafil is the Qatari foreign minister. He is also the Kafil of Al-Jazeera, the *Al-Quds al-Arabi* newspaper in London, and some smaller Cairo-based newspapers. Prince Khaled bin Sultan is the Kafil of Al-Hayat-LBC TV and newspaper. Prince Khalid Al-Faisal is the Kafil of the *Al-Watan* newspaper in Saudi Arabia, while Faisal bin Salman is the Kafil of *Asharq al-Awsat*. Every individual in the Arab world is under the tutelage and a client of a sponsor prince, sheikh, or a member of the ruling elite. Thus the system of Kafil, clientelism, permeates the whole social and political order.

In a clientelism system, neither professionalism nor independence can be realized. In fact there is a negative correlation between clientelism and professionalism and between clientelism and independence. Thus, if we want to talk about professionalizing the Arab media, the first step toward that is to undo the Kafil system. The main point here is that the Kafil system connects almost all social and political activity to the state. If one sees a newspaper or a TV satellite channel that looks private, one should not be hasty in assuming that it is in fact so. One should always ask who the Kafil behind it is. Who is the sponsor? An American public diplomacy officer would be wasting his time if he tried to persuade an editor-in-chief of a newspaper to change his mind about covering America fairly. One must talk directly to the Kafil. If he does not agree, then the editor-in-chief or producer cannot do anything about it. The editor-in-chief is a fall guy for the Kafil. He represents the TV station and newspaper in court whenever there is libel case. That's all.

The idea that there is an independent media in Saudi Arabia or in Qatar in the way we imagine it in the United States is a hoax. Even in Egypt, a different kind of regime, the rules of the Kafil system are at play. But here one must shift one's gaze to the world of Nageeb Mahfouz's novels and the racket system established by the fatwa of the Harra (the neighborhood bully). The Kafil system in Egypt is a relationship similar to Al-Mualim wal Sabbi, the realtionship between artisan and the apprentice in the medieval guild system of Mamluk Cairo. In this relationship, violence is the way to settle differences. The Mualim (the master) can beat up the apprentice if he fails to complete a task. You might call it unruly corporatism or a semi-authoritarian regime, but the reality is that it is a system determined by the

Mamluk. Equally whenever someone insists on using the label "mustaqila" (independent) on the front pages of his newspaper or in the logo of a TV station, it means one thing: that the Mukhabarat (state security intelligence) are in charge. This is the case for the *Sawt al-Umma* and *Al-Osbou'* in Cairo.[19] The clientelist system of the Arab world has metamorphosed many times and has taken different shapes, such as the military junta in Algeria or Nasser's regime in Egypt, but the basic underpinnings are the same. What looks modern on top is no different from the silver veneer on the dome of the Mohammed Ali Mosque in Cairo: a modern touch that covers a medieval structure underneath. Lebanon's system of Zamat or Qabaday is also of the world of Mahfouz's Futowa (the bully) racket system. The circles of the Kafil system are not just local. They usually widen to have a regional dimension. Newspapers in Morocco are sponsored by a Saudi Kafil, and TV stations in Lebanon and in Egypt are either directly or indirectly owned by a Saudi, Kuwaiti, Qatari, or even a Libyan Kafil. This is the case for Future TV and New TV; it is also the case for the London-based *Kul al-Arab* and *Al-Quds al-Arabi* newspapers.

Thus, a first step toward understanding the war of words in the Arab media is to look for the war between the Kafils. If there is no war between Kafils, one must then investigate the political differences amongst the squatters.

Today almost all Western governments talk about engaging with Islam and the Muslim world; before they do this it is advisable that they have a good understanding of the communication structures in these target places. They should be able to differentiate between the various media. The starting point would be to know who owns what and who works where and the ideological underpinning of the various communication venues. It is also important to place any television or radio station within the political context of the places that produced it. Essential for engaging with the Muslim world is knowledge of the field of engagement, the players, the symbols and the parameters. These pages are intended to provide such knowledge.

CHAPTER 1

NATIONAL PRESS ON THE EVE OF THE SATELLITE ERA

The Case of Egypt, Arab Nationalism on Radio, and Star Wars in the Making

One cannot understand the Arab media today without understanding the Egyptian media and its role in regional and national politics. For decades Egypt has been the trendsetter in Arab popular culture. The songs of the Egyptian diva Umm Kulthum,[1] the Elvis of the Arabs Abdul Haleem Hafiz, and the grand musician Mohamed Abdul Wahhab captured the hearts and minds of the Arabs, young and old alike. One only has to watch the Arab movie channel ART to realize that almost 90 percent of the movies aired are Egyptian in origin, including the black and white ones of the 1950s and 1960s. The Cairene dialect spoken by actors and actresses became a famil-iar—and at some points fashionable—way of speaking within elite Arab communities, especially in North Africa. Put simply, Cairo is the Hollywood of the Arab world and the center of gravity of the Arab media industry. The Egyptian laws and regulations that govern access to airwaves, patterns of media ownership, and various social and political taboos have been exported to countries throughout the Arab world. The Egyptian model of media shaped the vision of media development elsewhere in the Arabic-speaking world. Many producers and announcers in key news channels like Al-Jazeera and Al-Arabiya are Egyptians. The Egyptian Salah Nigm, for example, built up the newsroom of Al-Jazeera. When he left Al-Jazeera in 2000 to develop the newsroom of its rival Al-Arabiya, he left his position to his protégé Ibrahim Hilal, another Egyptian. After leaving Al-Arabiya in 2005, Nigm went to the BBC to start its Arabic TV station. As we will see in these chapters, the Egyptian experience at a variety of levels: personnel, ideology, and cosmology—shaped what we see on Arab televisions today.

After gaining their independence, the Arab states, particularly those in the Gulf, sought to emulate Egypt's media. This process was enabled in part by Egyptian migration to the Gulf region during the oil boom of the 1970s. Partly because of the harsh censorship policies at home,[2] and partly due to the oil boom, many Egyptian media professionals went to Kuwait, Saudi

Arabia, and Algeria to help the newly independent governments set up their media operations. These countries not only made use of Egyptian media professionals and borrowed programming content from Egypt, they also adopted the Egyptian approach to media control, ownership, and manage-ment. Egyptian sensibilities were also carried over by the broadcasters and journalists who manned and continue to operate Arab TV and radio stations. Today, we still find many Egyptians occupying key posts in pan-Arab satellite television. As I mentioned before, the directors of news at the most popular Arab news channels are Egyptians. Ibrahim Hilal, an Egyptian, directs news at Al-Jazeera and his countryman Salah Nigm directs news at Al-Arabiya. Although they were never able to establish a strong foothold in Lebanese media, Egyptians are a major presence in Dubai TV, Abu Dhabi TV, and ART. Clearly, the movement of media professionals from Egypt and their employment by the Gulf media and the Egyptian content and model of own-ership are very important to understanding the contemporary phenomena of Al-Jazeera and Al-Arabiya. The movement of journalists from Egypt to the Gulf is part of a general pattern of migration, and is governed by the same rules. So every individual has a sponsor (Kafil). The Kafil system in the case of men and Kafil and the system of muhrim in the case of women journalists shape news content and coverage. Thus it is important to look at journalism within the larger national and regional socio-political context. This chapter will look into the Egyptian model of ownership in print and television media, as well as the laws governing media to provide this wider context for understanding the Arab media that were inspired, if not outright shaped, by Egyptian media practices.

Who Controls the Egyptian Media?

"It does not concern me that the Head of the Shura Council Mr. Safwat Al-Sherif is planning a change in national press institutions that fall under his jurisdiction...However it is my right to preserve my dignity and self-respect and ask the Shura Council to accept my resignation," wrote Ibrahim Saeda in his last weekly column anticipating his dismissal as editor-in-chief of *Akhbar Al-Youm*.[3]

In July 2005 Safwat Al-Sherif dismissed the editors and head administra-tors of the main government newspapers and publishing houses in Egypt. These included Ibrahim Nafie of *Al-Ahram*, Jalal Dowidar of *Al-Akhbar*, Samir Ragab of *Al-Gomhuria*, and Makram Mohamad Ahmad of Dar Al-Hilal and *Al-Musawer*, as well as Ibrahim Saeda of *Akhbar Al-Youm*. These are no ordinary men that can be dismissed eas-ily, for they are not regular journalists. They are the men who Mubarak brought with him at the beginning of his rule and who dominated the Egyptian media scene for the last quarter of a century. Studying Ibrahim Saeda's letter of resignation helps us understand the complex nature of government–media relations in Egypt. Saeda's statement reveals a great deal about the nature of ownership and control of the Egyptian media. In theory, what we refer to as national media in Egypt is not a government institution per se, but a public enterprise, owned by the Shura Council (or Consultative Assembly), which controls the national press "on behalf of the people of Egypt." This is why Ibrahim Saeda addressed his letter of resignation to Safwat Al-Sherif, the head of the Shura Council. In the same column, Saeda criticized the manner in which the government handled the process of changing the heads of national newspapers. Important to this study is knowing who made the decision to dismiss the longest serving chief editors of national newspapers. Was it really the Shura Council, on behalf of the Egyptian people? Or was the decision made in a dark department of the Egyptian system, away from the Shura Council?

Name	Age	Publication	Position(s)	Served since	Replacement and previous position
Ibrahim Nafie	71	Al-Ahram	Editor-in-Chief and chair of Publishing House	1979 (Group Chair in 1984)	Salah Al Ghamri as chair (former chair of government-run National Distribution Company); Osama Saraya as Editor-in-Chief (former Editor-in-Chief of the state-run Al-Ahram Al-Arabi)
Ibrahim Saeda	68	Al-Akhbar	Chair of publishing House and Editor-in-Chief of the weekly Akhbar Al-Yom	1980s	Mohamed Fadli (former General Manager of the Akhbar Al Yom Publishing house) as chair and Momtaz El-Qott (former Cabinet correspondent for Akhbar Al-Yom) as Editor-in-Chief of the weekly Akhbar Al-Yom
Samir Ragab	68	Al-Gomhuria	Editor-in-Chief and chair of Publishing	Early 1990s	Mohamed Abul-Hadid (former managing editor of Al-Gomhuria) as

(continued)

Continued

Name	Age	Publication	Position(s)	Served since	Replacement and previous position
			House		chair and Mohamed Ali Ibrahim (former editor of the government-run *Egyptian Gazette*) as Editor-in-Chief
Makram Mohamed Ahmed	70	*Al-Musawer*	Editor-in-Chief and chair	Mid-1980s	Abdul Qadir Shueib (*Al-Musawer* acting editor-in-chief)

Saeda's column offers some clues about who made the call. One key sentence in his letter tells us that Safwat Al-Sherif by himself would have not been able to enact these changes without receiving "the long-awaited 'green light' from the Policy Planning Committee of the National Democratic Party."[4] In saying this, Saeda leaves no doubt that the idea for change originated from those in charge. In other words, his vague reference could mean only one of two men in the Egyptian system: either President Husni Mubarak, or his son Gamal Mubarak. Those who understand the particulars of Egyptian politics would know that Safwat Al-Sherif, the secretary-general of the National Democratic Party (NDP), does not take orders except from the man who moved him from the position of minister of information to head of the Shura Council and secretary-general of the NDP. So Saeda's reference to the NDP Policy Planning Committee in this context means Gamal Mubarak, the chairman of the committee. This make sense in the context of the new corporate configuration of Egypt's system of governance. While President Mubarak is the undisputed chairman of the Board of Egypt, the actual CEO is his son Gamal Mubarak, who has risen to influential posts in the ruling party over the past few years. The young Mubarak and his men forced the change of the old guard.[5] The removal of the old guard of the Egyptian media was part of a larger change affecting both the rules of the game and the personnel managing the affairs of the state. Almost a year before this incident, Safwat Al-Sherif, a man in his seventies, was replaced as minister of information by Anas Al-Fiqi, a younger man in his forties. It was the same process of change that brought about the amendment of Article 76 of the constitution to allow for a multi-candidate presidential election, a first in Egyptian history. Throughout its history Egypt has protected the sanctity of the position of the Pharaoh at the top of the Egyptian pyramid of power. It was always the realm of the Gods, but now for the first time it was being contested by humans. This rev-olutionary change required a cultural change that would make it acceptable to the Egyptian mindset. The media were instrumental in creating a new dis-course and outlook that accommodated this major shift in the way Egyptian politics is perceived, even on a symbolic level. The change demanded the dismissal of the old guard whose job it had been to justify the rule of one man over the past 23 years. New men who would take their cues from Mubarak's son were needed for the institutionalization of such a change. The president and his son probably shared the perception that for the NDP to overcome the challenges of anti-regime campaigns, such as 'kifaya', it had to change some faces in the government-controlled press. It would be a mistake to think that the desire for change in Egypt came from within. It was pressure from the outside that encouraged the Kifaya movement to say "enough" to the older Mubarak's rule. The outside world also encouraged people like Ayman Nour to contest the presidency. A change in the global environment led to these changes in Egyptian politics.

In this chapter, I will explain the methods of control that the Egyptian government has used to regulate its media. As the episode described above illustrates, the government has managed to develop a sophisticated system of management of the media over the years, adopting tactics that blur the lines of censorship and control. These tactics are observed in the government's relationship with both the print and visual media. I will explain the institutional and legal structures that the government uses to keep a lid on dissent within the Egyptian media sector. I will also provide some examples of the state's use of intimidation and repression as instruments of press regulation.

Types of Pressure and Control

The Egyptian government's control over its media follows three models. A common denominator among them is ambiguity. Government–media relations are part of a complex system of ownership that makes it difficult to track who exactly calls the shots in the Egyptian media. In this section, I will give a brief overview of the various types of state control of the media. One or two of these types, or sometimes a mixture of all three, have been was adopted by other governments in the region.

One type of media regulation direct ownership and control. This type is used in the case with television and radio. All national television and public radio personnel are employees of the Egyptian government. Thus any one who dares to cross the so-called "redline", whether a presenter, a reporter, or a producer, will face immediate dismissal. The threat of job termination extends to Egyptians working in foreign and Arab media. For example, Egyptians working for Voice of America usually retain their employment at state-owned audio or visual media by taking a leave of absence from their Egyptian employer.[6] Thus, even when Egyptians work for institutions like VOA, the BBC or Al-Hurra, or even Al-Jazeera or Al-Arabiya, they are still governed by the fear of losing their employment benefits in Egypt should they ever decide to cross the redlines of the Egyptian government.

Another type is second-degree control, and an example of such an approach can be observed in government influence over the national press, including *Al-Ahram*, *Al-Akhbar*, *Al-Gomhuria*, and *Al-Musawer*. As mentioned previously, all these papers are supposedly owned by the Shura Council on behalf of the people of Egypt. In official terms, the hiring and firing of the heads and editors of those publications falls under the jurisdiction of the Shura Council and its head. In reality, however, the Shura Council is a front for the president's office. The president dictates to the head of the Council and NDP leaders, who gets these posts, and usually the lucky ones are journalists who maintain close ties with Mubarak and his office. As in most sectors of the Egyptian political system, the substance of politics in state–press relations is not usually in the formal structures, but in the informal and patrimonial networks.

As for independent newspapers and those sponsored by opposition political parties, they are kept in check through indirect control. All independent newspapers must obtain a license from the Higher Press Council, another government-controlled body (described in detail below), and, in the case of party newspapers, a license for starting up a political party, an even harder task the two processes fall under government jurisdiction, the state is able to select which political voices can or cannot be heard in the Egyptian media arena. Moreover, party-sponsored and independent newspapers do not own their own their own printing facilities. In fact, most of them rely on the state-controlled Al-Ahram Publishing House's facilities for printing. Al-Ahram, virtually controlled by the state, retains the right to block the printing of papers if they go too far in their criticism of the country's top politicians. The government may also punish dissenting papers by depriving them of valuable revenues from government ministries' advertisements. The state also resorts to outright repression and intimidation of dissenting journalists. There are countless cases of Egyptian journalists subjected to beating, jail, and even death and disappearance.

Finally, privately owned satellite television, a relatively new phenomenon in the Egyptian media sector, stations such as Dream TV and Al-Mehwar, are all controlled by the government through business links between the ruling elite and owners of these stations. The example of Dream TV, whose owner Ahmad Bahgat pressured a number of dissenting presenters and journalists to leave the channel to avoid the government's wrath, is discussed in detail below. In this case, the government was able to influence the editorial policies of the channel in return for aiding Ahmad Bahgat, the chairman, with his financial difficulties.

The structure of media control in other Arab countries follows the Egyptian model of ambiguity, whereby the government is part-owner and controller, yet the media appears as if it were private. For example, Qatar dissolved its Ministry of Information, creating a more independent image for Al-Jazeera station, but still retains state control over it; Saudi Arabia launched Middle East Broadcasting Center (MBC), and later Al-Arabiya, but rather than asserting control through formal state-ownership, it does so through proxy owners. The late Prime Minister of Lebanon Rafiq Al-Hariri created his own station, Future TV, and controlled it, not through government ownership, but through his family and associates. Later on in this book we will see how Egyptian models of control are found with slight variations in other Arab countries. In the next two sections, I will describe how these types of control are used in the visual and print media in Egypt.

Television

Dream Television

Dream TV was founded in 2001 by the famous Egyptian businessman, Ahmad Bahgat. He is chair of the Bahgat Group that owns a number of Egyptian companies in the fields of electronics, communication networking, information technology, medical products, furniture, construction, and entertainment. The channel's history is of a dream that did not last long before it collided with the harsh realities of government control over media in Egypt. The satellite station was described as the first private Egyptian channel, but it turned out not to be anything of the sort. There is no such thing as private and public in the Arab media. For any media outlet to succeed it needs the political (and sometimes even financial) backing of the state or powerful actors, and the price for this support is high and usually expresses itself as constraints on the editorial policies of media.

Dream TV consists of three different channels with programmes ranging from youth-targeted entertainment to political talk shows. It was often said that the main purpose behind the creation of Dream TV was to serve as an advertisement board for Ahmad Bahgat's various companies and businesses. The channel's former vice president explains: " . . . [Bahgat] spends 40 million pounds [about $10 million] a year on advertising." So he got the idea of owning his own TV station where he could run his own ads. Three quarters of his annual budget for advertising could be used on his own station, with the double benefit of being able to target clients. The people who have a decoder and can watch Dream TV are his potential buyers.[7] The channel's start-up costs and annual budget are not officially disclosed. However, when asked how much money was needed to start a channel like Dream, Hala Sirhan, then its vice president, gave an estimate of 20–30 million Egyptian pounds.[8] In late 2002, Bahgat proclaimed that his assets amounted to 1.7 billion pounds.[9] It is not clear how the balance of costs and revenues workout, but given that the bulk of advertisements come from Bahgat Group's businesses and hence are free of charge, the station was clearly designed to serve more as a cost-saving than a profit-generating venture for Ahmad Bahgat.

Controversy began to encircle Dream TV after the launch of Dream 2, which featured controversial talk shows that tackled taboo social issues, including *urf* (customary) marriage and impotency. Before it was terminated, Hala Sirhan's show openly discussed issues of divorce and "masturbation and its effects on marital relationships."[10] Mohamed Hassanein Heikal, veteran Egyptian writer and thinker, crossed another redline in an appearance on

Dream TV in 2002 when he criticized the failures of Arab regimes in his comments on the ongoing Middle East crisis. In another appearance on Dream TV, Heikal not only voiced criticism of the Egyptian regime, but raised the issue of "hereditary succession" in Egypt.[11] Similar controversies were stirred by other talk show hosts like Hamdy Qandil (*Ra'is al-tahrir*) and Ibrahim Eissa (*'ala al-qahwa*), who were anything but diplomatic in discussing the short-comings of the Egyptian and, in some cases, Arab governments. In short, Bahgat's Dream was turning into the government's nightmare.

Despite the promising potential that the channel had when it was launched, the government still managed to tame the monster it had created by allowing Egyptian satellite channels to broadcast on ArabSat and NileSat. Only 2 years into its lifetime, signs of censorship began to appear on the screens of Dream TV. In 2003, Sirhan, Qandil, and Eissa were all suspended, with a common denominator linking the three cases: they all went too far in criticizing the Egyptian government. Sanaa' Mansour, Sirhan's successor as the channel's vice president, said in response to allegations that the channel was engaged in censorship on the demand of the Egyptian government, "We have no taboos— [the only material we reject] is whatever may be in conflict with religion, adversely affect national security, or lead to sectarian strife."[12] What is striking about this remark is that it resembles the usual PR line of Egyptian state media whenever eyebrows are raised at censorship procedures. Interestingly, Mansour had previously worked for the Egyptian Radio and Television Union (ERTU) as head of its satellite channels. This raises the question of who is really in charge at Dream TV: the state or Bahgat? We must try to offer an explanation of how the government was able to exert its influence over the editorial policies of the satellite station, ending the short-lived "dream" of an independent private media in Egypt. Understanding the Egyptian way of controlling supposedly private media will help us to understand how new media like Al-Arabiya and Al-Jazeera work.

Controlling the Site of Media Production

What is rarely revealed about Dream TV is the fact that Ahmad Bahgat does not hold sole ownership of the channel. Through the ERTU, the government owns 10 percent of the station. Thus the channel, despite claiming otherwise, is not independent. Hala Sirhan told the *TBS Journal* in 2004: "the problem lies in the fact that all the privately owned TV stations work with the assistance of the government. Hence they will never succeed in being objective. They will always be dependent and always seeking approval. Dream is a clear case in point."[13] Dream TV not only leased its access to ArabSat and NileSat from the Egyptian government, but is also part of the 6th October Media Production Free Zone.

The Media Production Free Zone consists of "areas where the government donates land and offers tax incentives to encourage private media companies to move in—complete with state-of-the art studios, stars and lucrative jobs."[14] Created in February 2000, the three-million-square meter city serves as a production site available for leasing by various types of media projects, whether cinema, television-show production, radio and television broadcast, or satellite television.[15] The Egyptian government provides tax exemptions for any project operating within the city's boundaries. This helps satellite channels cut down on normal costs of operation and start-up. However, such privileges are not without cost. Operating in this zone requires a license from a state body, namely the General Authority for Free Zones, which retains the right to revoke licenses. Although the satellite channels operating within this city are not subject to the censorship laws that govern state-controlled media, they are obligated to play by the rules of the city in which they operate. This puts their program content at the mercy of the General Authority for Free Zones.

As early as November 2002, Dream TV received a strong warning from the authority that "strict measures will be taken if the channel again tackles serious subjects in a sensational manner."[16] The station's success is highly dependent upon the government's resources, and by implication, its approval. For this reason the three controversial journalists were dismissed after they flirted one too many times with the understood limits of state criticism. Explaining that her dismissal from Dream was the result of state intervention, Sirhan states "My last episode discussed a hot topic, religious discourse. This was intolerable for them [the channel's management], it was too much. Their decision came after an accumulation of episodes on different issues. Of course, they never forgot that I was the one who pushed for Heikal's appearance on Dream."[17]

Another way the government was able to keep a lid on controversial programs on Dream TV was using its business links with Ahmad Bahgat himself. Bahgat, the biggest producer of television in the Middle East, dominates the Egyptian TV markets, and "is reputed to be a front man for well-placed interests within the regime, which may explain why the express road out to [his residential community] Dreamland were built in record time."[18] Ibrahim Eissa explains his own theory about his dismissal from Dream TV: "When I signed for Dream, I had my conditions: to be allowed to express myself freely and present what people are feeling, under a liberal-minded management like that of Hala Sirhan. Things were going perfectly, but after great success...their eyes were opened and the scissors of the editors had to start...when the prime minister himself insists on canceling my program in order to support Ahmed Bahgat in his financial troubles, this is really a question mark."[19] Bahgat denies that he has defaulted on any loans, and indicated in 2002 that his total assets (1.7 billion LE) were greater than the total sum he has borrowed in his lifetime (1.6 billion LE).[20] Even if Bahgat was not in a financially vulnerable position that necessitated the government's support of his business, it remains within the government's capacity to *put him in one*.[21] The success of Bahgat's businesses remains a function of the government's continued approval of his record and practices, and thus, he was faced with little choice but to suppress loud criticism of the state on the screens of Dream TV. Bahgat woke up from his dream.[22]

Al-Mehwar Television

Al-Mehwar TV, the other Egyptian satellite channel that inhabits so-called "private sphere," was founded in 2001 by Hassan Rateb. Like Ahmad Bahgat, Rateb is a successful businessman who has strong relations with the ruling regime. Like many of its counterparts in Egypt and the Arab world, Al-Mehwar defies the Western division of a private–public in the world of media, showing that a government-controlled media outlet can in fact exist in the private sector.

About 87 percent of Al-Mehwar (Arabic for axis) is divided between private shareholders, with 65 percent owned by Rateb, and 18 percent "divided among a group of prominent Egyptian business persons, including Hossam Badrawi, Raed Hashem, Nawal El-Digwi, Mostapha El-Salab and Samir El-Naggar."[23] Through ERTU, NileSat, and the 6th October media city, the government owns about 12 percent of Al-Mehwar.[24] Hence, ownership is divided between the government and private shareholders. Al-Mehwar's current capital amounts to more than $14 million. The composition of its board reveals the degree to which it is under the thumb of the state. For example, Hassan Hamed (head of ERTU), Amin Bassouny (head of NileSat), and Abdul Rahman Hafez (director of Media Production City) are all members of the board. These are direct employees of the government. Other members include major figures in the ruling NDP like Hossam Badrawi and Mustafa Al-Sallab, and they reflect the Party's control over this media. Put simply, the channel, at the very best, is a partnership between the government, pro-regime elites, and members of the ruling party in Egypt.[25]

Programming on Al-Mehwar began with a strong focus on entertainment and music. Recently, it has started to move toward enlivening its news-based shows and segments. However, it uses mostly reports from state-owned television channels.

Al-Mehwar did not attempt to cross the redlines in the same manner as Dream TV had done. Key to this situation is that Al-Mehwar remains under the same institutional and political constraints that limit the independence of Dream TV. It operates inside the government's Media Production City, and is subject to the same regulation banning "inflammatory programming that may affect national or state sovereignty" and "pornographic material." Rateb is close to the government and publicly acknowledged this association in an event celebrating the third anniversary of the channel, in which he awarded Safwat El-Sherif, head of Shura Council, and Anas El-Fiqi, the minister of information, honorary shields.[26] Moreover, the channel's coverage of the campaigns and events leading up to the presidential elections in October 2005 exhibited strong bias toward the ruling establishment. A report released by the Cairo Institute for Human Rights states that Al-Mehwar dedicated 41 percent of its coverage to Mubarak and his campaign, while each of the state-owned Channels 2 and 3 dedicated less than 30 percent of their respective coverage to NDP's candidate (Dream TV gave 69 percent of its coverage to Mubarak).[27]

In short, to argue that Al-Mehwar and Dream TV are independent of the control of the Egyptian state is like arguing that Lebanon enjoys complete independence from Syria. Although a "private ownership" label is attached to the channels, the structure of their ownership and content shows us that the Egyptian state remains in charge of managing and directing the Egyptian television media industry. The government is automatically awarded part of a "private" channel's ownership and this makes it very difficult for anyone wishing to set up an independent station to escape state regulations over programming content. While the opportunity to operate inside the government's Media Production City alleviates the financial burden of maintaining a private satellite channel,[28] this is not cost-free. In fact, as we have seen, it puts programming content at the mercy of the General Authority of Free Zones, which can revoke or threaten to revoke the license of any channel that goes too far in criticizing the government and its policies. Finally, the close association of the entrepreneurs behind these so-called "private channels" and the government creates strong incentives for self-censorship. As we have seen in the case of Dream TV, the government does not always resort to direct censorship. In this case, it merely used its banks to threaten Ahmad Bahgat's business. Dissent can backfire against the business interests of media entrepreneurs, if not against their channels directly. Additionally, the close association between these business elites and government makes state control prevalent in the private Egyptian media sector. Ever since the Nasserist period, civil society institutions such as the press, radio, and television have had close associations with the regime, and, arguably, have acted as its instruments in numerous cases.[29] The pattern is replicating itself even in the private satellite television industry, such that political and business interests have left little room for media owners to assert their independence from the state.

Print Media

Government regulation of the print media follows a pattern similar to that of television. In the case of television the government uses three forms of control: (1) direct ownership (this is the case with terrestrial broadcasting, which is monopolized by ERTU); (2) semi-ownership through business links with owners of television channels (as in the case of Ahmad Bahgat and his Dream TV), and also through laws that stipulate compulsory ownership of part of a private channel's shares to the government; and finally (3) indirect control (which means that the state controls licensing and Media Production City regulations, as well as controlling access to the Media Free Zone). In the case of the print media, the government uses similar means.

The rest of this section will examine the various bodies and methods of state control of the print media. These cannot be understood outside the political context of press–government relations. As I argued in the introduction, the Arab media is inherently political. They are not civil society institutions that balance against regime power, the media are an extension of the regime.[30]

The Egyptian Press under Nasser, Sadat, and Mubarak

As mentioned earlier, the political context of media outlets is key to understanding the nature of these media. Therefore, this section will be devoted to describing a political context that spanned the history of three regimes: those of Nasser, Sadat, and Mubarak.

Before the "Egyptian Revolution" of 1952, most of the Egyptian press was owned by wealthy families, the majority of which were foreign. On the eve of the revolution there were six major newspapers in Egypt. Some of these papers continued and others were shut down for political reasons. They included *Al-Ahram*, established in 1876 and owned by Salim and Bishara Taqla (Lebanese) and *Al-Muqatam*, an evening newspaper established in 1889 and shut down in 1954. *Al-Muqatam* was also owned by Lebanese partners (Ya'qoob Sarouf, Shaheen Makabous, and Faris Nimr). Another evening paper, *Al-Balagh* (1923–1953), was owned by Abdul Qader Hamza; *Al-Masri* (1936–1954), a morning daily, was owned by Egyptian partners, Mahmoud Abu al-Fatah, Muhamed al-Tabi'i, and Kareem Thabit. Two other newspapers were publishing on the eve of the revolution, *Al-Akhbar* (1952–present), owned by Mustapha and Ali Amin, and *Al-Zaman*, established in 1947 and closed in 1953, owned by another non-Egyptian, Edgar Jallad. Out of these six major papers only two remain in operation today, *Al-Ahram* and *Al-Akhbar*.[31]

The rise of Gamal Abdul Nasser in 1952, who distrusted foreigners, led to the nationalization of newspapers like *Al-Ahram* and *Al-Akhbar*, and to the growth of new publishing houses, like Dar Al-Tahrir, which still produces the most pro-government newspaper *Al-Gomhuria*. The Press Law of 1960 entrusted the main government institution, the National Union—and later Arab Socialist Union (ASU)—with licensing regulation and the appointment of newspaper editors and head administrators of their publishing houses.

During the Nasser years, the state was not only creating laws to hamper the freedom of the press, it also resorted to crude means of censorship. A new institution, the Ministry of Information, was created to ensure government control of the press through systematic censorship. The system of censorship included a censor's office in the Ministry of Interior. That office would contact the papers daily to enquire about the main stories and give them instructions concerning which were to be headlined and which played down.

The Sadat era witnessed the rise of opposition papers like *Al-Ahaly* and *Al-Ahrar*. This phenomenon came as part of Sadat's attempts to stave off pressure for a multiparty system without lifting the 1953 ban on political parties. In 1976, Sadat announced that three manabir[32] (quasi-political parties) would be permitted. Each of the three manabir began operating through its own newspaper: the centrist *Misr*, the rightist *Al-Ahrar*, and the leftist *Al-Ahaly*. *Misr* was virtually another mouthpiece for the government and *Al-Ahrar* offered little criticism. The only critical voice was the leftist *Al-Ahaly*, which came under government fire from day one.

Al-Ahaly became a stronghold for Sadat's critics, especially those who were displeased by Sadat's visit to Jerusalem in November 1977. Unable to tolerate criticism any longer, Sadat announced on May 21, 1978 that he would hold a referendum to ask the Egyptian people if "atheists," a code word for leftists and more specifically communists, should be barred from political life. As usual Sadat "won" the support of an overwhelming majority (98.2 percent). The most important item in this referendum was the infamous "Law of Shame" (Qanoon al-'Aib) which was aimed at "protect[ing] the basic social values from shameful conduct." In practical terms, the law prescribed punishment for any behavior the government deemed offensive. Following this so-called "victory," Sadat sharply intensified his regulation of the press.[33]

After his death in 1981, Sadat left behind a legacy both of institutions and regulations designed to curb press freedom in Egypt. Despite the greater press freedom of Mubarak's reign, the current Egyptian president has left the institutions restricting media activity intact. Today the government enjoys a host of institutional structures and legal privileges that allows it to block unfavorable speech and to punish its critics.[34] As one examines press regulating institutions, ones notices two things in particular: (1) the state's formal ownership of the media and censorship structures are more hidden than they were during the Nasser years; and (2) fear remains the main factor that shapes the media environment, due to the long legacy of legally sanctioned repression and brutality against dissenting journalists.

Institutional Instruments of Control

Two major institutions are entrusted with the issues of ownership and regulation of Egyptian media. These are the Shura Council and the Higher Press Council.

The current system of press ownership and regulation was established in 1980. A constitutional amendment created the Shura Council, a government body serving as an advisory council to the President and overwhelmingly dominated by Mubarak's National Democratic Party (NDP). The Shura Council assumed 51 percent ownership of the national press, theoretically "in trust" for the people. Apart from owning the national press, the Shura Council manages the press by appointing the chairmen of the board and the editors-in-chief of the national newspapers. The Shura Council owns the national press, which consists of the newspapers and magazines owned by and published by government-owned publishing houses.[35]

The Higher Press Council was first established by Sadat in 1975. As criticism mounted after Sadat's visit to Jerusalem, a new law was passed to further curtail press freedom, Law 148 of 1980, known as The Powers of the Press Act (Qanoon Soltat Al-Sahafa). Article 8 of this law gives the power to form or dissolve this body to the president of the republic.[36] The Higher Press Council is composed of the editors-in-chief and board chairmen of both the national and party papers, other heads of media agencies, and a number of "public figures concerned with press affairs," appointed by the Shura Council.[37] The chair of the Shura Council, Safwat El-Sherif, also chairs the Higher Press Council. The Higher Press Council is the government body responsible for licensing and regulating the press in Egypt.

No one may publish a newspaper without obtaining a license from the Higher Press Council.[38] In theory, Law 148 allows individuals to apply for press licenses. In practice, however, it is rare that someone can publish a paper under this law. Partly this is due to the enormous financial requirements imposed by Law 148. An individual—anyone other than parties, trade unions, and syndicates—must first form a stock company and must possess capital of 250,000 Egyptian pounds to publish a daily paper, or 100,000 Egyptian pounds to publish a weekly. No single family member may possess more than 500 Egyptian pounds worth of the capital value.[39]

To avoid the licensing requirements of Law 148, some organizations and individuals publish "irregular" newsletters or magazines rather than regular serials. According to an activist in a local women's group, an irregular publication cannot have a date on it and should not publish more than once a year. Moreover, it can be difficult to find a printer, as a lot of printers are afraid to publish irregular publications. The Higher Press Council is the government body that regulates the press in Egypt.

However, licensed political parties are permitted to publish a newspaper without meeting these capital requirements. Obtaining a political party license, then, is an important prerequisite for publishing a newspaper. Political parties receive their licenses from the Political Parties Committee, a committee of cabinet officials chaired, like the Higher Press Council, by the president of the Shura Council. Since its inception in 1977, the Political Parties Committee has approved only three out of sixty-six applications for party licensing.[40] All other parties that have been legalized have obtained their license by a court order after litigation challenging the Political Parties Committee's denial of their applications. For example, the Nasserist Party was legalized in April 1992 after a court battle and now publishes a weekly newspaper called Al-'Arabi.

Furthermore, according to the rules set forth by the Higher Press Council, no journalist is permitted to practice journalism without a license from the council. The Supreme Press Council also assigns newsprint to newspapers, sets prices, determines the amount of advertising, and grants permission for journalists to work for non-Egyptian media or overseas. Because of its hasty formation, "The council's authority is a mix of borrowed legislative, judicial, and executive powers that used to be in the hands of other institutions such as the prosecutor-general, ministers of the interior, the Journalist's Syndicate, and the State Information Service. This is in addition to powers supposed to be in the hands of the publishing houses themselves."[41] The Higher Press Council thus is the main authority that creates laws for the press, for journalists, and for everything else related to media in Egypt.[42]

This system of ownership does not entail formal direct government control over the management and content of newspapers. In reality, however, the state remains the main player, dictating the general guidelines for newspapers through its control over the Shura Council, and by default the Higher Press Council, not to mention the fact that all editors-in-chiefs of newspapers and magazines are essentially presidential appointees who act as PRs for the office of the president.

Legal Instruments

Egyptian law contains very weak guarantees of freedom of expression. Under the continuing state of emergency, the government maintains broad powers of censorship. Even the constitution appears not to provide for complete freedom for the press. This becomes obvious if one examines the guarantees and limitations on press freedom in Article 48 of the Egyptian Constitution:

> Freedom of the press and of printing, publishing and the information media is guaranteed. Administrative censorship, cautioning, suspension or prohibition of the publication of newspapers is not permissible. By way of exception, during a state of emergency or a time of war a limited censorship may be imposed on the newspapers, publications, and the information media in matters related to public safety or in the interests of national security, as provided by law.

Article 47 guarantees freedom of opinion in general but at the same time insists that freedom of expression should be "within the limits of the law." This requirement that all publications be "within the limits of the law" and Article 48's exception for emergency censorship severely restrict the scope of these freedoms. Although many Egyptians are proud of the constitutional provisions that guarantee limited press freedom, the fact that Egypt has been ruled by emergency law for nearly fifty years effectively nullifies them.

(i) Emergency Law   Based upon the British occupation laws of 1923, martial law was declared in December 1939, and has been in effect for all apart from approximately six years since then. Emergency law has been in place continuously since 1967, except between May 1980 and October 1981.[43]

The president exercises his emergency authority by decree. He may "impose restrictions on freedom of assembly, movement and residency, order the arrest and search of suspicious persons who pose a threat to security, [and] censor correspondence and the press." Moreover, the emergency law allows the president to try civilians in special state security courts for either violations of the emergency laws themselves and decrees promulgated under them, or for ordinary criminal violations. The president must ratify any judgment of these courts for it to become final. He therefore exercises a veto over any state security court decision. He may also order a retrial, even if the defendant was acquitted in the first trial.

Egyptian lawyers consider the emergency law as the greatest obstacle to freedom of the press and expression in general. For them, it represents "the suspension of any constitutional guarantees. Speaking of freedom or liberty of any sort is a mockery."[44]

Moreover, the Penal Code criminalizes a variety of self-expression, particularly criticism the state. This code is further strengthened by Article 97, known as the "anti-terrorism amendment," which was passed by the legislature in July 1992.

(ii) The Penal Code   One section of the Egyptian Penal Code concerns "crimes of the press." It prohibits publications that could be construed to: instigate hatred of the ruling system; humiliate the civil authorities; humiliate the armed services or the parliament; excite public opinion by propaganda; transmit false news; attack any of the three monotheistic religions; or propagate atheism. Under Article 98, it is unlawful to promote "opposition" or "hatred or contempt" for the "state's socialist system of government," or to "stir up resistance to public authorities." It is also unlawful to possess publications, or the means of producing publications, encouraging hatred or contempt for the state. Article 98 also penalizes any person who provides material support to these crimes, regardless of the person's intent to participate in the crime. A court may seize an offending publications or dissolve any association found to violate these provisions. Article 98(f) prohibits "exploitation of religion" to promote extremist ideas, or "disparaging...one of the divine religions."

Similar prohibitions, such as "promoting ideas that instigate public hatred of the existing regime," are also included under Article 174. Article 179 prohibit journalists from insulting the president. This kind of crime could lead to the arrest of a journalist and the closure of the newspaper. Article 188 punishes journalists for publishing "false news or false attribution." Article 195 puts the responsibility on the editor-in-chief of the newspaper for any crime committed by those working under him. The Penal Code authorizes the confiscation of written material if it is used to commit or incite certain crimes such as obscenity or intention to overthrow the government. However, the confiscation must follow due process. If the police suspect that such a crime has been committed through the press, they may seize the offending publication and take it to the *niyaba* (public prosecution), who makes the decision to confiscate.[45]

Repression and Intimidation

These legal structures have been used as tools of repression to enable governments to contain dissenters in the media arena. The historical evolution of state–media relations in Egypt explains the atmosphere of fear and intimidation that governs media outlets throughout the Arab world. In Egypt, government control over media outlets relaxes and tightens according to the domestic political climate. This is characteristic of the semi-authoritarian nature of most Arab regimes.[46] During the early to mid-1990s, for example, we find multiple cases of tough government retaliation against journalists due to the unstable environment created by the state's confrontation with Islamist militants. Today, with U.S. and internal pressures for reform and political openness, we find a relative relaxation of such measures has lessened both internal and international pressure for more serious reform. Nonetheless, the relaxation of the rules on the surface does not change the underlying realities that continue to govern the Arab press. People who work for nongovernmental media function in an atmosphere of fear that makes them practice self-censorship. Although the state at times may choose not to employ harsh punishments against dissident journalists, the long history of intimidation has created enough fear that the exercise of self-censorship has become well-established. Below are some examples of how the Egyptian government uses repressive means to silence its opponents in the media arena.

The most recent case was that of Abdul Halim Qandil, editor-in-chief of a newspaper, and a spokesman for the Kifaya movement. In November 2004 "four suited men swooped him off the street and into a speeding car. They blindfolded and beat him, stripped him naked, and tossed him on the Cairo–Suez highway, warning, 'This will teach you to talk about your masters (asyadak).'"[47] There is no doubt that the term "masters" in the last statement was a reference to Mubarak and his men, of whom Qandil had been very critical prior to the incident. Two weeks before his kidnapping he wrote, "no for re-extending Mubarak's presidency, and no to passing it on to Gamal Mubarak, and yes for a new president elected by the people...It is not enough to take down pictures of Gamal Mubarak from Al-Tahrir square, what is needed is to block his appearances in newspapers and television."[48] In the week of his beating, Qandil's column questioned the Ministry of Interior's claims about who conducted the terrorist attack in Taba earlier that same month.[49]

Qandil explained the following week that his kidnapping "was aimed at ending the discourse about 'the big guys,' at warning against criticism and setting an example through fear, and was aimed at instigating public fear."[50]

Al-Arabi journalists have suffered similar intimidation over the years. In November 1993, Mahmoud al-Maraghi, the paper's former editor-in-chief, was summoned by the state security prosecutor and interrogated for publishing an interview with the current Al-Qaeda No. 2, Ayman Al-Zawahiri, who at the time was one of the Islamic Group leaders. Al-Maraghi describes what happened:

> The SSI called me in and accused me of promoting terrorism because, according to police, I am contributing to portraying the Islamists' leaders as if they were national heroes. I answered that it is part of my job as a journalist to inform the public...By the end of the meeting, I was left with the impression that I could be recalled at any time and that next time they would not limit the investigation to this issue but they would bring up my whole file and review my whole career as a journalist. With the new "anti-terrorism laws," anyone who is accused of promoting terrorism should take the accusation very seriously.[51]

In 2001, the government closed down the *Al-Nabaa* newspaper, after it ran a controversial story about an excommunicated monk who allegedly ran a sex-and-blackmail ring. The ethno-religious polarization and protests that the story provoked caused the government to employ its press regulation instruments to stop the resulting political turbulence. Mustafa and Mahmoud Bakri of *Al-Osbou'* newspaper were jailed by a court order in 2003 after criticizing a leader of an opposition party who had been sentenced to prison by a state security court. Editor-in-chief of *Al-Ahrar*, Salah Qabadaya, and four other journalists from the paper were sentenced to six months in jail on grounds of slandering the chair of the government-owned Egypt Air company.[52] This is all, of course, in addition to the jailing of prominent figures who express dissent in public forums, including Saad Al-Din Ibrahim and more recently in 2005, Ayman Nour.

By the late 1990s, the government was able to consolidate an environment of fear inside the media arena. This was the product of over ten years of confrontation with dissenting journalists. The standoff between the state and *Al-Sha'ab* newspaper, which ended with the closing down of the paper in 2000, epitomizes the efforts of the government to contain free speech through force. The newspaper was published by the *Al-'Amal* party which had been allied with the banned Muslim Brotherhood since 1987. The six-month imprisonment of *Al-Sha'ab*[53] journalist Abdel Sattar Abu Hussein is one of the most visible expressions of the 1994 government campaign to silence critics of the regime. The charges against Abu Hussein were "endangering state security by reporting on the upcoming joint military training between Egyptian forces and American, French, and German forces."[54] According to Abu Hussein, "The news item was based on statements made by the minister of defense. I don't see any 'endangerment of state security' in publishing it." Other news organizations published the same item with no charge leveled against them. For example, two days after I was interrogated, *Al-Ahram* published the same news item.[55]

The Egyptian Model and Trend Setting in the Arab Media

As we saw earlier, the evolution of media control and pressure in Egypt provides useful clues about the nature of new media outlets like Al-Jazeera, Al-Arabiya, and Future TV. Throughout the rest of this book we find that variations on the Egyptian model have been employed by other states and political actors to exert control over their own media outlets. The ambiguity of the boundaries of media control by the Egyptian state is the same type of ambiguity employed by the owners of pan-Arab satellite channels to distance themselves from clear censorship mechanisms in exerting control over their own media outlets. The difference, however, is that questions of ownership and control in the Egyptian context are open secrets, while the same questions seem unresolved in the case of pan-Arab satellite media like Al-Jazeera and Al-Arabiya. The Egyptian model may help us to understand how other states have been able to utilize its methods and remold some of their features to fit their own interests and needs.

In Qatar, home to Al-Jazeera, and Saudi Arabia, the owner of Al-Arabiya, government–media relations, ownership, laws, and methods of control are not much different from those in Egypt. Reading Egyptian laws and restrictions, one would imagine that government discourse would dominate society and that the views of government are hegemonic. The reality is that the discourse of politics in Egypt is fragmented and if one wants to select a dominant discourse for the last 20 years, it would be that of the Islamists. The main reason for this is that control of modern media does not mean control of discourse. In a divided society like Egypt (part pre-modern and part modern) trusted communication happens in traditional institutions like the mosque or the souq. Face-to-face communication is more trusted than abstract communication from the newspapers, radio, or television. Radio and television lie on behalf of the ruling regime. A glaring example of this was in June 1967 when Radio Sawt Al-Arab told the Egyptians that their army was shooting down Israeli planes like flies and that the Israelis were defeated. A few days later, the Egyptians learned that their own army had been defeated. They did not know this just from the BBC or foreign media; they were told this by the returning soldiers (face-to-face communication).

However, the dominance of Islamic discourse has been the result of Islamist writers like Fahmy Howeidi, Ahmad Bahgat, Zaghloul Al-Najar, and the regular columns of Sheikh Al-Azhar, Dr. Mohamed Tantawi, and the Grand Mufti of Egypt, Dr. Ali Gomaa. Anyone who watches Egyptian television would notice the high number of religious talk shows and television series. One example is the daily show of the late Sheikh Mohamed

Metwally that aired for 20 years. Historical television series dramatizing the life of the Prophet and his companions are major forms of entertainment. Thus, at the level of producers, writers, and content, Islamic discourse has been dominant.

Media in the Arab world are part and parcel of politics. Television, radio, and the newspapers are sites of conflict between governments and their opponents at home. However, when it comes to foreign policy, the media is an extension of the regime. Reporters in Egypt do not question the policy of the regime. Instead, they become its advocates. Their main function is to vilify the regime's enemies at home and abroad. This was obvious in Nasser's media attacks on King Faisal of Saudi Arabia. It was also obvious in Saudi media attacks on Nasser.

Sawt Al-Arab was the most transparent example of media performing this function. Are Al-Jazeera and Al-Arabiya merely electronic versions of Sawt Al-Arab? Do the media laws in Saudi Arabia and Qatar follow the Egyptian example? Have the Islamists hijacked the media in the Gulf States in the same way the Islamists of Egypt penetrated the Egyptian media? These are the questions that the following chapters will try to answer.

CHAPTER 2

ARAB MEDIA AND INTERSTATE CONFLICT: QATAR VS. SAUDI ARABIA

Arab media is not shaped merely by an East vs. West conflict, which one might infer from the level of apparent anti-Americanism in Arab media programming. More importantly, it is driven by intra-regional conflicts, including rivalries between state actors, such as Egypt vs. Saudi Arabia, and more recently Saudi Arabia vs. Qatar and Syria vs. Lebanon, or even Morocco vs. Algeria. It is also susceptible to influence by political conflict within the state, as the case of Lebanon demonstrates in Chapter 3. This chapter presents an example of such rivalries, namely that between Qatar and Saudi Arabia, which pronounces itself in a less-than-subtle battle between the Qatari-government-owned Al-Jazeera and Saudi-sponsored media like Al-Arabiya. One has to look only at Al-Jazeera's documentaries against the Saudi royal family and Saudi media response to them to appreciate the point.

Media institutions are natural products of the societies in which they take form. When media institutions, laws, and practices do not reflect the societies in which they are produced, they appear like children that do not resemble their parents; doubts about their legitimacy abound. If we look at the Arab world, we find authoritarian regimes like Qatar, Saudi Arabia, and Tunisia, semi-authoritarian regimes like Egypt and Kuwait, semi-democratic but feudal regimes like Lebanon, and outright totalitarian regimes such as Syria. Yet from this region, the Al-Jazeera news network and Al-Arabiya satellite station seem to project a "free media." How can an authoritarian political order give birth to independent and free news channels? Is it possible or even justifiable to call Al-Arabiya and Al-Jazeera free and independent news channels? Are these channels legitimate expressions of their own societies? These are the questions that I try to answer in this chapter. My analysis is based on watching Al-Jazeera since its inception in 1996, and visiting its headquarters in Doha in 1997. I have interviewed many of the journalists who work there. It is also based on watching Al-Arabiya for the past two years, as well as on my participation as a frequent guest/commentator on both channels. In other words, my analysis is based on what anthropologists call "participant observation" as well as on analysis of programming and interviews with media professionals.

My main argument in this book has been that the Arab media is political and that we cannot understand it outside the historical, social, and political context in which it operates.[1] Through thick description and in-depth analysis of the political context and news coverage of Al-Jazeera and Al-Arabiya, I will try to explore the relationship between these satellite channels and the political and social order that produced them. I will also discuss the financial relationship between the two channels and the political regimes of Qatar and Saudi Arabia. The question here becomes "Are these channels indeed independent or are they mere tools in the intra-state conflict between Saudi Arabia and Qatar?"

We cannot understand the rise of Saudi and Qatari media without addressing the changes in the political landscape of the Arab world as a whole. Al-Jazeera and Al-Arabiya do not make commercial sense. They are losing enterprises. This being so, why do Saudi Arabia and Qatar spend all this money on them? Cleary, we cannot hope to understand these channels without understanding the motives of the states and regimes that finance them. To understand these motives we need to place them in the context of the historical evolution of the Arab media as instruments of power for Arab governments.

From Sawt Al-Arab to Al-Jazeera to Star Wars

As newly independent Arab states in the 1950s and 1960s tried to define themselves in the postcolonial era, the main role of their media became the consolidation of national identity, mobilizing people in support of the new regimes, and fashioning their own brands of Arab nationalism. The post-colonial media were used to legitimize the rule of the new indigenous regimes. The definition of Arab identity and Arab nationalism was essentially a battlefield between various centers of power.[2] The competition concerning who had the right to define what was Arab and what was not was reflected in media debates. For example, Egyptian President Gamal Abdul Nasser wanted an Arab identity fashioned after his own 1952 revolution and dominated by Egypt. In the Levant, the Ba'th party, with both its Syrian and Iraqi wings, wanted to define Arab identity in its own way. Finally, the Gulf monarchies led by Saudi Arabia wanted to define Arab identity with an Islamic color. This battle over the definition of Arab identity was in a sense a manifestation of an Arab Cold War that was brewing underneath the surface. From the very beginning media were transnational by nature: whatever the differences in spoken Arabic, a common educated tongue made it easy to spread ideas among elites. It is in this context that Radio Sawt Al-Arab (Voice of the Arab) emerged as Nasser's main tool to define the content of Arab nationalism.[3]

Sawt Al-Arab was founded by Nasser on July 4, 1953. It set the context for the development of media in the Middle East to the present day. At a time when illiteracy was common and information was passed on orally, radio was the perfect tool for reaching and influencing the masses.[4] Nasser was a revered figure of anticolonialism whose message many Arabs at the time were well disposed to listening to. He used the state-owned radio station to promote his policies both domestically and across the region. Sawt Al-Arab is often remembered as an influential weapon that galvanized the Arab masses, arousing Arab nationalist sentiments both in Egypt and throughout the Arab countries. It marked the real beginning of media politics in the Arab world.

The political function of Sawt Al-Arab during Nasser's reign was three-fold. First, the regime used it to gain legitimacy among the Egyptian public and to mobilize support for his revolution. He also used it to rally the Arabs in support of his brand of Arab nationalism. By playing up the theme of foreign hegemony and the oppression of Palestinians by the "Zionist Entity," Sawt Al-Arab boosted the popularity of Nasser. The language of the station used the rhetoric of Arab dignity and honor, two very dominant themes in Nasser's speeches that gained him greater support among the Arab masses both at home and abroad. Sawt Al-Arab was instrumental in Nasser's efforts to solidify support for his anti-Israeli and anti-Western stances.

Second, Nasser used Sawt Al-Arab to settle scores with Arab leaders who challenged Egypt's regional hegemonic ambitions. Egyptian commentator Ahmad Said, whose name was synonymous with Sawt Al-Arab, frequently vilified Nasser's enemies on air. The conservative regimes of the Gulf, particularly Saudi Arabia, were often the target of these attacks. For instance, Saudi Arabia came under sharp attack from Sawt Al-Arab during the Yemeni civil war, in which Egypt and Saudi Arabia supported opposing factions. Similarly, the station provoked anti-regime sentiments in Jordan during a power struggle between King Hussein and pro-Nasser elements within his government. Tunisian President Habib Bourguiba also became a target for Sawt Al-Arab when he called on Arabs to accept the division of Palestine into two states in accordance with the 1947 UN partition plan.[5]

A third function of Sawt Al-Arab and all of Nasser's media broadcasting was to redirect peoples' anger away from the failure of the policies of Nasser's regime toward an outside force beyond their reach and beyond national boundaries. Thus, instead of blaming Nasser for the deteriorating conditions that prevailed in Egypt at that time, media commentators designated the West as the main source of all the ills that had befallen Egyptian society, and by extension Arab society at large. Sawt Al-Arab's message dominated the airwaves of the Arab world. The station, armed with the cultural products of Egypt, especially the songs of the Arab diva, Umm Kulthum, and the Arab Elvis, Abdul Haleem Hafiz, captured the hearts and minds of Arab youth.[6] The Quran was recited on air in the sweet voice of Sheikh Abdul Baset Abdul Samad. It was a fantastic mix of songs, the

Quran, and nationalist rhetoric, that represented a serious threat to those who adopted a different worldview from that of Nasser. Saudi Arabia's King Faisal was Nasser's main challenger.

The Rise of Islamism and the Power of the Saudi Media

In 1967, Israel dealt Nasser's regime a very heavy blow. Israeli armies defeated the Arab armies of four countries in the Six Day War. As Arab armies were experiencing humiliating defeats at the hands of the Israeli army, Sawt Al-Arab continued to report on fictional military victories.[7] When people learned the truth about the magnitude of the defeat, this breach of trust created a chasm between Sawt Al-Arab and its audience. As people's faith in Arab nationalism and the Nasserite vision faded away, so did their interest in Sawt Al-Arab. One idea that dominated the Arab world after the defeat of 1967 was that Israel's religious piety, not its technological or military superiority, led to its victory over the Arabs. Thus, the remedy proposed was that for the Arabs to thrive and win the battle against their enemies, they had to return to the teachings of God. The media promoted this message: the Israelis won because they were closer to their God. If we are to win, we must emulate them. There was no mention of technological superiority or a better trained army or battle plans. It was all about God. The media of the Arab world at the time promoted symbols of this newly discovered religiosity. Men were shown on TV dressed in jallabiyas (a white Saudi style robe) to go to their Friday prayers. President Sadat himself adopted this "Islamic" dress during Friday prayers.[8] He even asked the media to refer to him as al-Raiyis al-Mumin ("The Believer President"), echoing the traditional Islamic title "Commander of the Faithful."

Media during this time, especially audiovisual media, delved into a new entertainment genre: the historical drama. These soap opera-like programs narrated the lives of Muslims during the glorious days of Islam. They made use of the new atmosphere of piety and the domains of Islam as a symbols of the collectivity. They also had interregional effects. In these shows, the attire approximated to that of the Gulf dress and the Arabic dialect moved away from the previously dominant Cairo dialect and closer to the dialect of the Gulf region, especially that of Saudi Arabia. We must remember that many workers from all over the Arab world had started to work in the Gulf due to the oil boom. They became familiarized with the habits and customs of the people of the Gulf. These traditional habits and customs were presented as authentically Islamic back home,[9] echoing the messages of the historical dramas. Gradually, Islamism started to take hold in most Arab societies.

In addition, a mix of Arab nationalism and Islamism came to dominate the airwaves. A new brand of Islamism emerged with the victory of Khomeini's revolution in Iran in 1979. The Iranian revolution was all about media. Everything was reported live on TV. The Arabs became more enthusiastic about their own brand of Islam when they saw the seat of Islam being moved from the lands of the Arabs to Persian land. Arab Islamism was not, as conventional wisdom has it, supportive of Khomeini. It was instead a response to what was seen as a Persian bid to take away the seat of Islam from its traditional place in Arabia, making Persia the new Islamic center of gravity.

The war was still between the traditional regional centers of power: Egypt, Persia, and Arabia. In the modern-day language of geopolitics, it was a battle for hegemony among Egypt, Saudi Arabia, and Iran. On the Arab front, Saudi Arabia asserted its dominance over Egypt, at least in the realm of media and finance. Saudi Arabia later enlisted Egypt and Iraq and the rest of the Arabs to battle the Persian bid for dominance of the Middle East. Saudi Arabia, armed with its particular brand of Islam and with oil money, became the center of Arab politics.[10] This trend was advanced by the increase in Saudi revenues, thanks to the oil boom of the 1970s.

Islamism as an ideology was further consolidated by the Arab victory over Israel in 1973.[11] Indeed, with a return to God Arabs could win; that was the message of the 1970s that dominated Arab media. Islamism as a viable ideology seemed to endure. In an effort to maintain the momentum of political Islamism, Saudi Arabia, as the self-designated seat of Islam, developed an elaborate media strategy to consolidate its position in Arab politics and to further undermine what remained of Nasser's Arab nationalism. As a result, throughout the late 1970s and 1980s, petro-dollars dominated the political scene and fashioned a new Arab imagination. The mix of Islam and oil money was Saudi Arabia's main tool to capture the hearts and minds of the Arab peoples.

Having observed and witnessed first-hand the power of the media, as illustrated by the success of Sawt Al-Arab, Saudi Arabia emulated Nasser's strategy by using the media to drive its own political objectives. Saudi-dominated media outlets include newspapers such as *Asharq Al-Awsat* (established in 1978), and *Al-Hayat* (a Lebanese newspaper bought by Saudi Prince Khaled bin Sultan in 1988), magazines such as *Al-Majalla*, and satellite television channels like the Middle East Broadcasting Center (MBC), which was launched in 1991. All of these outlets are based in London and are completely or partially owned by members of the Saudi royal family.[12]

The case of Arab Radio and Television (ART) illustrates Saudi Arabia's post-1967 quest for hegemony both in regional politics and in the world of Arab media. Take the pressure ART exerted on Arab governments by having exclusive rights to the World Cup in 2006. Governments and ministries of information throughout the Arab world were forced to put giant TV screens in the main squares to assuage their angry publics. Heads of states pleaded with Sheikh Kamel to let them watch the semifinal and final games free of cost. I was told that Kamel promised President Mubarak that he would give the two final games to Egyptian terrestrial TV free of cost. Of course Kamel would have got something in return. The point here is that Sheikh Saleh Kamel, a Saudi businessman, deals at the level of heads of states because of his media empire. Sheikh Saleh Kamel is also a proxy for the Saudi ruling elite. His regional influence translates to Saudi regional influence.

The story of ART started in 1993 when Saleh Kamel, a wealthy Saudi entrepreneur, joined forces with Saudi Prince Al-Waleed Bin Talal[13] to form ART, which has its main offices in Rome, Italy. ART is a group of television and radio channels broadcasting a mix of entertainment, news, and religious shows. Saleh Kamel was proud to announce, "All of these [channels] are 100 percent in conformity with Islamic values."[14] ART, although based outside Saudi Arabia, follows censorship rule similar to those of the official Saudi terrestrial television programming, which ban "criticism of religion, political systems or those in authority and forbade scenes showing smoking, dancing, consumption of alcohol, gambling, crime, non-Muslim religious symbols or places of worship, female singers or sports-women, unmarried couples alone together or people of the opposite sex showing affection for each other."[15] Sheikh Kamel's commitment to what he views as Islam-friendly television programming was symbolized by his decision to launch Iqra, "a comprehensive Islamic Arab channel, which presents a variety of programs covering religious, cultural, social, political, economic and recreational aspects of life."[16] Iraq is seen by Arab liberal intellectuals as a xenophobic television station. One Arab writer dubbed it "Ikrah," Arabic for hate. He accuses the channel of putting out programming that promotes hatred of non-Muslims.[17] The promotion of Saudi Islamism was clearly at the heart of the ART media project.

Like most of the other publications and television channels noted above, throughout its 12 years of existence, ART was anything but a profitable venture. Arabic *Forbes* reported recently that it was only in 2002 that ART was able to balance its books. Having poured in $250 million to add four more channels to the ART package without seeing an increase in advertising revenue, Kamel and Bin Talal were evidently not interested in running a profit-generating media venture. Hence, an invisible agenda must have guided their costly investment, and as the above discussion illustrates, a glance at the history of media politics in the Arab world suggests that promoting Saudi values, and by default hegemony, was at the top of this agenda. This is not to say, however, that Saudi Arabia's strategy to boost its political fortunes with government-backed media has encountered no resistance.

Saddam Hussein's Invasion of Kuwait and the Rise of Al-Jazeera and MBC

Even after the decline of Nasser's secular nationalism following the defeat of the Arab armies in the 1967 war, two Arab nationalist regimes of a Ba'thist hue did not automatically concede to Saudi leadership and to the dominance of Islamic discourse. Saddam Hussein's Ba'th regime in Iraq and

Hafiz Assad's in Syria remained the last bastions of Arab nationalism. The two regimes financed newspapers and magazines from Cairo to London to Paris to counter Saudi's growing dominance of the Arab media. Failing to assert his dominance over the Gulf states through soft power (i.e., through the media), Saddam Hussein resorted to military power in his bid for regional hegemony. On August 2, 1990, Iraq launched its invasion of Kuwait, marking Saddam's first attempt to challenge the Gulf monarchies militarily. Even after the liberation of Kuwait and the imposition of sanctions on Iraq, the invasion and its memory remained a harsh reminder to the small Gulf sheikhdoms of an important reality. It underscored their vulnerability to the hegemonic ambitions of large regional powers such as Iraq, Iran, and even Saudi Arabia. In their quest for greater security, countries like Kuwait, Qatar, Bahrain, and the UAE moved quickly to enhance bilateral defense relations with the United States. However, pure strategic considerations were not the only thing on their minds as they sought to protect themselves against perceived regional threats.

In almost every conversation I have with Kuwaitis about the invasion of 1990, I am struck by how they have managed to keep close track of who among governments, political groups, and individuals supported them and who abandoned their cause during *al-'edwan* (the invasion). Many of those who supported Saddam's invasion are barred from appearing on Kuwaiti television.[18] Indeed there were journalists and commentators who sided with Saddam Hussein and did not raise an eyebrow at talk of annexing Kuwait. Resentment is certainly one of the reactions that this created in the oil-rich Gulf, but, more importantly, this historical episode generated a strong feeling among the ruling elites of the region that something must be done to accommodate if not win the support of Arab public opinion. This feeling brought about greater investments in satellite media. Such investments were considered to be a way of exerting influence over public opinion, and more specifically, a way of mitigating the wrath of Palestinians and their cause and keeping it away from their own domestic politics. The case of Qatar and its launch of Al-Jazeera illustrates how those security concerns were addressed using satellite media.

The defeat of Saddam Hussein and his eviction from Kuwait in 1991 ended the last hope for secular Arab nationalism to dominate the region. Islamism, as an ideology, filled the vacuum. Even Saddam himself took on the image of an Islamist during the war. For the first time the phrase "Allah Akhbar" was written on the Iraqi flag and Saddam Hussein praying became a recurring image on Iraqi satellite TV.

The defeat of Saddam further consolidated the position of Saudi Arabia in the region in both soft and hard power terms. Smaller Gulf states felt vulnerable to both Saudi Arabia and Iran and always had the Iraqi invasion of Kuwait on their minds. Qatar, in particular, felt it might face a similar invasion like that of Kuwait, but the aggressor this time would be either Iran or Saudi Arabia. The conflict between Iran and Qatar over gas is almost a replica of the conflict between Kuwait and Iraq over oil before the invasion. In the same way that the Iraqis accused Kuwait of draining their oil fields, Iran also accused Qatar of draining its gas fields. This vulnerability led Qatar to contemplate its security. In the realm of hard power, Qatar looked to the United States as a guarantor of its security against its two powerful neighbors, Saudi Arabia and Iran. Qatar's insecurities were accentuated even further in 1995 when Emir Hamad bin Khalifa Al-Thani came to power after deposing his father in a bloodless coup. The coup was a source of escalating tension between Qatar and its neighbors in the Gulf during the subsequent years. In the beginning, Saudi and Egyptian newspapers did not support the new regime, claiming it went against Arab values and traditions. Some of the father's supporters fled to Egypt and others went to Saudi Arabia. This led to the feeling among the Qatari elite that Saudi Arabia and Egypt were trying to bring the deposed emir back.[19]

Already by the early 1990s, tensions between Doha and Riyadh were on the rise. In 1992, after confrontations between Bedouin on the Qatari–Saudi border, Qatar suspended a 1965 border agreement with Saudi Arabia. Continued border disputes between the two countries resulted in Qatar's boycott of the Gulf Cooperation Council (GCC) summit in 1994. A year later, Qatar protested the choice of a Saudi candidate for the post of secretary-general of the GCC and walked out of the GCC meeting. Moreover, Saudi Arabia raised its eyebrows at talk of Qatar's intent to supply gas to Israel in October 1995. It was later that same year that Saudi Arabia announced in public its welcoming of the deposed Qatari emir, angering the new regime in Doha even further.[20] The new emir rose to power in this context of Saudi–Qatari tension.

The new regime was vulnerable both militarily and politically. Most of its policies came as a response to these perceived threats on the military, economic, and cultural fronts. The new regime signed bilateral treaties with the United States to guarantee its security in terms of hard power. On the soft power front, it created a media equivalent of a super-gun under the name of Al-Jazeera to keep Iran, Saudi Arabia, and Egypt on the defensive, or at the very least to respond to attacks appearing in the Egyptian and Saudi Arabian media. The attacks and counterattacks between the Egyptian and Qatari media were vicious.[21] I was told that Al-Jazeera did not stop its attack on Egypt until the Egyptian minister of information sent his television crew to Geneva to record a six-hour interview with the deposed emir in which he made numerous embarrassing charges against the new regime in Doha. Egypt sent these tapes to Qatar and to Al-Jazeera and threatened to air them in their entirety on an Egyptian satellite channel if Al-Jazeera did not stop its attacks on Egypt.[22] This media battle culminated in 1997 when Egypt sent the head of its intelligence agency, Omar Suleiman, to Doha to respond to Qatar's constant Al-Jazeera attacks against Egypt.[23] Al-Jazeera finally ceased its attacks on Egypt. However, Saudi Arabia remained a thorn in the side of the new Qatari regime.

Al-Jazeera and the Vulnerabilities of the New Regime

Al-Jazeera television was founded by a Qatari royal decree on February 8, 1996. It was a response to regime vulnerabilities on the Islamic front as well as a means of legitimizing Qatar's military and economic pact with the United States in the years of angry Arab audiences. The Qatari emir provided Al-Jazeera with $137 million in start-up costs. Emir Hamad bin Khalifa Al-Thani, continues to fund Al-Jazeera from a line item in the budget of the emiri diwan (court) that reaches $300 million annually.[24] The head of Al-Jazeera's board of directors is Sheikh HamEad bin Tamer Al-Thani, the deputy minister of information.[25] The operating funds come from state finances and many of the people actually running the station are state officials, even after the dissolution of the ministry of information. Therefore, it is very difficult to claim that Al-Jazeera is independent.

This should not detract from the fact that Al-Jazeera has been known for its willingness to flirt with contentious issues that break longstanding taboos, not to mention its granting of airtime to controversial figures ranging from opposition leaders in Arab countries to Israeli officials. The popularity of Al-Jazeera can be traced to Operation Desert Fox in Iraq in 1998, when, as in the case of the Afghanistan war, Al-Jazeera was the only station covering the event from the scene.[26] It also gained popularity during the Palestinian Al-Aqsa Intifada. Al-Jazeera's raw coverage of the intifada and its consistent criticism of various Arab countries and leaders gave it instant appeal. The absence of another all-news channel in the Arab world contributed to the popularity of Al-Jazeera; its only competition was CNN in English.

Al-Jazeera has contributed to raising the ceiling of what can and cannot be said on pan-Arab television. However, this does not apply to local television stations inside each country. Al-Jazeera brought to Arab audiences Western-style political analysis through programs like *al-Ittijah al-Mu'akas* (The opposite direction) and *Akhar min–Ray* (More than one opinion), both of which took their inspiration from American programs like the *McLaughlin Group* and *Crossfire*. Yet those who applaud Al-Jazeera for its contribution to free speech fail to mention the extensive blacklist that Al-Jazeera has developed of Arab liberals or independent thinkers who do not bear allegiance to either the Islamist or Arab nationalist causes and who do not toe the official Qatari line.[27]

Watching Al-Jazeera, one might forget that September 11 ever happened, and think that the United States invaded Afghanistan for no reason other than to target Muslims. There is no mention of any crime committed by the Taliban regime. Bin Laden's and Al-Zawahiri's history of terror, both in the Arab world and globally, are forgotten. Instead, Bin Laden, Zawahiri, and the Taliban are portrayed as the victims.

Although there is a general understanding that Arab heads of state are not to be criticized in the Arab media, Al-Jazeera seems to violate this rule.

How is it, then, that Al-Jazeera can get away with scathing reports against Arab governments and leaders? The clichéd answer attributes this to the vigorous independence of Al-Jazeera. Such an explanation ignores the political context and the realities that really shape Arab media coverage. The truth is that Al-Jazeera's coverage is closely connected to the political freedom that Qatar gained by breaking away from its dependence on Arab neighbors for security. Politically Qatar has had to find a counter-weight to Saudi Arabia and Iran. Thus it has chosen a special military relationship with the United States to guard against a fate like that of Kuwait in 1990. However, Qatar remained culturally a vulnerable state. To fend off the influence of Saudi and Iranian Islamic credentials, Qatar "gave" part of Al-Jazeera to the Muslim Brotherhood. The director of the station, Waddah Khanfar, is a Muslim Brother, Sheikh Qaradawi, the TV star of the Muslim Brotherhood, has a regular show on Al-Jazeera, and another second-generation Muslim Brotherhood member, Ahmed Mansour, has two shows on Al-Jazeera: *Shahed ala al-Asre* (A witness to history) and *Bila Hudoud* (Without borders). Al-Jazeera glorifies Muslim Brotherhood founder Hassan Al-Bannah; the channel aired a two-part documentary on him in the months of January–February 2006.[28] The dominance of the Muslim Brotherhood in Al-Jazeera can only make sense if we realize that Saudi Arabia expelled most Muslim Brotherhood leaders when they did not endorse the Saudi position during the 1990 Gulf War. The Muslim Brothers can boost Qatar's Islamic credentials as well as serve as the spearhead in a media war against Saudi Arabia. Tension between Saudi Arabia and the Muslim Brotherhood is obvious in the comments of Prince Nayef bin Abde-Aziz, Saudi Arabia's minister of interior, in an interview with the Kuwait daily *Al-Siyasa*. In that interview, Prince Nayef accused the Muslim Brotherhood of being the source of all evil in the region, especially in Saudi Arabia.[29]

As we have seen, Qatar is vulnerable to its neighbors on a cultural level. Qatar and Saudi Arabia are both Wahhabi states, and the Wahhabi official doctrine of Qatar makes it subject to fatwas from Saudi Arabia. These fatwas, in addition to Saudi Arabia's strong religious standing as the home of the Muslim holy cities of Mecca and Medina, give Saudi Arabia power over Qatar. To protect itself from Saudi domi-nation in the religious arena, Qatar moved toward adopting elements of popular Islam. This included embracing Sheikh Yousef Al-Qaradawi. Al-Qaradawi is an Egyptian and the spiritual leader of the Muslim Brotherhood, and he has lived in Qatar for 20 years and has Qatari citi-zenship. Al-Qaradawi is also the favorite preacher of many members of the radical movements. In fact, in an interview with Al-Jazeera following September 11, he could not bring himself to condemn Bin Laden and his group. More recently, he was denied entrance to the UAE because of what he preaches.

Other Islamists who have appeared on Al-Jazeera are hosts such as Maher Abdullah (who died a year ago), Tayseer Alouni, and Ahmed Mansour, mentioned earlier. From the Balkans to South Asia, leaders of Islamist movements trust Mansour. Since 1988, he has served as Peshawar correspondent to many Arab papers. While in Pakistan, he cultivated an impressive network of relations that started with his close associations with Islamist leaders, ranging from Burhanuddin Rabbani to the Taliban. He was managing editor of *Al-Mujtama'a* (The society) magazine, a Kuwaiti weekly published by the Al-Islah group, an umbrella Islamist group whose members range from the Muslim Brotherhood to Salafi extremists.[30] Mansour was brought to Al-Jazeera in 1996 to produce and host an Islamist show *Al-Shari'a Wal-Haya* (Life and Islamic law), which later was hosted by Maher Abdullah and is now being hosted by the newly veiled Khadija bin Qina. Bin Qina, an Algerian newswoman, joined Al-Jazeera in 1997. When she interviewed me in 1997 at Al-Jazeera studio in Doha she struck me as a secular woman with Arab nationalist leanings. One would not expect such a woman to don the veil any time soon. In 2003, Bin Qina surprised her audience by appearing in the new fashion, "the Islamic" veil, as she read the newscast. This was big news in the Arab press. For the past ten years, these stories have made it to the front pages of Arab newspapers because of this trend that developed among celebrity women in the Arab world. Many female movie stars, such as Shams Al-Baroudi, whose profile in the Arab world is close to that of Angelina Jolie in the United States, have decided to wear the hijab and abandon their acting careers. These include stars such as Shadia, Shahera, and many others.[31] Analysts attributed the veiling of actresses and TV anchor women to a payoff of conservative Gulf money. As soon as she started wearing the hijab, Bin Qina became the main host of the *Al-Shari'a Wal-Haya* religious program. When I asked about the reason behind her veil, many Al-Jazeera journalists told me that it was the direct impact of her relationship with Al-Jazeera's Sheikh Yousef Al-Qaradawi.

The Islamist takeover of Al-Jazeera was slow, but deliberate. Not only did the personnel become Islamists, the content and also the reporting took on an Islamic coloring. One only has to refer to Ahmed Mansour's coverage of the American siege of Fallujah, in which he was crying at the top of his lungs about the necessity of jihad, to understand this transformation. Mansour was begging the Arabs to come and defend Fallujah and save its women and children from American barbarism. He went beyond being a reporter to being the jihadist that he was during the Afghan war in the 1980s.

Embracing Islamists allowed Qatar to build up its "Islamic," specifically Wahhabi, credentials against those of its Saudi rivals who derived much of their legitimacy from adherence to conservative Islamic codes and their efforts to promote Wahhabi values abroad. It also provided Qatar with the

Islamic leverage to stand up to the Islamic Republic of Iran. Relations between Qatar and Iran have been shaky at times. For example, in 1989, the Iranian oil minister issued a provocative statement claiming that a third of the natural gas of the North Field was in Iranian waters. More recently, Iranian clerics criticized Qatar for providing the United States with base-support for its military operations in Iraq.[32] The airtime that Al-Jazeera devotes to Osama Bin Laden and other Saudi oppositional figures can be explained in the context of Qatar's political goals vis-à-vis its confrontation against Saudi Arabia.

On the American front, Qatar and the United States signed a Defense Cooperation Agreement on June 23, 1992, giving the United States base-rights in Qatar, thereby officially including the Gulf sheikhdom under the U.S. security umbrella.[33] By 1996, Qatar had completed the building of Al-Udeid airbase, which the United States used for supply flights for Operation Enduring Freedom in Afghanistan. During the 2003 invasion of Iraq, Qatar served as headquarters for U.S. Central Command (CENT-COM). The expansion in U.S.–Qatari military relations was concomitant with the decline in U.S. military presence in Saudi Arabia, a major issue of contention that was used by Saudi opposition figures to discredit the ruling elite in the kingdom. Hence Qatar, along with its smaller neighbors, was moving toward limiting the role played by Saudi Arabia in the regional security formula, which was becoming less of a U.S.–Saudi venture and more of a set of individual partnerships between the United States and each of the small Gulf monarchies.

Qatar also tied itself to America economically. The country managed to compensate for the fact that it exported almost no oil to the United States by working with American companies such as Exxon Mobil, Occidental, and Pennzoil to develop its natural gas resources. Qatar's gas revenue is projected to outstrip oil revenues for the first time in 2007.[34] The government's eagerness to develop its natural gas resources came at a time when it was trying to distance itself from the dominance of oil-rich Saudi Arabia, which holds a considerable amount of leverage in the OPEC. In comparison, Qatar's oil production is small, and the country's oil resources are likely to run out by 2020.[35] Qatar's strategy to exploit its vast natural gas resources as a foreign policy instrument is helped by the absence of international regulation of natural gas production levels. "From the Qatari perspective, the shift in its energy export portfolio to natural gas has allowed it to move to a commodity less influenced by Saudi Arabia's leadership than oil, since the kingdom had no plans to export natural gas abroad."[36] When asked if there would ever be an OPEC to regulate the natural gas market, Abdullah Bin Hamad Al-Attiyah, Qatar's minister of energy, industry water and electricity, answered that this would never happen.[37] Thus Qatar was able to consolidate its independence from Saudi Arabia and strengthen its ties with the United States by playing the natural gas card.[38]

Saudi–Qatari Conflict and the Bin Laden Tapes

Many Western analysts have focused exclusively on the anti-American message of Osama Bin Laden's audio and video tapes aired on Al-Jazeera. This is part of the interpretive context of Bin Laden's tape but certainly not a comprehensive way of understanding those tapes. The missing context is that of Saudi–Qatari tension. Bin Laden was first and foremost an enemy of the Saudi state even before he turned his jihad against U.S. targets and interests. The airing of Bin Laden's messages on Al-Jazeera reveals a great deal about Qatar's policies vis-à-vis Saudi Arabia.

Bin Laden's frequent appearances on Al-Jazeera is part of a tacit understanding between Qatar and Bin Laden whereby Al-Jazeera airs his anti-American statements that give him global stature, while Qatar has the exclusive use of Bin Laden's tapes in its media war with Saudi Arabia. In Qatar's conflict with Saudi Arabia Bin Laden is the only credible force that could undermine the Saudi royal family. His speeches may be dominated by anti-American and anti-Western rhetoric, but the actual airing of Bin Laden's tapes by Al-Jazeera is directed more at Saudi Arabia than America. Consider the following excerpt from Bin Laden's statements that Al-Jazeera airs repeatedly:

> We also stress to honest Muslims that they should move, incite, and mobilize the [Islamic] nation, amid such grave events and hot atmosphere so as to liberate themselves from those unjust and renegade ruling regimes, which are enslaved by the United States.
>
> They should also do so to establish the rule of God on earth.
>
> The most qualified regions for liberation are Jordan, Morocco, Nigeria, Pakistan, the land of the two holy mosques [Saudi Arabia], and Yemen.[39]

Part of the intellectual coherence of Bin Laden's message is that it builds on the previous messages and fatwas that he has issued. The underpinning of his message is his break with Saudi Arabia in 1990. The fatwas that followed it targeted the Saudi regime. Al-Qaeda was formed to fight the far enemy as a way of undermining the near enemy. Saudi Arabia is both Bin Laden's and Qatar's enemy. Superficially, it is very surprising that Bin Laden criticizes the American presence in Saudi Arabia, while ignoring American military bases elsewhere in the Gulf region like Qatar, where the U.S. Central Command was based at the time of the Iraq invasion in 2003. But if one understands the Qatar–Bin Laden tacit agreement, Bin Laden's reluctance to criticize the American presence in Qatar becomes comprehensible.

Bin Laden is by no means the only Saudi oppositional figure who appears on Al-Jazeera. Al-Jazeera often interviews anti-regime figures such as Sa'd Al-Faqih, Mohamed Al-Masari, Mabrook Al-Saleh, Abdullah Al-Hamad, and many more. This trend has also been replicated by some American media outlets that unwittingly played into the hands of Al-Jazeera by re-airing Bin Laden's statements under the impression that they have a primarily anti-American message. The American-sponsored Al-Hurra copied Al-Jazeera practices by giving airtime to Saudi opposition figures.

The main point here is that we cannot interpret the media campaign of Bin Laden through the prism of the U.S. confrontation against international terrorism. The dynamics of the Arab media (Qatar–Saudi media rivalry in this case) play a great role in shaping the anti-American message on Arab television screens and paper. When we watch Bin Laden's videotapes on Western television stations with the Al-Jazeera logo in the corner of the screen, we must bear in mind that what is at play is not simply an anti-American dynamic. There are two agendas at work: First, Bin Laden's own goals of undermining U.S. interests and rallying support for his confrontation with the West. Second, there is his more direct campaign to undermine the Saudi royal family. In this, Bin Laden and Qatar see eye-to-eye. Saudi Arabia is their common enemy. This is an alliance based on shared interests as well as on ideological connection.

As shown above, Al-Jazeera is essentially Qatar's tool for pursuing political its objectives in the region. Qatar's political, economic, and military alliances with the United States freed the country—and Al-Jazeera—from any Arab obligation. The confidence Qatari leaders had acquired due to the American military's presence on the ground emboldened them to the point that they did not fear Arab reactions to Al-Jazeera's reports. Similarly, despite its close relationship with America, Qatar still allowed members of the Muslim Brotherhood to openly criticize the United States on Al-Jazeera as a way of maintaining its strong relationship with "popular Islam" in its efforts to bolster itself vis-à-vis the Islamic credentials of its neighbors, mainly those of Saudi Arabia and Iran. In short, Qatar gave the airstrip to the Americans and the airwaves to the Islamists and the Arab nationalists.

How Independent Is Al-Jazeera?

The Arabic-language *Forbes* reported recently that the operational costs of Al-Jazeera are no less than $100 million, then there is the $50 million per year that will be spent on the newly launched Al-Jazeera sports channel.[40] The channel's advertisement revenues, which are supplemented by revenues generated by selling original footage and leasing equipments, although growing, are not sufficient to give Al-Jazeera full financial autonomy from Qatar's government.[41]

Al-Jazeera remains a Qatari government enterprise. Sheikh Hamad bin Tamer Al-Thani, the current chairman of Al-Jazeera, was the under-secretary at the Qatari Ministry of Information and Culture before it was dismantled. Al-Jazeera's managing director, Jasim Al-Ali, was the director of Qatar TV when it was still controlled by the government.[42] It is obvious from all of this that Al-Jazeera is simply Qatar's Information Ministry with a new name and a new agenda. Al-Jazeera's courage in its negative coverage of Arab governments is a result of Qatar's breakaway from the Arab regional security system and its complete dependence on the United States. Al-Jazeera's freedom and editorial independence will only be proven when it reports critically on the internal affairs of Qatar. Thus far the state of Qatar and Qatari affairs are off-limits to Al-Jazeera. The day Al-Jazeera airs a documentary on how the current emir deposed his father will be when we can say that Al-Jazeera is free.

Al-Arabiya: Saudi Response to Al-Jazeera?

Within the context of the Saudi–Qatari conflict, Al-Jazeera did not stay unchallenged for long. As a response to Qatar's media attacks, Saudi Arabia launched the Al-Arabiya all-news channel in 2003. Al-Arabiya is part of the Middle East Broadcasting Centre (MBC), which consists of MBC 1, 2, 3 and Al-Arabiya, known as MBC4. MBC was founded by King Fahd's brother-in-law Walid Al-Ibrahim, commonly seen as the front-man for the King's son Prince Abdel-Aziz. Saudi Arabia launched Al-Arabiya after 8 years of relentless attacks by Al-Jazeera on the Saudi political order and the Saudi royal family. Al-Arabiya's programming shows that the station is more than an alternative to Al-Jazeera; it is a counter-missile directed at the Qatari news channel itself. Al-Arabiya is known for picking up the slack in areas that Al-Jazeera is less willing to explore in its "censorship-free" reporting, such as the relations between Qatar and Israel.

Just as the regional insecurities felt by the Qatari regime gave rise to Al-Jazeera, the rise of MBC in 1991 can also be viewed as the Saudi royal family's response to the insecurities induced by the Iraqi invasion of Kuwait. A startling fact of Saddam's invasion of Kuwait was that, with the exception of the Gulf populations, the Arab public supported Saddam. The Gulf monarchies were shocked by the reaction of Arabs to Saddam's invasion of Kuwait. Throughout North Africa, Saddam was the champion. Saddam's propaganda, the Saudis thought, carried the day. Indeed Saddam financed many newspapers and kept many Arab journalists on his payroll. A partial list of the names of these journalists was published in the Iraqi *Al-Mada* newspaper after the collapse of Saddam's regime.[43] Palestinians marched in the streets carrying pictures of Saddam, the man who told them that he would liberate Palestine through Kuwait. The reaction in Jordan was totally anti-Kuwaiti and the population supported the annexation of Kuwait. The Jordanian response was so overwhelming that King Hussein himself had to oppose the United States to keep his throne. These shocking realities convinced the Saudis that their media campaign against Saddam had failed and that they must create a television station to convince the Arabs to support the liberation of Kuwait and defense of Saudi Arabia.

Indeed, a glance at the modern history of the region shows that hegemonic states have often managed to justify their aggressions against smaller states using media propaganda. Iraq's aggression in Kuwait, like Nasser's intervention in Yemen, is a case in point.

Within this context, MBC was founded in London in 1991. ARA Group International, the Saudi founding organization, aimed at providing Arab audiences with a mixture of entertainment and news.[44] The main founders included Sheikh Saleh Kamel, a famous Saudi businessman, and Walid Al-Ibrahim, King Fahd's brother-in-law and uncle of the King's youngest son Abde-Aziz, along with his brother Abde-Aziz Al-Ibrahim. Differences in policy, however, led principal backers to buy out Kamel's 37.5 percent share. MBC1 is the biggest money maker of the channels and has the largest audience. MBC2, launched in 2002 and devoted to movies and subtitled English language programming, is watched all over the region, including a large audience in Iran. MBC3, dedicated to children's programming, was launched in 2004 and has a smaller audience.[45] MBC4 airs a combination of talk shows, sitcoms, and news, much of it subtitled. This is a result of a recent contract between MBC and CBS and ABC News that granted MBC the rights to air all content and programming.[46] In 2003, with start-up capital of $300 million, MBC set up the 24-hour news channel Al-Arabiya with headquarters in Dubai, attracting shareholders from the governments of Saudi Arabia, Jordan, Kuwait and Bahrain, along with then Prime Minister of Lebanon Rafiq Hariri.[47] Walid Al-Ibrahim is known to be backed by King Fahd's $28 billion fortune. In addition to the ARA Group, he is also owner of ANA Radio and Television, and the news wire service ME News. He also acquired United Press International (UPI) at a bankruptcy court auction in New York in 1992.

As we have seen, Al-Arabiya was largely the Saudi reaction to the growing dominance of Al-Jazeera. The latter was viewed by Al-Saud as a danger, as it gave airtime to Osama Bin Laden and the enemies of the Saudi royal family.[48] It is also widely believed that Al-Ibrahim's decision to pour $300 million into the launching of Al-Arabiya was an attempt by the Saudi elite to reassert its influence over the Arab satellite television industry after losing much of that power following the rise in Al-Jazeera's global profile and popularity. Al-Arabiya is still nowhere near balancing its costs and revenues. Its yearly costs are estimated at $70 million, and advertisement revenues are a little more than $10 million.[49]

Al-Jazeera vs. Al-Arabiya: Saudi and Qatar

The content of Al-Jazeera and Al-Arabiya vividly reflects the political rivalry between Qatar and Saudi Arabia. In my study of Arab media content, I observed a pattern in their news reporting suggesting that the two channels often exchange blows on behalf of their respective governments.

For example, on February 25, 2005 Al-Jazeera reported on a State Department human rights report, emphasizing the poor Saudi human rights record highlighted in the report. This report on the conditions of human rights worldwide was reduced by Al-Jazeera to being a report about Saudi Arabia. There was no mention of what it said about Qatar.[50]

A few minutes after this report, Al-Arabiya responded by reporting on the "secret visit" of the Israeli deputy minister of education to Qatar. This was an embarrassment to the state of Qatar and to Al-Jazeera, which prides itself on being anti-Israeli in public. Al-Arabiya had a field day catching the Qataris conducting secret meetings with the Israelis, thus showing to their audience the "hypocrisy" of Al-Jazeera and Qatar. The style of reporting was very suggestive. It stated that the wife of the emir of Qatar suggestion secretly invited the Israeli deputy secretary of education to visit Qatar. The suggestion of secrecy implied a furtive liaison with sexual overtones between a Jewish male (the Israeli official) and an Arab female (the wife of the emir). When I asked Mr. Abdul Rahman Al-Rashed, the director of Al-Arabiya about this, he said "we got them this time." He explained to me that his aggressive reporting had forced Al-Jazeera spokesperson Jihad Balout and the new public relations person for Al-Jazeera, the famed Tim Sebastian, the anchor of the English show *Hard Talk*, to address the story. Al-Rashed pointed out that Sebastian denied the connection between the Israeli deputy minister of education and the wife of the emir. "We challenged them by bringing the Israeli deputy minister on air on Arabiya several minutes later. He confirmed our story and told us that he was invited by the very foundation headed by the wife of the emir of Qatar. We got them big, I tell you,"[51] Al-Rashed said with great joy in his voice.

Al-Jazeera then responded with a report on the Saudi political prisoner Sheikh Said bin Zuair. The report claimed that he was suffering from very poor health and that the Arab Organization for Human Rights hold the Saudi authorities responsible for his fate.[52] Any observer of the two channels familiar with the underlying tension between Saudi Arabia and Qatar and its reflections on Al-Arabiya and Al-Jazeera cannot help but see these "news" shows as little more than entertainment.

Another example of how the content of Al-Jazeera and Al-Arabiya reflects the rivalry between Qatar and Saudi Arabia is the recent coverage of the meeting of U.S. President George Bush and the then Arabia's Crown Prince of Saudi, Abdullah bin Abdel-Aziz Al-Saud, in Crawford, Texas on April 25, 2005. On the day of the visit, Al-Jazeera feautred a statement from Human Rights Watch that called on President Bush to intervene on the issue of three members of the Saudi opposition who were arrested more than a year ago in Saudi Arabia.[53] Al-Jazeera noted that the Human Rights Watch statement also asked Bush to put pressure on the Saudi government to put an end to the death penalty and to appoint women to local councils. On the same day, Al-Arabiya responded with a scathing report on a member of the Qatari royal family who was accused of having sexual relations with underage girls in Prague.[54] Recent reports from Al-Arabiya include one on the lawsuit launched on behalf of the wife of the emir of Qatar, Sheikha Muza al-Masnad, against the Iraqi-owned and London-based daily *Al-Zaman*. The Qataris, according to the Al-Arabiya report, accused *Al-Zaman* of being a "Saudi mouthpiece."[55] In the sections below, I shall describe some of the main themes of the two stations' news programming and how these themes relate to and reinforce the rivalry between Saudi Arabia and Qatar. They can be divided into ones directly related to Qatar and Saudi Arabia, i.e., negative coverage of Saudi Arabia on Al-Jazeera and negative coverage of Qatar on Al-Arabiya, and themes that reflect the competing approaches of the two states in their relations with countries such as Syria, Lebanon, and Libya.

Al-Jazeera's airtime generosity to Saudi opposition figures other than Bin Laden himself is also a product of the Saudi–Qatari political rift. One figure who has benefited from this eagerness to feature Saudi dissidents is Mohsen Al-Awaji, who has often appeared on shows such as Ahmed Mansour's *Bila Hudoud*. In May 2003, Mansour interviewed Al-Awaji to discuss the problems of the Saudi system.[56] What is interesting about such interviews is that Mansour usually gives Al-Awaji the positive title of a reformer rather than using neutral terms such as oppositionist.[57] Al-Awaji also took part in a panel on the ascendancy of terrorism in the Arab world moderated by Ghassan Bin Jeddo in 2004.[58] Mansour devoted a program to Salman Al-Auda (a Saudi dissident clerk) in 2004.[59] Moreover, Al-Jazeera has given a great deal of coverage to the exiled Saudi oppositionist Sa'd Al-Faqih, who was added to the international list of terrorists in 2004.[60] In 2003, Al-Jazeera gave positive coverage to Al-Faqih's allegations that the Saudi government tried to kidnap him.[61]

An Al-Jazeera report in 2006 covered border problems between Yemen and Saudi Arabia. The report, which was put together by Ahmad Al-Sahalfi from the Yemini side of the border, exaggerated the problem of families that had been divided by the current border configuration. It presented the problem as if it were similar to the border problem between the occupied Golan Heights and Syria.[62]

Al-Arabiya on the other hand picks up what Al-Jazeera is reluctant to report. The station's director, Abdul Rahman Al-Rashed, once said in reference to its reporting of Qatari affairs, "we did not exaggerate and we did not create the stories ourselves. We simply conveyed real stories...We know that the Qatari visual and print media ignores them (those stories), but that is their own problem."[63] What Al-Rashed was referring to was Qatar's dirty laundry, namely its low-profile relationship with Israel, the royal family's scandals, the country's cooperation with the U.S. military, and its democratic shortcomings.

Qatari–Israeli Relations

Al-Arabiya's programming contains a great deal about Qatar's covert relationship with Israel. In February 2005, Al-Arabiya relayed a report from an Israeli newspaper about a secret visit by the Israeli deputy minister of education to Qatar, suggesting that this was a sign of efforts to normalize relations between the two countries.[64] Two days later it ran a segment about the Arab reaction to the Israeli minister's visit to Doha, adding that he met secretly with the wife of Qatar's emir secretly.[65] Al-Arabiya also reported the controversy that arose because of its own coverage of the story.[66] In another story, Al-Arabiya reported in May 2005 that Qatar requested that Israel support its nomination for membership to the United Nations Security Council.[67] In August of the same year, it aired a news segment that said Qatar's emir would donate $10 million to an Israeli soccer team,[68] and the following month it reported that the Qatari government would provide financial aid to a project to build a stadium in Israel.[69] On September 15, Al-Arabiya reported a meeting between the Israeli and the Qatari foreign ministers in New York.[70]

Qatar's Relations with the United States

Another recurring theme in Al-Arabiya's programming is Qatar's close association with the United States. For example, the station covered a statement from the Qatari foreign minister expressing acceptance of the U.S.–Middle East Partnership Initiative, which has been declared by Washington as the main umbrella for democracy promotion in the Arab world.[71] Another report in the same year suggested that Saddam Hussein was imprisoned in Qatar without the knowledge of the government.[72] U.S.–Qatari military cooperation is often the topic of Al-Arabiya shows, highlighting the presence of American troops in Qatar and the small sheikhdom's role in the 2003 invasion of Iraq.[73]

The Al-Murrah Tribe Story

Another batch of Qatari dirty laundry that Al-Arabiya brandished was is the incident of the Al-Murrah tribe. The government of Qatar deprived 5,000 members of the Al-Murrah tribe of their Qatari citizenship for their alleged support for the deposed former emir.[74] This story was discussed in depth both in news reports,[75] and talk shows on Al-Arabiya.[76] The station followed the story for almost three months.[77]

Qatari Royal Scandals

Al-Arabiya has also taken the lead in reporting on the scandals of Qatari royals. In one story, Al-Arabiya interviewed a media analyst who spoke against a British court's ruling against an Iraqi newspaper made on the grounds that it defamed the Qatari emir's wife.[78] Al-Arabiya was also active in bringing to light a corruption scandal involving the head of the Qatari National Council for Culture, Art and Antiquities, a member of the royal family. Prince Saud bin Mohamed Al-Thani was allegedly fired because of illegal spending practices. Al-Arabiya ran a report asserting that the Qatari media had provided little coverage of the scandal.[79]

The point here is that both a London-based Arab analyst and Al-Arabiya know that the accusations and counter-accusations are between the two states and their proxies and not a media war between Al-Jazeera and Al-Arabiya. According to Al-Arabiya, "Saudi Arabia has been exposed for decades to media campaigns through newspapers, books, and television, and this whole Qatari attack is something that is not new."[80] Another scandal that has been aired on Al-Arabiya is that of the Qatari royal who was accused of having sexual relations with underage girls in the Czech Republic. Al-Arabiya was keen on following the court case in Prague, where Sheikh Hamed bin Abdullah Al-Thani was put on trial.[81] Al-Arabiya quoted a Czech news agency saying that some 25 young Czech girls under the age of 15 had sex with the accused Qatari man.[82] Such reports may not be the most important news story of the day as far as the audience is concerned, but they are designed to embarrass the Qatari royal family. Al-Jazeera counters by featuring Saudi dissidents who accuse the Saudi royal family of corruption and mismanagement of the country. They also highlight the status of women in Saudi Arabia and abuses of human rights in Saudi Arabia.

Al-Jazeera and Al-Arabiya on Syria–Lebanon

Another story that demonstrates the Saudi–Qatari rivalry in the respective programming content of Al-Jazeera and Al-Arabiya is that of Syria, its involvement with Lebanese politics and the assassination of former Prime Minister of Lebanon Rafiq Al-Hariri, and the Asad regime's standoff with the international community on these two issues. We find that Al-Jazeera's programming is more favorable to, if not directly sympathetic with, the Syrian regime. Al-Arabiya's programming is more critical of Syria and sympathetic to Lebanese aspirations for independence. Once again, politics is at the heart of this discrepancy between the two channels' coverage. Al-Arabiya's sponsor, Saudi Arabia, has publicly taken a hard-line against Syrian policy in Lebanon since the assassination of Al-Hariri, a Saudi citizen and a close associate of King Fahd since the 1980s. Syria's alliance with Iran and its support of Shi'a dominated Hezbollah is certainly a source of great discomfort for Riyadh. Qatar's policy in managing its rivalry with Saudi is to stay on the opposite side of Riyadh on any given issue. It also has close relations with Syria. It was reported in 2006 that Qatar had become Syria's number one trading partner, with $800 million in trading volume in 2006.[83] Content analysis of the channel's coverage of Syrian and Lebanese affairs from December 2005 until the end of February 2006 is illustrative of the Saudi–Qatari political rivalry that takes place in the satellite space.

Assassination of Jibran Tueini

The two channel coverage of the assassination of Jibran Tueini, an anti-Syrian Lebanese journalist and politician, is reflective of Al-Arabiya's pro-Lebanese stance and Al-Jazeera's sympathy with the Syrian regime that was accused of his murder. Al-Jazeera reported the death in a short segment:

> The assassination of the Lebanese journalist politician Jibran Tueini as a result of a car explosion in the Melks area. The Lebanese ruling majority was quick to accuse Syria, and the Druze leader Walid Jumblatt was quick to accuse Damascus, claiming that [the assassination] meant to serve as a message from Syria, especially after the latest statements by President Bashar Al-Asad. Pro-Syrian circles have criticized the haste in accusing Syria, and spoke of an international-Israeli project to implicate Syria.[84]

With Al-Arabiya, we find much more sophisticated coverage. Al-Arabiya's reports did cite Syrian denial of any involvement in the assassination, however, they provided a more sophisticated look at the Lebanese reaction. The station quoted very dramatic and serious statements from Lebanon's Prime Minister Fouad Al-Saniora:

> He [Al-Saniora] said the government "will not give in" adding that "the criminals have kept killing us one after the other and we will not give in." Al-Saniora indicated in a following statement "We will not give in, we will not give in. The criminals have kept killing us one after the other and we will not give in no matter how many times the hands of the criminals will hit our leaders."[85]

The same report quotes Javier Solana, EU Higher Representative, condemning the assassination and expressing the EU's commitment to investigate the murder. It reports opposition leader Walid Jumblatt's accusation of Syria in his interview with the BBC. The report offers a biography of Tueini and discusses his courage in advocating Lebanese independence and free speech.[86] Additionally, Al-Arabiya provided a series of follow-up stories that cited accusations against Syria.[87] Al-Arabiya chose to keep the assassination as a developing story throughout the month, while Al-Jazeera dealt with it only briefly.

Al-Arabiya and Syria

Another story that demonstrates the chasm between Al-Arabiya and Al-Jazeera's coverage of Syrian affairs is that of Abdul Halim Khaddam, former Syrian vice president who resigned last year and went into self-imposed exile in Paris. Between December 2005 and January 2006, Khaddam made some damning statements about the Asad regime, and, by doing so, instigated a new point of news rivalry between Al-Jazeera and Al-Arabiya.

Al-Arabiya ran an exclusive interview with Khaddam, in which he strongly criticized the Syrian regime and suggested the nearing of its collapse.[88] A week later, Al-Arabiya reported on another statement made by

Khaddam in which he claimed that he would form a new government. Al-Jazeera responded by reporting the same statement and adding that "an Al-Jazeera correspondent in Paris learned that an official French delegation traveled to Syria on a special mission to Saudi Arabia to explore the possibility of moving Abdul Halim Khaddam former Syrian vice president there [to the kingdom]."[89] Unsurprisingly, many of the talk shows featured guests critical of Khaddam and his statements.[90] Moreover, Al-Jazeera reported on the same day that Al-Arabiya ran the interview that "the Syrian parliament called for the trying of Abdul Halim Khaddam on grounds of grand treason."[91]

In response to Al-Arabiya's interview with Khaddam, and another interview by Saudi-owned *Asharq Al-Awsat* with the former Syrian vice president,[92] the Syrian government voiced its objections to the government of Saudi Arabia. In a move to reassure Damascus and convince Asad to cooperate with the international investigation of Hariri's death, Riyadh agreed to "ask all Saudi media institutions to refrain from broadcasting Khaddam interviews or statements."[93]

American news stories on both Al-Jazeera and Al-Arabiya are not designed solely to generate hatred for the United States. The primary function of anti-American stories is to provide a cover for what otherwise could be seen as "sleaze stories" aimed at embarrassing other countries' royal families. Given this, one should not expect this portion of anti-Americanism to go away anytime soon, no matter how aggressive the efforts of U.S. public diplomacy might be. Anti-American programs are an integral part of the underlying tension between Saudi Arabia and Qatar and should be understood in that spirit.

Hezbollah's 33-day War with Israel

During Hezbollah's 33-day war with Israel, Arabs were watching two different versions of the war in Lebanon and reading two scripts about winners and losers. From day one, the Arab world was watching a split screen and an (un)civil war of words between two camps that helped to shape the geopolitical scene in the Middle East. The two halves of the split screen were Al-Jazeera and Al-Arabiya. While outsiders focused on the war between Hezbollah and Israel, the Arabs were glued to their screens watching a mudslinging match between representatives of various states, various sects, and various groups. It was a war within the Arab world. If not quite reflecting a civil war in the making within Islam and Arabism, certainly this kind of reporting helped to accelerate this particular war. The first of the two camps is led by Saudi Arabia, Egypt, and Jordan, while the second is made up of Syria, Qatar, Iran, and Hezbollah. As Qatar and Saudi Arabia own the two all news-channels that dominate the Arab airwaves, the Saudi–Qatari tension was reflected on the screens in the coverage of the Hezbollah–Israel war.

While Saudi Arabia called the war at the start "an uncalculated risk," (mughamara), Qatar and its Syrian and Iranian allies called it a "pre-planned war against Hezbollah (Muamara), conspiracy." Thus, it was a war of words between the camps of Mughamara and Muamara. The two camps also represented the Sunni–Shia divide within Islam. The Shia are represented by Syria and Iran, and adopted and highlighted by Al-Jazeera, while the Sunni camp is represented by Egypt, Jordan, and Saudi Arabia, with Al-Arabiya as their main gun in the war of words. Thus, the story of the war as the Arabs watched it followed the political positions of the owners of the media outlets. At the beginning of the war, Al-Jazeera aired an exclusive interview with Hassan Nasrallah conducted by its bureau chief in Lebanon, Ghassan bin Jeddo. In this interview, Nasrallah blamed Egypt and Saudi Arabia for providing cover for the Israeli attack on Lebanon. This sound bite became part of Al-Jazeera's promo for the war. The rest of this promo included showing U.S. Secretary of State Condoleezza Rice saying that she cared about the suffering of the civilians as pictures of dead and maimed children flashed across the screen. As Rice talks about how worried she is about Lebanese infrastructure, a bridge is blown up in the background. Then Nasrallah's image appears telling Arab leaders, "if you do not support us, at least be neutral."

Nasrallah gave two interviews to Al-Jazeera and to Bin Jeddo exclusively and gave none to Al-Arabiya or any other channel except Al-Manar TV, Hezbollah's own TV station, where he made all his battle statements, and the Iranian state-owned, Arabic-speaking Al-Alam TV that is extensively watched by the Iraqi and Syrian Shia populations. One Lebanese journalist told me that Bin Jeddo is "a card-carrying member of Hezbollah. His relationship with Nasrallah is like that of Tayseer Alouni with Bin Laden." This is a reference to the Al-Jazeera correspondent who was imprisoned in Spain for his ties with Al-Qaeda.

Al-Jazeera also ran two interviews with Hamad bin Jasim bin Jabar Al-Thani, the foreign minister of Qatar. In both interviews, Al-Thani blasted Saudi Arabia for saying that Hezbollah's kidnapping of soldiers was mughamara (miscalculation). He blamed Saudi Arabia and Egypt for providing a "political cover" for Israel to wage its war against Lebanon, echoing Nasrallah's interviews.

Al-Arabiya did not let these accusations go unanswered. While Al-Jazeera presented Nasrallah as the presiding force of Lebanon, Al-Arabiya focused on Fouad Al-Saniora, the current prime minister, and on his speech to the Arab League Foreign Ministers. While Al-Jazeera supported Hezbollah and its state-within-a-state, Al-Arabiya focused on the formal state of Lebanon. It interviewed Saad Al-Hariri, the son of the assassinated former prime minister, and it broadcast the speeches of Saniora live with sympathetic commentary. Al-Jazeera, by contrast, broadcast live the speech of Syrian president Bashar Al-Asad in which he accused Arab leaders of the opposing camp "half-men". The station's commentary on Asad's the speech depended very heavily on Syrian officials such as Emad al-Shuaibi, among others. Al-Jazeera's cheerleading of the speech as he talked about the victory of Hezbollah made the station sound and look like Syrian state television.

Al-Arabiya also devoted some time to responding to Qatari accusations and to what it dubbed Qatari "hypocrisy". One Saudi commentator expressed his bewilderment Qatar's policy—he wondered how it was that "Qatar gives its airstrips to the Americans and its airwaves to Hezbollah." The theme of Qatari hypocrisy was the subject of many Al-Arabiya programs, especially their primetime show *Panorama*, hosted by the Jordanian Montaha al-Rumahi. In response to the accusations of the Qatari foreign minister against Saudi Arabia, Al-Arabiya and the Saudi-owned *Asharq Al-Awsat* newspaper, ran three stories about Qatar's relationship with Israel. The first was about the transfer of American "smart bombs" to Israel from the U.S. base in Qatar. This one brought an immediate response from Al-Jazeera, who interviewed the foreign minister who said that he had no knowledge of the bombs being transferred from Qatar to Israel. He told his host Mohammed Kreeshan, "If you knew the source of this information, you would know that it is false." Al-Arabiya also ran a story about the Israeli commercial office in Qatar. Its commentators made the point that if Qatar urges Egypt and Jordan who have formal peace treaties with Israel, to cut off their diplomatic relations, it should lead by closing the Israeli commercial office in Doha. The point of the coverage was that although Sheikh Hamad and Al-Jazeera were calling upon all the Arabs to rise up against the Israelis and the Americans, Qatar itself was being protected by the American bases and by its special alliance with Israel. *Asharq Al-Awsat* ran a story by its Israel correspondent, Nazeer Mujali, saying that the Qatari foreign minister flew to the Arab foreign ministers' meeting in Beirut from Israel and that his plane was escorted by two Israeli fighter jets. The Saudi newspaper wondered why Al-Jazeera did not cover such stories.[94]

In response Al-Jazeera created a special one-hour daily program called *Saut al-Nass* (Voice of the people), a supposed call-in show that one of the journalists at Al-Jazeera told me was in fact a call-out. This means that Al-Jazeera operators call select people from various Arab countries. This is because many of these people cannot afford the cost of international calls. The show allows all kinds of insults to be aired without any intervention from the host. For example on the 4th August, 2006 Fairuz Zaiyani, the hostess of the show, accepted a call from a man who called Condoleezza Rice an "an old black witch"; another referred to her using the "N" word. Zaiyani did not intervene or apologize to her audience for what they heard. But this is the nature of Al-Jazeera. Faisal Al-Qasim who has a show called *Al-Itijah Al-Muakish*, hosted a program on August 8, 2006 on the differences between Israel and Nazi Germany and Olmert and Hitler. He featured on it a man called Ibrahim Aloush who stated that it was an injustice for Nazism to be compared with Zionism. "Zionism is far worse."[95]

On the *Voice of the People* show on Al-Jazeera, it is open season on Saudi, Arabia and its leadership. Many of the callers are supposedly Saudis critical of the Saudi position and the royal family. One woman called Omm Saad described Saudi Arabia, on Al-Jazeera, as the "occupied land of the two holy mosques." Other supposed Saudis expressed shame over the attitude of their country toward Hezbollah.

The Arab media failed to show us anything about Hezbollah fighters in the Israel-Hezbollah war. Only on the Monday, after the ceasefire did one Hezbollah fighter give an interview to the Al-Jazeera correspondent Abbas Nasser. None for any other channel. Hezbollah saw Al-Arabiya as amplifying its own TV station Al-Manar. When I asked a Lebanese journalist on the ground about the lack of coverage of Hezbollah's activities, he said that everything in Lebanon was monitored by Hezbollah men who accompany journalists on their motor scooters. They make sure that nothing but the human suffering is reported. He told me that he had been taken to shelters and told who to talk to and who not. Hezbollah fed the world its own version of the story. He said, "If you look at any BBC or CNN report from South Beirut, you can see the men on their motor scooters in the background. They threatened journalists and confiscated pictures." He also added that if you watch Al-Jazeera you get the feeling that Israeli planes only target men and women over sixty and children under ten. These are the pictures that you see on Arab screens.

As the war wound down we saw the competition again between Al-Jazeera and Al-Arabiya over writing the final script: a victory or a defeat for Hezbollah?

In his recent show "from Lebanon," Al-Jazeera's Beirut bureau chief Ghassan Bin Jeddo presented an hour of Hezbollah supporters writing the script of victory and raising the flag of Hezbollah and pictures of Hassan Nasrallah. Although he presented them as ordinary people telling the audience that they are ready to sacrifice their children for Nasrallah and Hezbollah, it was obvious that all the people had to be selected very carefully and that the stage was prepared. In the background, there were the destroyed buildings of Al-Dahiya (southern Beirut), with a white banner covering a large part of the background with the words "America is the real terrorist" written on it. The show intended to demonstrate that even the Christians of Lebanon, who represent 30 percent of the population, are supporters of Hezbollah. As this lengthy show was celebrating Hezbollah's victory, Al-Arabiya's correspondent from Marjeyoon near the Lebanese–Israeli border was the level of destruction and the Israeli soldiers still in control of the south. Al-Arabiya was covering a story about the possible existence of Israeli soldiers in some of the buildings of this destroyed town and its correspondent was asking locals whether they had seen any Israelis there since the beginning of the ceasefire. The correspondent was looking for verification of Israeli withdrawal by asking the local people. His segment was showing the misery and suffering of the people who were returning to their destroyed homes. None of them praised the victory of Nasrallah, as did those appearing Al-Jazeera.

This is the story of two channels and the two sponsors of these channels who held different positions on the war. The rest of the Arab media were somewhere in between. This uncivil war of words endorsed by the latest speeches of Syrian president Bashar Al-Asad and Iranian president Ahmadinejad is likely to bring about a real war between the two camps, and may be sooner than many would expect. I hope that the above examples, have shown clearly the link between media ownership, the political and economic concerns of media owners, and media content.

Anti-Americanism on Al-Jazeera and Al-Arabiya

How do we understand anti-Americanism in the context of the conflict between Saudi Arabia and Qatar that is represented by Al-Jazeera and Al-Arabiya? First, I would like to suggest that anti-Americanism in the Arab media is a complex phenomenon that is integrated into the very nature of the reporting of the Iraqi and the Palestinian stories. These two stories dominate Arab media such as Al-Jazeera and Al-Arabiya, which target wide audiences from Morocco to Oman. The main message that all Arabs understand is that America supports Israel in its occupation of the Palestinian territories (Arab land), and that America itself is involved in occupying an Arab country, Iraq.

Anti-Americanism is also related to who is doing the reporting, producing, and editing of Arab media. A great many Arab journalists working on Al-Arabiya and Al-Jazeera are either Palestinians or Western nationals of Arab origin. For example, Faisal Al Qasim, a major talk-show host on Al-Jazeera, is a British Syrian, and Sami Haddad, another talk-show host, is British Palestinian. Hafiz Al-Mirazi, the station's Washington bureau chief, is American Egyptian, Ahmed Alshouli, the news editor, is Palestinian, and Eman Banora, the main anchorwoman on Al-Jazeera, is Palestinian. I devote a chapter to the relationship between journalists' backgrounds and their reporting (see Chapter 4). My point here is not that a Palestinian bias generates anti-Americanism on Al-Jazeera. Rather, these Palestinians and diaspora journalists know the Palestinian story very well from almost all sides—American, Israeli, and Arab. This allows them to be able to improvise on the air, for they do not need directions from a producer. While well versed in the Palestinian story, these same people do not know the local stories of Morocco, Egypt, or Tunisia, let alone of Mauritania or Libya. This leads me to believe that over-reporting the Palestinian story and over-discussing it on talk-shows is due to the fact that many editors, correspondents, and also many talk-show hosts are Palestinians themselves. Content is shaped by what those who produce the Arab media know. It is also shaped by their ideological orientations, be they Islamists or Arab nationalists. In this particular package, anti-Americanism is always part of the story, part of reporting, and part of the picture. I dedicate a chapter to the role of journalists in shaping Arab media coverage and as transnational actors.

This, however, is not true whenever there is a major local story. Palestine and Iraq were not the dominant stories on Lebanese TV stations for forty days after the death of Prime Minister Hariri. Following the Al-Hariri assassination, Palestine and Iraq were taken off the screen because journalists who were reporting the Al-Hariri story were Lebanese. They knew their story very well and therefore did not need Palestinian journalists to produce solid TV programming. Also, both America and Israel were nowhere to be seen on any of the Lebanese TV channels during Hariri's assassination and its aftermath.

The fact that local stories are not covered on Al-Jazeera and Al-Arabiya allows for the dominance of pan-Arab, and therefore anti-American, stories to dominate the airwaves. This does not mean that Al-Arabiya and Al-Jazeera did not report the Hariri story. They did, but according to the agendas of their sponsors. Al-Arabiya took the side of the Hariri family and the Lebanese opposition, while Al-Jazeera took the pro-Syrian side. The conflict between Qatar and Saudi Arabia manifested itself on the Lebanese media scene as well.

The competition of Al-Jazeera and Al-Arabiya is, as we have seen, part of a larger conflict between Saudi Arabia and Qatar. This conflict is multilayered. It involves the Saudi brand of Islam vs. the Islam of Qatar and the Muslim Brotherhood. It is a conflict between oil represented by Saudi Arabia and gas represented by Qatar. It is a conflict between Egyptian journalists and Lebanese journalists. It is a conflict between Bin Laden and the Saudi royal family on Al-Jazeera and between the Al-Murrah tribe and the Qatari royal family on Al-Arabiya. Each of the satellite television channels acts on behalf of its Kafil (sponsor). While Al-Jazeera does the bidding of Qatar, Al-Arabiya is accountable to the Saudi state. To interpret these two channels outside the context of Saudi–Qatari tension is to be misled about the nature of both Al-Jazeera and Al-Arabiya.

CHAPTER 3

ARAB MEDIA AND INTRA-STATE CONFLICT: THE CASE OF LEBANON

It is common to think of media in terms of state vs. private ownership. It is often argued that the lack of freedom of speech that is apparent in the Arab world is the result of years of state monopoly on the ownership and production of the mass media. In the preceding chapters, I have shown that Al-Jazeera and Al-Arabiya are not in reality privately owned channels: they are controlled by the states of Qatar and Saudi Arabia respectively. This financial and political control is reflected in the content of these television channels and their use as tools of foreign policy. Although both channels appear to be private, commercial enterprises, they are in fact political ventures. This needs to be taken into account in analyzing their impact on the Arab world as a whole, and their possible role as catalysts and shapers of public opinion, and in any analysis of the relationship between Qatar and Saudi Arabia and interstate relations in the Gulf in general. Nonetheless, does clarifying the confusion over the public/private in the cases of Al-Jazeera and Al-Arabiya allow one to hypothesize that all transnational Arab media are political tools in the hands of governments? Perhaps these two channels are special cases that have taken root in particularly authoritarian states. What about the Arab media in democratic or semi-democratic states like Kuwait and Lebanon where the media appears to be wholly private? In seeking an answer to this question, I will explore media content, ownership, and politics in Lebanon. I will analyze the programming, ownership, and political links of four television channels: Lebanese Broadcasting Corporation (LBC), Hezbollah TV (Al-Manar), Amal TV, also known as the National Broadcasting Network (NBN), and Hariri's TV station, Future TV, in terms of their significance in intra-state ethnic and political conflicts. This is clearly an essential aspect of their importance and it merits in-depth examination. Yet, the divisions between the channels are also played out in the realm of international politics, as well as in intra-state conflicts. Interstate conflicts between Syria, Iran, Saudi Arabia, and Qatar are woven into the very fabric of the Lebanese media. This was especially clear in the coverage of the assassination of former prime minister Rafiq Hariri and the events that followed his death. I examine television coverage during these events to show how each of the four channels answers to a variety of political masters both within and outside Lebanon. This chain of command is apparent in the content of news programming as well as in ownership structures. It shows that in spite of the clearly confessional and ethnic basis of the channels and their attachment to the Lebanese nation, like Al-Jazeera and Al-Arabiya they fail to conform to the "apolitical" or "free speech" criteria that promoters of objective journalism often thought would be the result of private ownership of the media. Like state-run television, these media outlets are first and foremost political institutions. The purpose of this analysis is to place the Lebanese media into its broader political and cultural context.

The current audiovisual media of Lebanon has been largely shaped by the legacy of the civil war (1975–1990). The political ties that are apparent in the LBC, Hezbollah TV (Al-Manar), Amal TV NBN, and Hariri's TV station (Future TV) can be traced to the civil war period when each political group felt it necessary to have its media outlet to rally its supporters and relay its political propaganda. There was no mechanism to regulate who should put what on the air, due to the general collapse of the authority of the Lebanese government, which also led to the collapse of television licensing and regulating authority. During that time there were between 150 to 300 unlicensed radio and TV stations on the air. This chaos was brought under control after the fighting parties of the civil war reached an accord in Taif, Saudi Arabia, in 1989. As the dust settled, the Lebanese government enacted the Audio-Visual Media Law in 1994. According to this law, the government has the right to fine journalists and publishers and even detain them for slandering the head of state or inciting sectarian strife. This law is used erratically against foreign newspapers or those who fall out of favor with key figures in the Lebanese government such as the president, the prime minister or the speaker of the parliament. It was used in 1999 when President Emile Lahud punished the pan-Arab newspaper *Asharq Al-Awsat* by banning it for a while; and when he banned Murr TV in 2002. Despite the fact that the Audio-Visual Law is used solely against the government's political opponents, it still sets up a frame of reference for the media in post-civil war Lebanon.

Media laws are indeed important to comprehend, but in order to understand the media environment in Lebanon, it is more important to pay attention to the de facto activities that set the rules of the game. Laws may not have any bearing on what is happening on the ground. In this chapter, I am more interested in de facto than de jure analysis. In a country crisscrossed by ethnic and religious divisions, it is of no surprise that these differences are reflected in its media. There are many ways of classifying Lebanese media depending on one's objective. It can be classified according to religious affiliation and its representation of local groups, or it can be classified according to external involvement in the affairs of Lebanon. For example, although there are Lebanese laws that grant television channels a Category 1 license allowing them to have both terrestrial and satellite broadcasting, the reality is that these laws are irrelevant if a group has political clout. Most Lebanese TV stations represent the various confessional interests as reflected in the make-up of the government. Future TV was given a license to operate both as a terrestrial and as a satellite station because it belonged to the Sunni prime minister Rafiq Al-Hariri, the NBN was given license before it actually came into existence as an operational station because it belonged to the Shia speaker of parliament, Nabih Berri. Jokingly, some in Lebanon interpret NBN to mean Nabih Berri Network. The Shia minister of information during the 1990s, Bassem Al-Sabaa, also made sure that the Shia community had another station— belonged to Hezbollah which—Al-Manar TV. Despite the fact that Al-Manar does not have the Category 1 license that would allow it to broadcast news, under the political influence of Berri and Al-Sabaa, the station was exempted from this condition on the pretext that it provided a counter-balance to the Catholic Church's Télé-Lumiere that operated without a license. No one in this religious political culture dares question the operation of Télé-Lumiere, because it has the backing of a religious community. MTV, or Murr TV, was given a license because it belonged to Gabriel Murr (brother of the ex-minister of the interior Michel Murr and uncle of Michel's son, who also became an interior minister after his father and who is the son-in-law of the current president of Lebanon, Emile Lahud). Even when MTV was closed, the closure was not carried out on the grounds of the station's violation of press laws. The Lebanese government under Lahud closed it temporarily because of an inter-family feud between Gabriel and Michel Murr.

Understanding Lebanese media requires an understanding of Lebanon's political and social make-up. Lebanon is a mosaic of confessional groups: Shia Muslims, Sunni Muslims, Maronite Christians, Orthodox Christians, and Druze. We can analyze the media in terms of interstate rivalries and balancing. In terms of the impact of outside forces, the pro-Syrian/anti-Syrian divide provides another way of categorizing Lebanese media, especially after the assassination of Hariri. The anti-Syrian group includes LBC, Future TV, and the *Al-Nahar* newspaper, all owned by members of the Lebanese elite who at present support the oppositionist position against Syria and the current Lebanese government. It is wrong to assume that the anti-Syrian rhetoric transmitted by these outlets has been constant throughout the past decade. In fact, Future TV station was the most pro-Syrian and Arab nationalist TV station until the moment Hariri was assassinated. The Syrian hold over Future TV was very strong prior to Hariri's death. The station's programming and news coverage always showed what political leaders in Damascus wanted to see. In other words, Future TV was a latecomer to the anti-Syrian camp on the media arena. The pro-Syrian group includes Al-Manar and NBN, which are owned by prominent members of Hezbollah and the Amal party respectively, the two groups that dominate Lebanon's Shia cultural domain. Like their respective owners, these stations are known to be supportive of a Syrian presence in Lebanon, and this support is often mirrored in their programming. These two broad categories of Lebanese media can be used as an analytical device to make the story simpler and to capture the external influence that would be difficult to grasp in terms of the ethnic and religious categorization mentioned earlier.

Audiovisual media can also be classified in terms of outlets that are allowed to broadcast political news and commentary and those who do not enjoy that privilege. The first category consists mainly of channels controlled by the government or by some powerful political faction. These include the government-owned Télé Liban, Hariri's Future TV, the minister of the interior's Murr TV (MTV), the speaker of Parliament's National Broadcasting Network (NBN), and the Lebanese Broadcasting Company International (LBCI), the strongest wartime station originally established by the Christian militia. Radio stations allowed to broadcast political news and commentary are owned by the same forces. The only media that show some degree of independence, although connected to political forces inside Lebanon or outside it, are the print media such as the *Al-Nahar*, *Al-Safir*, and *Al-Hayat* newspapers. Political forces involved in the media business know that in Lebanon audiovisual media have a greater impact on the public. Newspapers are less influential.

I will start with a detailed overview of the ownership of media and the political players behind each of these media outlets. I will follow this with an analysis of Lebanese media coverage of the assassination of Rafiq Al-Hariri and its aftermath to illustrate how issues of ownership, political linkages, and cultural identity shape news coverage in Lebanon. I will also address the involvement of external players such as Syria, Iran, and Israel in the Lebanese media environment. Most importantly, I will also discuss how the Qatari/Saudi rivalry expressed through Al-Jazeera and Al-Arabiya spills over into the Lebanese media context.

The Lebanese Broadcasting Corporation

In the Lebanese national allocation of television station to various religious and ethnic groups, the LBC is the station of the Maronite Christians, one of the major factions of the civil war period. Although outnumbered by the Shia in today's Lebanon, the Maronites were the largest among the 17 different religious and ethnic groups that make up Lebanon. On several occasions, after chatting with Lebanese Maronites, I have been left with the impression that Lebanon is a Maronite country. Many Maronites are sure to remind you that they were the main drivers of Lebanese independence. While the premiership of Lebanon belongs to the Sunnis and the speaker of parliament position belongs to the Shia, the maronites hold presidency and the leadership of the armed forces, and LBC is their media platform.

According to the history posted on their website, LBC began terrestrial broadcasting on August 23, 1985, in the midst of the civil war. Although they describe themselves as the first private television station in Lebanon, as I show below, the station is owned by a mix of Maronites and Orthodox Christians. LBC continues to be chaired by a Maronite Christian, Pierre El-Daher.[1] In 1989, due to Michele Aoun's "war of liberation," LBC had to evacuate its office as a result of shelling six months' uninterrupted. This continued throughout the 1990s. LBC was targeted because it was seen as a party to the conflict. With the launch of LBCSAT in 1996 through ART's production and satellite facilities in Italy, LBC moved from being a terrestrial channel to a satellite channel that could be viewed in the Arab world, North America, and Australia.[2] To gain an audience throughout the Arab world, LBC's programming was a mix of news and entertainment. Very quickly it became famous throughout the Arab world because of the "soft-porn" nature of its entertainment. Shows like *Ma Ilak ila Hayfa* ("Hayfa is the only one for you") exposed Arab audiences to scantily clad young Lebanese female dancers. The show is very popular throughout the Gulf States, where women are rarely seen in short clothing. In fact, in places like Saudi Arabia women are completely covered from head to toe.

Following the conclusion of the civil war, and with Syria and its loyalists gaining control over the country, the channel experienced strong waves of Syrian influence—which was simply a reflection of Syrian political hegemony over the country's various political factions, including the Maronite community. Many members of the LBC's board of directors are closely associated with the Syrian regime, and thus hold sway over the station's occasional ventures into politically sensitive territory. Board members affiliated with the Syrians include Suleiman Franjieh (health minister under Hariri), the wealthy MP Issam Faris, and businessman Nabil Boustani. LBC has also been the target of Syrian intimidation. In August of 1998, a long-standing friend of Syria's military intelligence chief in Lebanon was appointed to supervise LBC's coverage. Rumors circulate that the appointment was ordered by the Syrian government after it felt that LBC had performed poorly in its coverage of President Hafiz Al-Asad's visit to France that year.[3] Earlier in the year, the government had banned LBC, along with Future TV, from transmitting news, seemingly because of LBC's interview with a Najah Wakim, one of pro-Syria Lebanese politicians, that included allegations of government corruption. Of course, Syria's ability to censor LBC was no longer apparent following the assassination of Hariri, as the station joined its counterparts among the oppositionist channels in its open and thorough coverage of the assassination and the subsequent demonstrations that called on Syria to end its 29-year occupation of Lebanon.

Even before the assassination LBC was seeking an alliance that would shield it from Syrian pressure. One such alliance was with two leading Saudi media entrepreneurs Princes Khaled bin Sultan and Al-Waleed bin Talal. Already Saudi businessman Saleh Kamel was connected to LBC through ART's parent company, Arab Media Corporation. Kamel went on record saying that he had managed to "influence" LBC's programming, hinting that he was able to curb the flamboyant and "un-Islamic" nature of some of its shows.[4] The Saudi connection was crystallized in 2002 as LBC and the *Al-Hayat* newspaper (which is owned by Prince Khaled bin Sultan) launched a joint venture, whereby they cooperated in producing a televised newscast. According to Jihad Al-Khazen, editor-in-chief of *Al-Hayat*, he was contacted by LBC chair El-Daher after 9/11, who expressed interest in launching such a venture with the daily newspaper.[5] Prior to this project, LBC's news coverage had been limited due to the diversity of its 24-hour programming, which encompassed movies, music, sports, talk-shows, and mini-series. But the rise of professional talk shows over the years had helped to create a political dimension to the channel's programming. These shows included Shatha Omar's *Naharkom Saeed* and Mai Shydaq's *Al-Hadath*, in which I personally participated three times.

The Saudi role increased after Saudi Prince Al-Waleed bin Talal bin Abdel-Aziz bought 49 percent of the station's shares in 2003. Traditionally, foreigners are not allowed to own shares in Lebanese media institutions, but, because of Al-Waleed's prominence, coupled with his relation to the Riyad Al-Solh (his grandfather and the first prime minister of Lebanon), an exception was made. In addition to the Saudi influence, reflected in the allocation of shares shown in the table below, we can also see that Maronite power is heavily represented, through Pierre El-Daher, the original founder of the station, and his associates. Syrian control is exhibited by the shares of Issam Faris and Nabil Boustani, who, as mentioned above, are pro-Syrian.

Pierre El-Daher	9 percent
Rima Yankoush	8 percent
Nabil Boustani	4 percent
Issam Faris	10 percent
Najjad Isam Fares	10 percent
Al-Waleed bin Talal*	49 percent
Marcel El-Daher*	10 percent

* Figures taken from "Arab Media Moguls" *Forbes Arabiya* (Jan 2005).

Future TV

At its inception in 1993, Future TV was seen by many as the Sunni counterweight to the Maronite-dominated LBC. The Lebanon-based channel was founded by the Lebanese prime minister Rafiq Al-Hariri and began its satellite broadcasting in October 1994. In 1996, Hariri, the largest shareholder in Future TV, had to sell a considerable number of his shares to comply with Law 382 of 1994, the Audio-Visual Law, which in addition to breaking the broadcasting monopoly of Télé Liban, also prohibited any individual from owning more than 10 percent of a given television station.[6] However, the move did not challenge Hariri's control over the station, as most of the shares were still owned by his family members and associates, as shown below:

Distribution of Shares in 2005: Future TV[7]

Name of shareholder	Relationship to Rafiq Hariri	Percent share
Nazik Hariri	Wife	10
Bahya Hariri	Sister	10
Ghaleb al-Shama'	Close family friend	8
Saadeddin Hariri	Son	8
Bahaeddin Hariri	Son	8
Shafeeq Hariri	Brother	7
Mustafa Rizian	Chairman of the Board of the Hariri-owned Mediterranean Investment Bank	1
	Total	**52**

Hariri's prominence in Lebanon began with his appointment as King Fahd's emissary to Lebanon during the 1980s; a role that allowed him to gain standing within Lebanon's political spheres and within Syrian circles of power. After playing a major role in the events that ended the Lebanese civil war, Hariri was prime minister from 1992 until 1998. He regained the position again in 2000 and held on to it until he resigned in October 2004, a few months before his assassination in February 2005. *Forbes* estimated Hariri's wealth in 2005 at $4.3 billion. In addition to virtually owning Future TV, Hariri was known to have owned shares in *Al-Nahar* and *Asafir* newspapers.

During Hariri's first premiership, Future TV was essentially a marketing tool being used by the prime minister to present Lebanon as a center of civil peace in the region and to advertise the country as a thriving business center complete with tourist attractions worthy of hefty investments from Gulf Arabs.[8] Such an approach very closely resembles that of government-owned Arab satellite television channels, such as the Egyptian Space Channel and Nile TV, which were used by the Egyptian government as means to enhance their tourism industry and to encourage foreign investment. Although it is unclear whether Future TV's advertisement revenues cover the station's costs, it is unreasonable to assume that the venture was able to sustain financial independence throughout the past twelve years. In 1997, Nadim Munla, chairman of Future TV, complained of low advertising revenues in the satellite media industry.[9]

Future TV's programming throughout the 1990s correlated with Hariri's political career very nicely. From 1992 to 1998, the station refrained from directing any substantial criticism against the government. During the period between 1998 and 2000, the two years that marked Hariri's absence from the post of prime minister, the channel became more adamant in advancing the "cause of freedom of speech," by voicing disapproval with the policies of Hariri's replacement, Selim Al-Hoss.[10] Thus, even though there is no evidence to refute Future TV's financial self-sufficiency, there is much evidence that it has never achieved full autonomy from the politics and personal influence of Hariri himself.

Future TV's programming content also reflected Hariri's political and personal connections. For example, Hariri's closeness to Syria at certain times could explain Future TV's occasional self-censorship and deference to Damascus. Prior to the death of Hariri, Future TV's programming exhibited a mixture of Arab nationalism and anti-Americanism, emphasizing the pan-Arab causes of the Palestinian–Israeli dispute and the American occupation of Iraq. Iraq, Palestine, and Hezbollah dominated its news coverage. For forty days following Hariri's assassination, Future TV dropped Iraq and Palestine from their coverage and focused on the assassination and its aftermath. As the sections that follow will illustrate, Future TV changed its agenda according to the political position of its owners. It was a pro-Syrian Arab nationalist station when Hariri was in government and changed its position when Hariri became a member of the opposition. It further changed its position after Hariri's assassination, completely dropping its coverage of the two most sacred pan-Arab causes. Future TV may claim to be commercial TV, but when it is tested it becomes obvious that it is a political station of Sunni persuasion.

Shiite TV Stations: Al-Manar and NBN

In 1991, Al-Manar emerged as a representative of the Shiites in the Lebanese media war. It is essentially the station of Hezbollah (Party of God), the Iran-supported Shiite movement that holds a number of elected seats in the Lebanese government but also appears on the U.S. terrorism list. Al-Manar aims to "preserve the Islamic values and to enhance the civilized role of the Arab and Islamic community." It claims to do so by presenting a combination of religious programming, international and local news, sports, politics, society, culture, and children's shows. In 1997, Al-Manar registered under the name of the "Lebanese Media Group Company," but Muhammad 'Afif Ahmad, the station's second general manager, asserted in an interview that Al-Manar has belonged to Hezbollah "culturally and politically" from its very establishment.[11] Hezbollah's authority over Al-Manar is demonstrated by the station's geographical location in the Shiite neighborhood of Harat Hurayk, south of Beirut, where it is surrounded by armed Hezbollah guards.

Because it produces most of its own content, Al-Manar is one of the most expensive channels operating in the Middle East. The majority of it funding comes directly from shareholders, who are leaders in the party. According to Nayef Krayem, Al-Manar's previous general manager and chairman of its board, Hezbollah and Al-Manar "breathe life into one another. Each provides the other with inspiration. Hezbollah uses Al-Manar to express its stands and its views, etc. Al-Manar in turn receives political support for its continuation."[12]

Many reports have estimated Iranian financial support to Hezbollah at somewhere between $100 and $200 million a year.[13] Some of this money goes directly to Al-Manar. The station received much of its original funding from Iran, and reports indicate that Iran still helps to finance it, although Al-Manar officials have said the station does not receive funds from any government because it would be against Lebanese law. Jorisch suggests that Al-Manar gets round the law by taking money from Hezbollah—in Lebanon—which in turn gets the funding from Iran.[14] Additional finance for the station comes from Shiite communities and other Arabs and Muslims who support Hezbollah's mission with the station. It has been said that large amounts of money have been deposited into Hezbollah's bank accounts by Muslim groups in Europe, Canada, and the United States.[15] Syria also backs Hezbollah and has played a political role at the station since its inception. According to Jorisch, Hezbollah sent a delegation to Damascus in an attempt to convince the then-president of Syria, Hafez al-Asad, to give them broadcasting permission, and on September 18, 1996, at the request of the Lebanese president, the cabinet decided to grant Al-Manar an operating license.[16]

Al-Manar is said to have inaugurated the approach of "reality television" to media programming in Lebanon. The phrase "reality television" was used by many journalists and media analysts to describe the style adopted by Lebanese opposition media outlets in their coverage of Hariri's assassination, as they all competed to convey to their viewer the situation on the ground. The concept was first introduced by Al-Manar when it offered its viewers video clips of Hezbollah members as they conducted operations against the Israeli army in southern Lebanon. Sawsan Al-Abtah, a prominent Lebanese writer and journalist, writes that over the years the station was able to use sharp vocabulary and candid images to achieve three goals: rallying support within Lebanon for Hezbollah's resistance against Israel (and by implication support for Hezbollah's legitimacy itself); providing moral support for the Palestinian resistance inside the territories; and demoralizing Israeli army personnel.[17] The last objective was often pursued through the airing of anti-Israeli ads in Hebrew, in addition to television programming presenting Israel in the role of the aggressor, and Hezbollah members as the heroes who sacrifice themselves for the sake of justice.[18] Hezbollah's relationship with Syriag helps it to work toward these objectives, and the Syrian presence in Lebanon has been essential to the success of the Shiite group. Hence, Al-Manar, through its connection with Hezbollah, is an open supporter of both Syria and its presence in Lebanon.

A more moderate Shiite media player in the Lebanese media war is NBN, privately owned by Nabih Berri, speaker of the Lebanese parliament and head of the Amal party, a moderate Shiite organization and Hezbollah's competitor in the Shiite community. "Amal" means "hope" in Arabic and is also an acronym for Afwaj al-Muqawama al-Lubnaniya—Lebanese Resistance Brigades. Unlike the Amal movement's founder, Iran-born Imam Musa Sadr, Berri is not a cleric. A lawyer, he was born in Sierra Leone, later studied in Beirut and then built his career in the United States. Bassem Sabba, former minister of information and also a Shia, played a key role in ensuring that NBN received a license. Berri's associates at NBN include the Shia former minister of economy, Yassin Jaber. The station's CEO is Nassir Saffieddin. Furthermore, according to *Forbes*, unconfirmed reports indicate that Issam Faris, an Orthodox Christian from north Lebanon who currently lives in the United States, used to own more than a third of NBN, but he later abandoned it because it turned out to be a financial burden.[19] According to *I Monthly*, Issue 5, November 2002, the major stakeholders in NBN were:

Ahmad Mohammed El-Safadi	6.24 percent
Samira Assi	7.18 percent
Amina Berri	6.18 percent
Ali Fran	7.5 percent
Ahmad Hussein	6.09 percent

Most of these shareholders are close affiliates of Berri or members of his family. Samira Assi, the sister of Nabih Berri's wife, made her fortune through a contract with Libyan leader Moammar Qadhafi that allowed her to print one million copies of Qadhafi's "Green Book."[20] She is a prominent member of the Lebanese Shiite community.

NBN generally supports the Syrian position and the current government in Lebanon. Berri believes that because of the presence of Syrian troops in the country and its aid to Lebanon, Lebanon's closest ally is Syria. The Amal party has had close ties with Damascus since the mid-1970s, but this relationship has grown stronger under Berri's leadership.[21] In February 1982, Berri announced that Amal's goals included "the definition of special military, security, economic and cultural relations between Lebanon and Syria."[22] Also, "In the late 1980s, Berri supported the efforts of Syria to oust the constitutional government headed by Interim Prime Minister Michel Aoun. Berri endorsed Syria against Aoun despite the strong support that Aoun enjoyed in the Shiite community."[23]

Lebanese Media Politics and the Assassination of Hariri

The discussion above has shown that the media environment in Lebanon is intrinsically linked to the fractious political situation in the country, whereby each station is owned and controlled by key individuals with their own political affiliations and specific agendas for the country. Programming is designed to promote the interests of these individuals, as we saw with the media coverage of the assassination of Rafiq Al-Hariri, where the opposition media challenged the Lebanese government and called for Syrian withdrawal from the country while the Shiite stations supported the Syrian government and maintained that Syria should stay in Lebanon. The connection between media ownership and programming content could not have been more visible.

For example, the fact that Hariri essentially owned Future TV explains the station's defiant position against Syria and pro-Syrian government in Lebanon, mainly after the assassination. One columnist, Fared Hashshan, railed against the government in Future's weekly publication.

> There is a consensus in the country that it is impossible to trust that the failed government will be capable of investigating (the assassination) and providing answers, because even if it is innocent of this act of terrorism, it bears full responsibility for what happened (the assassination)... The that Lebanese authorities had profited from Hariri's death. "For months these authorities have been inciting to assassinate Al-Hariri, and they benefit from his disappearance."[24]

Future TV became a platform for the anti-Syrian Lebanese opposition. It featured stories about the life of Hariri, interviews with leading figures of the Lebanese opposition such as Waleed Jumblatt, Waleed Iydu, and Marwan Hamada, who was the target of an assassination attempt months before Hariri's murder. The coverage always carried the slogan of "...li ajl Lebanon" ("...for Lebanon"), with various phrases such as "The truth" and "Freedom" and so on filling the blanks before "for Lebanon". Programs were littered with clips of Hariri's speeches and appearances. In fact, so many clips and speeches were played on Future TV on the 30th anniversary of the Lebanese civil war that people began joking that Hariri was still alive, and that it was his friend who had died in the blast (as the literal translation of "Rafiq Al-Hariri" in Arabic can be interpreted as "Hariri's friend"). Sawsan Al-Abtah writes:

> On the 30th anniversary of the beginning of the civil war, 59 days after his death, Hariri came back to life on television. Future TV played clips of him saying "do not believe all what your ears hear and believe what your eyes see, and leave the rest for your brain to process...using your brain is the way to knowing the truth that some are trying to hide." In other words, the man was not dead, but—thanks to Future Television—he was virtually walking in the middle of Beirut, celebrating with the Lebanese people the memory of the war. This was part of a unique tactic employed by the channel: after it had convinced the viewers that the death of Hariri was the death of Lebanon, it began telling the public that Hariri is alive, and therefore using the same logic, Lebanon is alive.[25]

Coverage on Future TV, as well as on fellow opposition station LBC, focused on opposition demonstrations, using zooming techniques to emphasize the large size of the crowds and supplementing images with dramatic commentaries in an anything but subtle manner. In one incident the anchor invited viewers to join the opposition demonstration: "Here we are waiting for you as you come from all around of Lebanon. Do not lose hope; here are your compatriots who arrived despite all the obstacles and hindrances. We are waiting for you. You will certainly find the way here."[26] In contrast, Future TV and LBC offered only limited coverage to pro-Syrian rallies.[27]

In the opposite sector of the media arena—and hence on the other side of the political spectrum—Al-Manar and NBN devoted only limited airtime to the "Lebanon Spring" demonstration of March 14, 2005, ignoring "the hours-long buildup and the human avalanche pouring in from around the country—and provid[ing] in-studio commentary and voice-overs on split screens to minimize the impact of the swelling numbers."[28] At the same time, the pro-Syrian stations embellished the Hezbollah-organized rally in Riad Al-Solh Square, reporting that 1.5 million people were present at the event. To reciprocate, Future TV argued that the pro-Syrian rally numbers "were beefed up by Syrians bussed in the night before—something Al-Manar denied."[29] Al-Manar, moreover, replayed Syrian president Bashar Al-Asad's speech of March 5;[30] a speech that was aired by LBC only on split screens, presenting his words along images of Lebanese crowds demanding immediate and full withdrawal.[31]

LBC followed the same approach as Future TV and freed itself from the self-censorship that had made its news programming in the past favor Syria and its supporters in Lebanon. Its coverage of the assassination tended to support the position of the opposition on behalf of the Maronite Christians. It did so by exaggerating the numbers involved in opposition protests and outwardly blaming Syria for the assassination.[32] Former minister for the economy, Marwan Hamadeh, was quoted on LBC TV as saying, "Responsibility for this ugly crime is known. It begins in Damascus and passes through the Lebanese presidential palace in Baabda, the Lebanese government and the Lebanese intelligence apparatus."[33]

The thrust of the opposition's coverage (i.e., that of Future and LBC) was that Syria and the Lebanese government were responsible for the assassination of Hariri. Thus, it was of no surprise that Future TV received threats from pro-Syrian forces in Lebanon. Pro-Syrian groups distributed pamphlets accusing what used to be an Arab nationalist channel of having becoming Zionist TV. Forty days after Hariri's assassination, in response to these threats, the chairman of the station, Dr. Nadeem Munla, appeared on Zahi Wahbi's show *Khaleek bil Bayt* or "Stay at Home," explaining the policy of his station and attempting to calm his Syrian critics, in particular Faiz Al-Saygh, the editor-in-chief of the Syrian regime's newspaper *Al-Thawra*. Wahbi got Mr. Saygh on the phone from Damascus to air the accusations about Future TV that he had published in his article in *al-Thawra* a week earlier. Al-Munla explained that the station would return to its earlier programming and champion pan-Arab causes again. He also discussed the accusation that Future had become the opposition television station. He said, "We invite the Muwalat (the pro-Syrian elements in the parliament and in government) and they do not want to appear on our shows." He also issued an invitation on the air to Hassan Nasrallah, the head of Hezbollah, to appear on Future TV.[34]

The change in programming and tone forty days after the assassination was a result of the Syrian withdrawal from Beirut, and pressure from other Arab states that were uncomfortable with American involvement in Lebanon. Furthermore, it came about as a result of fear. On the same program Al-Munla contemplated moving Future TV to Dubai if the threats continued. He reminded the audience that Future TV was hit by two rockets months before the Hariri's assassination. That was during the period when Hariri had become an opposition figure after he left the government. Many in Lebanon see this rocket attack as a precursor to Hariri's assassination.

Hariri's influence at *Al-Nahar* was also clear in the newspaper's coverage of his assassination. In blaming Syria for the crime, Ali Hamada wrote on February 15, 2005, "Just as they assassinated Kamal Jumblatt and threw him bleeding into the street in 1977, so they blew up half of the city and assassinated Rafiq Al-Hariri, turning his body into coal."[35] He added, "Rafiq Al-Hariri, who fell as a martyr for the sake of independence, is not the first in the series of crimes and perhaps is not the last; thus it is necessary that his blood not be spilled in vain, and that Lebanon not be captive from here on, in the hands of this kind of mafia behavior."[36]

In response to the anti-Syrian positions taken by LBC, Future TV, and *Al-Nahar*, the Shiite channels of NBN and Al-Manar have continued to take the position of Al-Muwala, those allied with Syria and the pro-Syrian Lebanese government. Programming on the two stations has oscillated between two elements: (1) a less than courageous defense of Syria; and (2) attempts to avoid giving complete coverage to the opposition.

Nabih Berri has used NBN to cast doubt on the legitimacy of accusations against Syria. He recently told journalists: "Revealing the circumstances of this crime is our number one priority, not just because it is a national duty but also because it calms people's spirits and stops false accusations being made."[37] As Hazim Al-Amin observed in a column in *Asharq Al-Awsat*, and as we have already seen, Al-Manar has also become a forum for supporting Syria's role in Lebanon.[38] The station has been used by Hezbollah to show how Syrians in Lebanon have been affected by Hariri's death. "I have information that 20 to 30 Syrian workers have been killed recently…This is a disgrace," Sheikh Hassan Nasrallah told Al-Manar.[39] He went on to describe how the workers were killed in Lebanon in anti-Syrian attacks following the assassination of the former prime minister. Al-Manar was also keen on providing almost instant analysis of anti-Syrian statements made by any politician, and "analysis" in this context is not really the sort of analysis one gets from Western news stations like CNN or the BBC. "Analysis" here means "subtle denial. In other words, the analytical approach allowed the channel to call into question the accusations against Syria. One of the major themes played on the station's programming was that the death of Hariri gave the Americans the opportunity to increase pressure on Syria to implement UN Security Council Resolution 1559. Additionally, the theory that the assassination of Hariri was part of an American–Zionist plot was often explored by Imad Marmal on *Hadith Al Sa'a* and Omar Nasef on *Madha Ba'd*. On one occasion, Marmal's comments that an international investigation of Hariri's death would constitute a violation of Lebanese sovereignty caused Bahya Al-Hariri to call in live on air asking the anchor to stay off this topic.[40] Such tactics were supplemented by attempts to downplay the strenght of anti-Syrian sentiment in Lebanon. An example was seen when NBN avoided covering the rally outside the parliament as Prime Minister Omar Karami announced his resignation inside the chamber.[41] As there was nothing but bad news for Syria inside Lebanon during this period, NBN and Al-Manar resorted to devoting an unusually large amount of programming to Israel–Palestine, Iraq, and Afghanistan, ironically, at a time when non-Lebanese stations were preoccupied with nothing but events in Lebanon.

In short, the Lebanese media arena is the site of political battles between the competing groups inside the country. The politico-ethnic loyalties of a media outlet constrain the content of its programming, especially its news coverage. This tendency could have not been more pronounced following the death of Hariri. Future TV, controlled by the Hariri family and the Tayar Al-Mustaqbal front, switched the content of its programming to become the leading opposition channel in the country, airing anti-Syrian accusations and rallies, in addition to glorifying Hariri's personality and legacy. As the Maronite community freed themselves of the constraints imposed by Syrian control, the Maronite-controlled LBC did the same. Similarly, programming on the pro-Syrian Shia stations NBN and Al-Manar mirrored the political discourse of Syrian loyalists.

Spillover of Qatari/Saudi Arabian Competition in the Lebanese Context

The regional spillover of the Qatar/Saudi Arabia rivalry also manifests itself on the Lebanese media scene. While Future TV, owned by the Hariri family, is allied with Saudi Arabia, Tahseen Khayet, the owner of New TV, is an ally of Qatar. The accusations and counter-accusations between Future TV and New TV before the assassination of Hariri replicated this Saudi/Qatari animosity, with a Lebanese tinge. Fittingly, Mr. Khayet lives in a fortress-like mansion befitting a multi-millionaire in a place outside Beirut called Doha. Lebanese often make wry remarks about which Doha he really lives in.

Future TV is also in competition with LBC, a rivalry between the Sunnis and the Maronites on one level, and the Islamists (Saudi) and the Arab nationalists on another. The rivalry was also between Mr. Hariri and Mr. Pierre El-Daher, the owner of LBC. While Future TV adopted a pan-Arab, anti-American discourse before the assassination of Hariri, LBC adopted a more pro-American stance. Future TV accused LBC of doing this to gratify the Americans because LBC was given the contract by the Pentagon to construct an Iraqi TV station call Al-Iraqiya. It was Arab nationalist Sunnis vs. Westernized pro-American Maronites. LBC was accused of corrupting the Lebanese and Arab youth by broadcasting shows such as *Ms. Lebanon*, in which TV cameras were turned on scantily clad young women twenty-four hours a day. This show, which involved audience voting with text messaging, generated a lot of money for the station, but it also generated an Islamic fatwa from Saudi Arabia against LBC. The substance of the accusations was that LBC was being anti-Arab, for entering into a contractual relationship with the Pentagon to build the Iraqi station, and anti-Islamic for showing semi-naked women on screen. LBC adopted a dual strategy to minimise the effect of these accusations. It entered into a partnership with the *Al-Hayat* newspaper, owned by Prince Khaled bin Sultan, to secure Saudi political cover against the accusation that it was anti-Islamic. Although the news part of LBC did not generate any money, its viability as a political cover warranted the expense. To stop the station being labeled anti-Arab, its controllers resorted to Arab nationalist rhetoric. Anti-Americanism is a very integral part of this discourse and was a way for LBC to distance itself from the rumors that it was influenced by the Pentagon or the U.S. administration.

Clearly, the Lebanese media are inherently political and play an influential role in the intra-state conflicts of the country. And as the news coverage of the assassination of Rafiq Al-Hariri makes clear, the media have become the primary vehicle for political players to battle among themselves and rally public support for their positions. Lebanese media may be privately owned, but that has not resulted in an atmosphere of editorial freedom or objective journalism. On the contrary, the Lebanese media are scarcely different from the government-owned media found in other parts of the Middle East.

Connections Between Television and Other Media

Al-Nahar newspaper, established in 1933, represents the Greek Orthodox opposition voice in Lebanon that for decades has publicly denounced Syria's presence in the country. In 1999, Jibran Tueini succeeded his father as managing editor and chairman of the board at the newspaper. Tueini spent three years exiled in France for the outspoken role he played in the multi-sectarian, populist movement that backed Prime Minister Michel Aoun's 1989–1900 attempt to expel Syrian military forces from Lebanon. His *Al-Nahar* editorials and "open letters" to President Hafez Al-Asad have also sparked heated controversy among the Lebanese political elite.

Tueini's political career began with his appointment as general secretary of the Lebanese Front (1990). He was also a founding member of the "Movement de Soutien à la Liberation," established to support former prime minister General Michel Aoun (1989). Tueini is currently a member of the moderate center-right, Christian Qornet Shehwan political grouping, which is close to Patriarch Sfeir and advocates dialogue as a prelude to the accurate implementation of the Taif Agreement, specifically the provisions that relate to the redeployment of Syrian troops.

More recently, Tueini has focused on uniting the Lebanese against the Syrians. Tueini was later assassinated, but before the assassination, an Associated Press (AP) article quoted him saying:

> Those who are saying that [the bond will break] are being brainwashed by the Syrians and the [Lebanese] regime who want to find a pretext to bring the Syrians back into the country by claiming we cannot sit together around the same table...The plurality of the opposition is very important, and we want to keep it this way...We want to restore democracy so we can compete the way people do in other countries.[42]

Following Hariri's death, the former prime minister's shares in the paper were bought by Prince Al-Waleed bin Talal, who had already purchased 10 percent of the shares in May 2002.[43] This Saudi purchase has further extended Saudi Arabia's already tremendous leverage over the Lebanese press on behalf of the Sunnis. A recent article in *Asharq Al-Awsat* suggested that *Al-Nahar* has reclaimed its position as the voice of the opposition in Lebanon.[44]

CHAPTER 4

ARAB JOURNALISTS AS TRANSNATIONAL ACTORS

The previous chapters examined why the Arab media covers events in the way that it does. For example, Chapter 2 showed that the political differences between the governments of Qatar and Saudi Arabia drive the coverage of Saudi affairs on Al-Jazeera and Qatari affairs on Al-Arabiya. This is a direct result of the impact of ownership on the content of Arab media. In short, conflict between Qatar and Saudi Arabia manifests itself through the media war between Al-Jazeera and Al-Arabiya. While the Gulf media show the impact of government on coverage, the Lebanese media reveal the impact of confessional and ethnic groups on the media outlet(s) they control. Future TV, a Hariri family enterprise, is but one of many examples of ethnicity-driven media. Analyzing media coverage in the first forty days following the assassination of the former Lebanese prime minister, I found that Future TV took on an active political role that mirrored the loyalty of the channel to its main owners. Other media outlets like LBC and NBN took a political stance reflective of that of their respective owners and the confessional groups they represent. As we turn our attention to other salient features in Arab media news coverage, such as anti-Americanism, anti-Semitism, and the focus on Iraq and Palestine, we find that the variables we have discussed thus far—states, ethnic groups, funding, and ownership—are not enough to explain the totality of these phenomena. Thus, for the picture to be complete, other variables must be taken into consideration. In this chapter, I will examine the role of the journalists themselves in shaping media coverage of particular stories. Where do those journalists come from? How do their backgrounds affect their understanding of the issues they report? And what is the manner in which they discuss these issues on the screen or on paper? The role of journalists and TV producers in shaping what Arabs see or read cannot be ignored.

To begin with, Arab journalists who dominate pan-Arab media are mostly nationals of a few specific countries and their backgrounds affect the way they report issues. Currently, most Arab journalists come from four countries: Egypt, Sudan, Palestine, and Lebanon. It is no coincidence that these are the same countries that provide the bulk of expatriate labor in the

Gulf region, particularly in the educational sector and the service industries. The media can be seen as another service sector dominated by expatriate workers. It is part of the general pattern of movement of people, labor, and ideas, in that part of the world.

Along with the centrifugal direction of this trend, globalization has contributed to greater movement of people. Many workers left populous poor countries like Egypt, Sudan, and Morocco for work in the oil-rich Gulf states. Others left for Europe and the United States. Journalists are part of this pattern. The rules governing the relationship between the worker and their sponsor or Kafil in the Gulf states also apply to journalists. Arab media is part and parcel of Arab life and the practices of journalists and the way they are hired are not different from other social practices in a system based primarily on patronage. In the media context, the owner of the outlet is essentially the Kafil who provides the expatriate journalists working under him with a forum through which they can pursue their own agenda as long it does not conflict with the larger agendas of the Kafil. In the case of the media, the Kafil is usually a government member or a proxy for the government or the ruling family. The role of the media Kafils has been explained in detail in previous chapters. What has not been explained is the role of his workers who decide program content on a host of social and political issues.

Arab immigration to Europe, especially from North African countries to France and Britain, is both visible and significant in the host countries. Some of these immigrants are journalists. The civil war in Algeria during the 1990s drove many secular Algerian journalists away, for they were prime targets of Islamists.[1] Some of these journalists were the best in the business. Many of them went to work for the French press, others for the Arab press in Paris or London. Those who went to Europe acquired citizenship of European countries. Some worked for organizations like *Al-Hayat*, *Asharq Al-Awsat* and Al-Jazeera. Others worked for Arabic services of the BBC, Radio Monte Carlo, and more recently Al-Hurra and Sawa. Though they escaped the arbitrary local Kafil system, they are still part of this patron–client relationship.

The way Arab journalists inhabit media space is very similar to the way they inhabit physical space. Journalists nested in media islands like Al-Jazeera, Al-Arabiya, *Asharq Al-Awsat*, and *Al-Hayat*, is in a way similar to how every Arab nationality clusters in specific neighborhoods in Paris and London. For example, Sudanese tend to gravitate toward *Asharq Al-Awsat* newspaper, while Lebanese go to *Al-Hayat*. Palestinians tend to be more present in Al-Jazeera, while Egyptians are more visible in Al-Arabiya. In fact, as the Washington bureau chief of *Al-Hayat* told me that there is a tacit understanding within the Maronite community that runs the paper that Egyptians are not welcome to work there. With the exception of the Cairo correspondent, *Al-Hayat* has no Egyptian editors or correspondents.[2] The experience, the hopes, and fears of these journalists determine the way they narrate a story to their audience. Thus, it is fair to ask whether the place of origin and the ideology of these diaspora journalists and producers affects the editorial choices they make, as well as the narration of the stories they put on air. To investigate this point, I look at how the Arab media covered political violence in the Palestinian occupied territories, Islamist violence in Algeria and Egypt in the 1990s, post-Hariri civil unrest in Lebanon, and the coverage of the killing in Darfur, Sudan.

It is almost impossible to pick up an Arab newspaper or tune in to any Arab radio or television station without hearing a news item or a talk show about Palestine. The issue grabs the attention of Arab audiences. The coverage of Palestine ranges from plain reporting about developments in the territories or Israel proper to violent clashes between Palestinians and Israeli soldiers, and statements made by Israeli or Palestinian officials, or those made by Arab officials. The latter are usually expressions of a continued commitment to resolving the conflict and aiding the Palestinian side. Hamas and Islamic Jihad statements get more air play on Arab television, especially in Al-Jazeera, than statements made by Mahmoud Abbas or any other Arab leaders. Al-Arabiya and Al-Jazeera introduced to Arab television the concept of documentaries examining the harsh conditions under which Palestinians are forced to live. The nature of coverage may vary from one news outlet to the other, but the issue remains central at all times for almost every television channel, newspaper, and radio station.

In addition to Palestine, Iraq has emerged as the second pan-Arab issue that occupies a central position on Arab media screens. Although the story in the Western media is about Iraq's liberation from the dictatorial regime of Saddam Hussein, the narrative of Arab Diaspora journalists has focused on the American occupation of Iraq. They have created a symmetry between the American occupation of Iraq and the Israeli occupation of Palestinian territories, and in many cases, the images on the screen and the words chosen for moqawama (resistance) or shahid (martyr) are interchangeable. Many people whom I interviewed in Cairo, Kuwait, and Riyadh claimed if you mute your television you cannot tell with certainty whether what you are watching on the screen is Iraq or Palestine or whether the soldier entering a home is American or Israeli.

Why Palestine and Iraq?

What explains the obsessive focus of the Arab media on issues like Palestine and Iraq? The easy answer that Arab media executives give to Western analysts and diplomats is: audience preference. This would be an accurate answer if Arab media outlets were fully commercial enterprises, motivated by the principle that the larger the audience, the greater the profits to be made from advertising. Under this logic, ratings would drive program content, which would consequently focus on issues like Palestine and Iraq, which are thought of as causes that bind the Arabs from Rabat to Muscat. Yet my analysis shows that this motivation cannot be the main factor shaping the coverage. This is because, as we saw earlier, the gap between advertising revenue and operating costs of Arab media reaches $13.5 billion every year. Such a gap forces us to ask the question: If the Kafils really cares about profits, why do they continue to operate a financially burdensome project? When such huge losses are tolerated, advertising revenues are not useful clues to what shapes Arab media content.

What covers this deficit is advertising of a different sort, namely political advertising, which seems to generate greater profits than advertising as we know it. We regularly see political advertisements on news reports, as the Arab news media treat us on a daily basis to what a particular king, president or emir did or did not do at any given moment. This is why the emir of Qatar, for example, subsidizes Al-Jazeera with $60 million annually to cover its costs.[3] Thus the dominance of Palestine and Iraq cannot be exclusively examined through the prism of audience and ratings alone.

Palestine and Iraq dominate coverage for a variety reasons. For one, these stories are safe stories that allow journalists to show their talent for vilifying the occupying force in eloquent Arabic with very little political cost. Furthermore, as I stated in the introduction, the Arab media is free under occupation. That is, the Israelis and the Americans allow the Arab media to report freely or at least with greater freedom than the journalists would enjoy if they were to report about Arab governments. It is easier for Al-Jazeera to cover what is taking place in Gaza than it is for it to cover the Kurdish riots in Qameshli in Syria. Thirdly, many Arab journalists have the protection of democratic Western states by virtue of their citizenship of the United States, European countries, or even Israel in case of Palestinian reporters reporting for Al-Jazeera from the West Bank. Fourthly, coverage of these issues gives these journalists instant stardom among their audiences. It also helps them avoid covering pressing and yet politically risky internal Arab issues.

In this environment, journalists avoid stories with high political risks that anger those who financially underwrite their media organization. Thus stories of no or little political risk are taken on: stories like the U.S. occupation of Iraq or Israeli actions in occupied territories. Any Arab journalist who spends 15 or 20 minutes on the air blasting America or Israel is not likely to be met with anger from the audience or government. Rather he knows that he will be praised by both. Arab journalists who try to provide any thought-provoking analysis of U.S. or Israeli policies end up paying the price either in the form of punishments from their sponsoring state(s) or in the form of lost subsidies to their station or newspaper from their financers.

Palestinian journalists covering Palestinian stories display an emotional closeness to their own people. They tend to know all the minute details about the networks connecting political factions, leaders, and ideological movements. And being on the screen provide these journalists with something akin to a leadership role. Palestinian journalists appearing on Al-Arabiya and Al-Jazeera are looked upon, and in some cases perceive themselves, as stars in their own communities. This star status cannot be preserved unless they color their stories with passionate statements about the "cause" and tough remarks about the enemy and the support it receives from the United States. If they criticize, if not actually curse, Israel and the United States, they gain the admiration of audiences among Palestinians and Arabs worldwide. One has to watch the rhetoric of Palestinians like Sami Haddad, Jamal Rayyan, and Abdul Bari Atwan on Al-Jazeera to have a sense of this passionate anti-American, anti-Israeli rhetoric. If their cost-free tirades against Israel and the United States were substituted by criticism of any Arab regime, the political cost would be certainly high. Palestinian journalists are not alone in shaping this trend. While Palestinians provide anti-Israeli and anti-American drives on Al-Jazeera, anti-Syrian rhetoric is provided by the Lebanese journalists manning Al-Arabiya and other Lebanese stations.

Journalists will also address themselves to the supporters of political and religious ideologies as well as to national communities, as in the case of Islamist journalists. The rise of Islamism and Islamic movements as non-state actors in the Middle East was accompanied by the rise of the Islamic media, especially satellite channels such as the Saudi Iqra and Al-Majd, Islamic media research centers, and Islamic journalists and writers. As Islamist forces failed to capture the apparatus of the state in their own countries, whether through political organization or violence, they began directing their efforts toward hijacking Arab media outlets. In doing so, they followed a three-tier strategy. They inserted Islamic journalists in almost every Arab media outlet to narrate stories from their Islamic perspective; they created research centers and cultivated experts that provide tame journalists with information about Islamic causes. They also have their own columnists, frequent op-ed contributors and guests available for media appearances and writing in the Arab press.

While some Islamists thrust themselves into the journalistic community as practicing journalists, others presented themselves as talk-show hosts or columnists. Unfortunately, Western journalists often seem poorly informed about the relationship between some of these Islamist journalists and Islamic organizations. There is the famous case of Tayseer Alouni, member of the Syrian Muslim Brotherhood and Al-Jazeera reporter, who stayed in Afghanistan after the end of Taliban rule. Alouni was recently arrested in Spain and charged with being a collaborator with Al-Qaeda.

He was found guilty and sentenced to seven years in prison.[4] During America's war on the Taliban regime, Alouni was interviewed on CNN by none other than Paula Zahn on a morning show, and was treated as the war correspondent who stayed behind after the collapse of the Taliban. What Zahn did not know was that Alouni was able to stay in Afghanistan only due to his special connections with the Taliban and with Al-Qaeda. Zahn also failed to recognize that she was being fed Taliban and Al-Qaeda propaganda through this "war correspondent." Zahn is not alone. A similar situation occurred after the 7/7 bombing in London when MSNBC's Tucker Carlson hosted "Islamic scholar" Azzam Al-Tamimi to comment on the attack. Carlson did not know that Mr. Tamimi was the spokesperson of Hamas in London.[5] These examples illustrate how Islamist journalists have been successful in not only hijacking Arab media stations, but also in fooling Western journalists into thinking that they are dealing with fellow journalists and not political activists and agents of suspect organizations.

There are numerous examples of how Islamists were able to gain a platform in the Arab media by presenting themselves as talk-show hosts, commentators, and columnists. Members of the Egyptian Muslim Brotherhood have presented themselves as talk-show hosts, for instance Ahmed Mansour, while others such as Essam Al-Eryan and Abdul Mondeim Abu Al-Fotuh have posed as regular commentators. A commentator who frequently appears on Al-Arabiya and Al-Jazeera, as well as on Lebanese TV is Montasser Al-Zayat, the lawyer of Egypt's Islamic Group, which was responsible for the Luxor massacre of 1997. Notwithstanding his affiliation, Al-Zayat is presented to the Arab audience as a dispassionate, objective commentator. We also find many Arab writers, such as the Egyptian Fahmy Howeidi, who describe themselves as Katib Islami, or Islamic writers. Howeidi is a columnist for *Al-Ahram* and *Asharq Al-Awsat*, and a syndicated columnist known throughout the Arab world. Although Howeidi's prominence inside the Muslim Brotherhood is similar to that of Sheikh Yousef Al-Qaradawi, the Arab media have given him the image of an Arab Tom Friedman. We can analyze Howeidi's articles in *Asharq Al-Awsat* in terms of their treatment of three areas: anti-Americanism, Palestinian issues, and the promotion of Islamist thought.[6] Sheikh Al-Qaradawi, an influential voice inside the Egyptian Muslim Brotherhood and a naturalized Qatari, is a regular guest on the Al-Jazeera show *Al-Shari'a Wal-Hayat*. At its inception the show was hosted by another member of the Egyptian Muslim Brotherhood, Ahmed Mansour. Mansour was later assigned to lead other shows on Al-Jazeera: *Bila Hudoud* ("Without Borders") and *Shahid Ala Al' Asr* ("Witness to History"). Another figure who hosted *Al-Shari'a Wal Hayat* was the late Maher Abdullah, a member of the Palestinian Muslim Brotherhood. Now the show is hosted by Khadija bin Qinnah, a recently Islamized Algerian. This pattern shows that even when an Islamist leaves a talk-show, he makes sure that his successor is another Islamist with the same ideological commitment, if not a member of the same Islamist group. There are also Islamic talk-show hosts who resemble American evangelists like Pat Robinson and Jerry Falwell. One such host is the young Egyptian preacher Amre Khaled, who appears on all ART channels.

Another element of the Islamist strategy to shape media coverage in the Arab world is "Islamic research centers," and their affiliated experts. One example is the Al-Maqrizi Center for Historical Studies, a London-based institution founded and directed by the Egyptian leader of an Islamic group Hani al-Siba'i, which specializes in providing Arab media with ready-for-publication stories and arranges for journalists to interview jailed Islamists in Egypt, London, or Pakistan. Al-Siba'i and his center serve as a liaison between Western and Arab media and Islamists from Morocco to Pakistan. Looking at most stories about Islamists in the biggest two pan-Arab newspapers, *Al-Hayat* and *Asharq Al-Awsat*, one cannot help but notice that both Mohamed Salah of *Al-Hayat* and Mohamed Al-Shaf'i of *Asharq Al-Awsat* relay heavily in their reporting on this center and its experts like Montasser Al-Zayat and Al-Siba'i himself.

Another such organization is that of Jamal Sultan and Mohamed Mitwaly; the Egyptian International Center for Studies and Research. The center provides Islamist writers with ready-made columns for them to sign and publish. It prepares articles for Islamist writers like Mr. Abdul Razzaq Al-Shaijy and often provides misleading information about the activities of Al-Qaeda and other Islamist groups.[7]

In London, there is the Institute for Islamic Political Thought, which is run by Azzam Al-Tamimi, the Hamas spokesperson in London. Sitting on the supervisory board are Hamas member Basheer Nafi, Mohamed Selim Al-Awa (Egyptian Muslim Brotherhood), and Abdelwahab El-Affendi (Sudanese journalists). The Institute's board of advisors includes visible Islamist figures such as Yousef Al-Qaradawi. Like many such Islamic centers, the Institute serves as a public relations machine for Hamas and affiliated Islamic organizations.

Another center that employs media-based strategies to promote Islamist causes is the World and Islam Studies Enterprise (WISE), based in Tampa, Florida. The organization was shut down after a federal investigation linked its founder Sami El-Eryan to the Palestinian Islamic Jihad group, which is on the U.S.'s list of terrorist groups. Prior to the shutdown, WISE published a journal titled *Qara'at Siyasiya* (Political Readings) in which various Islamist figures presented their views and perspectives. The journal was edited by Ramadan Abdullah Shallah, secretary-general of the Palestinian branch of Islamic Jihad.

With the advent of satellite media not directly owned by governments, Islamists have finally made their way in to the media arena after years of exile from state-owned media outlets. Al-Jazeera is a quintessential example of this phenomenon: The station has given members and supporters of the Muslim Brotherhood airtime. As I explained in Chapter 2, in order for Qatar to bolster its Islamic credentials against the two biggest Islamic states in the region, Iran and Saudi Arabia, Muslim Brothers were used as willing pawns in the interstate media war. Qatar is using the Muslim Brotherhood and various Islamist forces to counterbalance Saudi power just as Saudi Arabia used them in the 1960s and early 1970s to combat Nasser and his brand of Arab nationalism. Other transnational Islamists and even terrorists like Osama Bin Laden have found an opportunity to deliver their anti-Saudi and anti-Western statements on television to a broad range of audiences. This was unthinkable when media outlets were entirely local and state-owned.

Who Is Behind Anti-Americanism?

There are various factors shaping anti-Americanism that we need to comprehend in order to understand the phenomenon. The first is the residue of Soviet propaganda adopted by Arab nationalist regimes like that of Nasser. Throughout the 1960s and 1970s Nasser and his radio station Sawt Al-Arab filled the airwaves with anti-American and anti-colonial rhetoric. Arab journalists dug out the discourse that their predecessors were using against the British and the French and directed it toward the Americans. Pro-Soviet propaganda of the Cold War and the colonial legacy underpin the anti-Americanism of today.

Other factors relate to the local regimes and local movements and their view of U.S. policies. Another has to do with the U.S. democratization initiative. It is an easy strategy for some of the authoritarian Arab regimes to use anti-U.S. rhetoric to deflect criticism from their own failed policies and blame them on the outside world, namely the imperialist West and Zionist conspiracies. Anti-Americanism also stems from the consequences of American policies in the region and the kind of enemies they create. Here I do not mean America's policy toward the Arab–Israeli conflict, though this is a contributing factor. The particular brand of anti-Americanism we see today is a result of actions by the American administration that earned the animosity of Arab nationalists, the radical Islamists, and the ruling elite all at the same time. By attacking Iraq and undermining the Ba'th regime of Saddam Hussein, Americans angered the Arab nationalists. By attacking the Taliban and Bin Laden, the administration angered the Islamists. By adopting reform as the only way to change the political environment in the Middle East, the United States angers the ruling elite. Thus, America is hated by the Islamists, Arab nationalists, and regimes at the same time. Who is left to support the United States? Only genuine liberals who care about reforming their societies. But these are the people the U.S. administration does not talk to. They are not cheerleaders for America but potential allies who seek to reform the Middle East and transform it into a democratic or at least semi-democratic region. When we think about addressing the issue of anti-Americanism in the Middle East, we must be fully cognizant of these factors and have the ability to disentangle them instead of lumping them together.

Anti-Americanism in the Arab media can partly be traced to the rise of transnational journalism and ideological pockets inside media outlets. Although the governments and political groups that own media outlets like Al-Arabiya and Al-Jazeera are all allies of the United States, the people who operate these outlets are interested in stories that carry an anti-American rhetoric: American occupation of Iraq, the "U.S.-backed" Israeli occupation of Palestinian territories, along with the discourses of angry Islamist groups. These issues are easy stories that require no qualifications and little research. If one compares the Arab media's coverage of political issues with its coverage of economic ones, the lack of training among Arab journalists becomes obvious. Economic journalism in the Arab world is almost nonexistent.

Anti-Americanism and anti-Israeli stories, despite the controversy they stir in Western societies, are considered as "safe" issues that journalists or analysts can talk about. Put simply, the political cost of anti-Americanism is nil from the perspective of an Arab journalist. Being critical of American policy and U.S. support, unlike criticizing the regime that owns the station, will not incur any personal costs for the anchor or journalists. On the other hand, criticizing local forces, whether local regimes or Islamist groups, means in many cases losing one's life. Thus most producers opt for covering safe issues like anti-occupation and other anti-American issues that turn them into heroes in the eyes of their audience.

Ironically, most journalists and TV talk-show hosts who produce anti-American and anti-Western propaganda are nationals of Western nations. Many of them hold citizenship of one or more Western nation along with their original Arab nationality. Faisal Al-Qasim and Sami Haddad of Al-Jazeera are both British nationals. Also from Al-Jazeera, the Washington-based talk-show host Hafiz Al-Mirazi is a naturalized U.S. citizen. His colleague, the famous anchorwoman Iman Ayad (before 2005 she went by the name of Iman Banoura) is also an American citizen. Many of the Tunisian and Algerian journalists working for pan-Arab media outlets hold French citizenship. The two London-based Arab newspapers, *Asharq Al-Awsat* and *Al-Hayat*, employ a host of British Arabs. So the anti-Western element we find in their reporting is not the result of their "misunderstanding" of Western culture, as many have argued. Rather, it is derived from their proximity to Western society. A classic example of an extreme case of this phenomenon is that of Sayyid Qutb, the second founder of the Muslim Brotherhood, and the source of a great deal of spiritual guidance for contemporary violent Islamist movements. Many have argued that Qutb's experience in the United States during the late 1940s were instrumental in the formulation of his anti-Western feelings.[8] In the modern context, Arab journalists living on the borderline between the Arab world and the West have reacted to their experience in the West by turning against it, albeit much more moderately than Qutb. These Arab journalists live in Western societies, but as marginalized members, and hence, their attitude toward the Western world, particularly their country of residence, becomes negative if not hostile. Therefore, their commentaries oscillate like a pendulum: one minute they will talk about the failures of the Arab world and the shortcomings of its governments, the next, they will criticize the West for what they view as imperialistic and arrogant policies. One advantage they have over local journalists is the legal protection provided to them by their adopted Western countries. The American, British, and French passports they hold allows them to express loudly their grievances against the West, while enjoying the legal protection of free-speech codes enshrined in the constitutions of the countries they criticize.

In the following sections, I will detail the impact of specific groups of journalists on Arab media coverage. I begin with the implications of the national origin of journalists: principally Lebanese, Sudanese, Palestinian, and Egyptian. I follow this with a discussion of the impact of the ideological leanings of journalists to show how they affect the programming content of the Arab media.

Lebanon

The growth of Lebanese journalist diasporas can be attributed to two important developments that occurred in the 1970s. The first is the Lebanese civil war in 1975 and the subsequent migration of Lebanese journalists to Europe, and the second is the soaring of oil revenues in the Gulf region earlier that same decade, particularly in Saudi Arabia. The interplay between these events created an alliance between wealth and manpower; one that remains alive and well, as the screens of Al-Arabiya and the pages of *Asharq Al-Awsat* demonstrate. Put differently, "the imposing presence of Arab and especially Lebanese journalists in Europe has facilitated the alliance between Lebanese journalists and the Saudi emirs who came to control much of the media."[9] Given that most Saudi-funded media enterprises, like *Asharq Al-Awsat*, *Al-Hayat*, and MBC were based in Europe, the Lebanese–Saudi alliance took the form of a marriage of convenience. Yet even after pan-Arab media outlets such as MBC relocated to the Middle East and new media outlets like Al-Arabiya were launched with head-quarters in the Arab world, the alliance remained intact. On Saudi-backed Al-Arabiya we find a strong Lebanese presence, including Ellie Nakozy, Gisele Khoury, Gisele Abu Joudah, Hisham Mehlem, and Mohamed Noun. *Asharq Al-Awsat*'s editorial team and list of columnists features several prominent Lebanese names such as Iyad Abu-Shaqra, Samir Atallah, Houad Matar, Sawsan Al-Abtah, Hoda Al-Husseiny, and Diana Moglad. A similar pattern is observed at *Al-Hayat* where the editor-in-chief, his deputy, and two out of three managing editors are all Lebanese.[10] This is certainly a reflection of a broader pattern inside pan-Arab media outlets, where Lebanese journalists have been able to secure a strong representation in influential positions, whether as writers, anchors, producers, or managers.

Regardless of the roots of this phenomenon, the significant Lebanese presence inside the Arab media is a reality that must not be ignored when we analyze the coverage of issues that relate to the ideologies and back-grounds of those journalists. Let us take for instance Al-Arabiya's coverage of the assassination of Rafiq Al-Hariri in February, 2005. Veteran Lebanese journalist Sanaa Al-Jacques observes, "Al-Arabiya proved its Lebanese identity with great professionalism," covering the assassination and its aftermath in a manner similar to that of opposition channels like LBC and Future TV, leaving little doubt in the minds of viewers that Syria was guilty of the crime. "Under the heading of 'Stories-related to Lebanon' Al-Arabiya displayed some drama-stirring headlines: America withdraws its ambassador from Syria in light of Hariri's assassination; Hariri's assassina-tion and a dramatic impact on the Lebanese economy; Paris demands an international investigation to reveal the truth behind Hariri's assassination; Al-Jamil: Syria is guilty." All this was accompanied by little coverage of the statements and activities of the pro-Syrian Lebanese government.[11] Meanwhile, Al-Arabiya gave a considerable amount of airtime to opposi-tion voices, such as Bah Al-Hariri, the sister of the late Lebanese prime minister.

The Lebanese-style coverage is even more noticeable, when we compare Al-Arabiya's programming on post-Hariri Lebanon to that of Al-Jazeera, where fewer Lebanese presenters work.[12] Al-Jazeera, adher-ing to its traditional pan-Arab and anti-Western stances, provided cover-age that was more supportive of Syria and its loyalists. The best example of this was its repeated airing of "a seemingly fabricated tape by a self-styled Islamist who claimed responsibility for Al-Hariri's death,"[13] which rather suggested that some one was trying to keep the heat off the Syrian regime.

Could it be that the high proportion of Lebanese among the influential staff of Al-Arabiya compared to that of Al-Jazeera was a decisive factor in determining the respective slants of the stations in their coverage of this event?

A case could be made for a link between the Hariri family's ownership of shares in Al-Arabiya and the station's coverage of the assassination, but the picture remains incomplete unless we examine carefully the background of the journalists involved and how it affected their interpretation of the issues. The Saudi–Qatari rivalry, or the rivalry of the owners of the stations, may explain a great deal about Al-Jazeera and Al-Arabiya's coverage of Saudi and Qatari politics, but leaves us with little explanation for the position the channels took on issues that are not directly related to the interstate/inter-owner conflict.

As much as Al-Arabiya's programming was influenced by the politics and ideologies of its employees in this episode, Al-Jazeera's coverage was similarly derived from the distinct set of ideologies and values defined by the background of its journalists. So what values and ideologies were at play when Al-Jazeera refused to take an anti-Syrian line in its coverage?

Pan-Arabism

Recently in late 2006, President Asad visited Qatar to solicit Qatar's help in facilitating a dialogue between Syria and the United States. Syria and Qatar also worked together in Lebanon to counterbalance the Saudi dominance of Lebanese politics through Rafiq al-Hariri. In addition to the recent emergence of this special relationship between Qatar and Syria, the ideology and origin of journalists has also played a role.

Then there is Al-Jazeera's pan-Arab identity; one that is not so much attributable to the financers of the channel (or the Kafil) as to the journalists working for the station. Hence, understanding the channel's recruitment policies in comparison with that of outlets like Al-Arabiya is important. The organizational culture of Al-Jazeera, which makes its employees regard themselves primarily as Arabs working for an Arab station, elevates the importance of Arab nationalism. Thus, we find a strong Arab nationalist rhetoric in the content of programming. Take for instance the example of Faisal Al-Kasim, a Syrian journalist who hosts the famous show *Al Ittijah Al-Mo'akes*, or the "Opposite Direction." The show often features advocates of Arab nationalist causes, and "slogans referring to the Arab nation or Arab solidarity are often invoked, and images that suggest the nationalists' struggle against colonialism or Zionism are frequently evoked."[14] Comparing Al-Jazeera to the Nasser-backed Sawt Al-Arab, Al-Kasim himself wrote, "If anything satellite talk-shows have brought the Arab masses together and given them a pan-Arab identity. In other words, to a certain extent they have played a nationalist role by narrowing and sometimes bridging divides. In fact, one might argue that popular talk-shows on Al-Jazeera and other channels have succeeded where Gamal Abdul Nasser failed. Debate programs and live talks on satellite broadcasting are watched avidly by millions of Arabs and are contributing a great deal to the formation of pan-Arab public opinion over many issues."[15]

In the context of Hariri's assassination, the pan-Arabist ideology of Al-Kasim's description of shows like the one he hosts was illustrated by a reluctance to oppose a country that calls itself Arabism's beating heart.

Where would Arab nationalism stand, the logic goes, if Al-Jazeera behaved like a Maronite station and began to question whether Syria was involved in Hariri's assassination? Al-Jazeera was the first to report the Abu Addas story, where a Palestinian from the refugee camps claimed responsibility for Hariri's assassination. This was Al-Jazeera's way of absolving Syria from any responsibility.

Qatar's own geo-strategic considerations are important, but the picture is not complete unless we consider the role of the journalists themselves. Their Arab nationalist discourse serves as a divertion from American pressure in Qatar. This is why talk-show hosts like Al-Kasim were able to find a friendly base of operations in Al-Jazeera.

Sudan

Sudanese journalists have maintained a strong presence inside pan-Arab media outlets. Sudan is known for the protracted conflict between the Islamic government in Khartoum and the rebellious and non-Muslim south. The civil war led to an economic collapse that pushed many Sudanese to seek job opportunities elsewhere in the Arab world. We find a considerable community of Sudanese journalists working for *Asharq Al-Awsat* and for Al-Jazeera. Qassem Ja'far, a board member of Al-Jazeera, indicates that the channel is host to many Sudanese nationals, who constitute a remarkable portion of the station's employees.[16] Although figures are not precise, he claimed that Sudanese represent at least 25 percent of Al-Jazeera's manpower, including writers, bookers, and producers. One has to point only to teh Islamist Nizar Daw Al-Naeem who produces several programs at Al-Jazeera.

Sudanese diaspora journalists are mostly Arabs and Muslims. Their ability to speak and write in Arabic qualifies them to work for the various Arab media outlets. The Sudanese journalistic community displays two broad ideological trends. Some of them are Arab nationalists who are obsessed with the Arab character of the Sudanese nation. For them, the non-Arab southerners must learn Arabic and become more integrated and accept the Arab character of the Sudanese state. The other trend is Islamist. For this group, Sudan is an Islamic state and the southern animists and Christians are but a small minority that should accept Islamic law as the law of the land. Thus, for both these factions, the story of the southerners is not worth narrating. Although these journalists might oppose the government of Omar Al-Bashir in Khartoum, their Islamic and Arab sentiments make them for the most part indifferent toward the plight of the southerners.

Sudanese diaspora journalists are representative of Sudanese society. Most of them come from northern Sudan, where Arabic speakers are more abundant than in the south where people speak either English or local dialects. This ethnic imbalance inside media outlets leads to skewed coverage of Sudanese politics, as illustrated by the coverage of the recent Darfur crisis. The reporting of these Arabic-speaking, mostly northern journalists is less critical of the Sudanese government than that of journalists at other stations.

In the case of the Darfur atrocities, we find that Arab media have demonstrated little interest in moving the issue to the forefront of political debates in the Arab street as Iraq and Palestine have been. For example, when Al-Jazeera was reporting the Abuja negotiations between the government of Sudan and the southern rebels, it began the story with seven killed in Darfur and the Africans' criticism of the rebels.[17] Another item also took the point of view of the Islamic government of Khartoum. The story reads: "Khartoum accuses Darfur rebels of attacking a city in the north."[18] The point of view of the southern Sudanese is rarely expressed or treated fairly and objectively. As the international community, particularly human rights groups, criticized Arab journalists for shedding little light on this critical humanitarian crisis, and as accusations of Arab racism against southern Sudanese increased, the frequency of reports on Darfur increased slightly. But the bias toward the Sudanese government remained. A common tactic employed by journalists in covering the subject was to modify the dimensions of the problem in a manner favorable to the government of Sudan. Put differently, many media outlets, instead of presenting the Darfur issue as a crisis characterized by genocide and human suffering, transformed the issue into a question of imperialism. The Darfur story, as told by the Arab media, was a problem of Western intervention, of which the government of Sudan was a victim. For example, a commentator wrote in Egypt's *Akhbar Al-Youm* "George Bush and Tony Blair . . . are now both planning another adventure in Africa, this time in Sudan's Darfur, with different pretexts from those they used in the invasion of Iraq."[19] In a late response to the atrocities of Darfur, the Union of Arab Journalists pledged to produce a report on the truth behind the crisis in Sudan—an implicit recognition that little has been done by the Arab media to investigate the story. The head of the delegation that was dispatched to compile the report expressed in a statement his support for the "unity" of Sudan, and condemned "visible and covert foreign interventions in Darfur."[20] For the likes of him, the Sudanese government is not guilty of any atrocities. The problem originates in the designs of the American imperialists.

Al-Jazeera, notwithstanding the courage shown by its employees on battlefields in Iraq, Afghanistan, and Palestine, did not send any of its correspondents to Darfur.[21] An Arab observer laments:

> . . . Al-Jazeera aired the reports of Egyptian doctors returning from Darfur asserting there was no famine, rapes or murders. Why did the benevolent Al-Jazeera fail to send any of its correspondents there,

especially when its correspondents have gone into the heart of the battles of the murderers and transmitted their pictures as they hailed the Iraqi leader Saddam?[22]

Al-Arabiya, where fewer Sudanese journalists work, did not exhibit the same bias as Al-Jazeera, where pro-government Sudanese journalists enjoy greater control over the production of news. On the other hand, Al-Arabiya employs more Lebanese Christians, who empathized with the plight of the Christian south in Sudan. Thus we find more stories focusing on the testimonials of victims from Darfur, along with statements of condemnations from international organizations and bodies.[23]

Under Palestinian Siege

Othman Al-Omer, a veteran Arab journalist, once told me, "The solution to the Arab media problem lies in the dismantlement of the Palestinian settlements in Arab television and newspapers."[24] Al-Omer, who was the editor of *Asharq Al-Awsat* and owner of online news service Elaph, explained: "dismantling those Palestinian settlements is important for the sake of fair reporting and in order to allow other Arab issues to make it to the front-page of a newspaper. But this is easier said than done." This is simply because, he goes on, the number of Palestinians who are in journalism is greater than those from other Arab countries, and they are better trained, in addition to having a high human capital in terms of literacy and educational attainment. The adult literacy rate among Palestinians is 55.6 percent, while the Arab world's most populous country, Egypt, has a literacy rate of 51.4 percent.[25] Thus it is only natural that those who control the world of Arab journalism and visual media in terms of talents should be Palestinians.

Indeed the number of Palestinian journalists working in Arabic television and newspapers is higher than that of journalists of Arab nationality, including owners of television channels and newspapers. Al-Omer of course is speaking from experience, for the number of Palestinians in the *Asharq Al-Awsat* newspaper during his tenure as editor-in-chief was very high. At the top, he had Abdul Bari Atwan as his managing editor, and Bakr Oweida as his assistant editor and the editor of the opinion page. To date 20 percent of the total number of journalists working for *Asharq Al-Awsat* have been Palestinians.

There is no better way of illustrating this predominance than by investigating the number of Palestinians working for the Arab world's most-watched satellite television station, Al-Jazeera. Of all news anchors, talk-show hosts, and correspondents listed on the station's website, more than 22 percent identify themselves as Palestinian or Palestinian-born. Egyptians, Syrians, and Jordanians are ranked next, with about 12 percent each. When we take into account the populations of those countries, Egypt being home to 70 million people, compared to 3 million Palestinians, we find that the Palestinians are disproportionately represented in Al-Jazeera's staff. Visible Palestinian figures working for Al-Jazeera include Iman Banoura/Ad, Tawfiq Taha, Jamal Rayyan, and Farah Al-Barqawi. The Palestinians among correspondents include Heba Akiyla, Waleed Al-Amry, Jivara Al-Bouderi, Sherin Abu-Aqla, and Ahmad Barakat. Reporters like Sherin Abu-Aqla, Waleed Al-Amry, and Jivara Al-Boudeiri report from the occupied territories and shape what the Arabs see or do not see about Palestinian affairs. Almost all Arab television stations and newspapers use Palestinian journalists to report from the occupied territories. When I asked some of the executives at Al-Arabiya and Al-Jazeera why they do not have journalists from the Gulf region or from other Arab countries covering Palestinian affairs, the answer was the same from both stations: Many Arab journalists and Arab countries boycott Israel and therefore the only choice we have is to use Palestinians. Of course this is a convenient answer, but in fact I have met many Arab journalists who work for Al-Jazeera and Al-Arabiya and report from Israel or the occupied territories. One Egyptian journalist, Nabil Sharaf Al-Din, who writes for Elaph news agency, told me he does not mind working as a correspondent for either of these stations from Israel itself. The disproportionate number of Palestinian anchors and correspondents at Al-Jazeera is small compared to the number of Palestinians among producers and behind-the-scenes aides. When I interviewed Qassem Ja'far, a board member of Al-Jazeera and a political advisor to Sheikh Hamad bin Jasim, the foreign minister of Qatar and allegedly the man behind the Al-Jazeera operation, he told me that Palestinian producers and aides constitute more than 40 percent of the total workforce of the station.[26]

We find Palestinian journalists spread throughout news outlets in Western and Arab media. To name a few, Sawsan Ghosheh is a producer at CNN. Oktaviya Nasr is a senior Arab affairs analyst at CNN. Many Palestinians can be found at United Press International, Associated Press, and AFP. Mohamed Daraghmeh is a known Associated Press journalist. The existence of a Palestinian diaspora throughout the Arab world has created a parallel diaspora inside Arab media outlets. Again, hiring practices that favor Palestinians, whether attributed to intentional policies of the press and media organization or to unintended circumstances, is certainly a factor that continues to shape how Palestinian affairs and concerns are presented in print and on TV by the Arab media. They have helped in maintaining the Palestinian issue as a topic of central concern on the Arab street, in addition to playing a major role in influencing the way Arab audiences interpret the issues.

What does the case of Al-Jazeera tell us about the influence of Palestinian diaspora journalists on television programming in the Arab world? It illustrates that the influence of Palestinian journalists on programming is strong. Palestinian journalists at Al-Jazeera blur the line between news and editorials, between journalism and political activism whenever the topic of discussion is remotely related to Palestine.

For example, Jamal Rayyan, a Palestinian anchor on Al-Jazeera, hosted a sixty-minute program entitled *Palestinians under Israeli Siege*. The program was designed to rally viewers in support of a Palestinian viewpoint that supports armed resistance. For the untrained Western eye, Mr. Rayyan's call-in show appears similar to something that CNN might air. However, there is one significant difference: that Al-Jazeera's call-in is in fact call-out. I know from experience, as well as from interviewing various people who participated in Al-Jazeera programs, that the way the station conducts the call-in show is in fact by calling out. In other words, the producers identify certain activists and call them and put them on air as if it were a spontaneous call from a passionate viewer, while in fact it is a previously agreed-on conversation. As illustrated below, when Mr. Rayyan does not intervene or stop unsubstantiated claims from a particular person, it is because he and his producers have agreed on what is going to be said. It is only when people veer off the agreed script that they are corrected. This practise does not only work for the Palestinian cause and rally support for the resistance, it also manufactures praise for Al-Jazeera itself. For instance, the first caller on the show, Nidal Al-Sabe', started his call by praising Al-Jazeera TV. Another caller, Abu Samed, praised Al-Jazeera as the channel of Arab unity and the only lit candle in these dark times for the Arabs. Of course, nobody knows who Abu Samed is. Most of the names used by these callers from Morocco to Brazil are aliases. Throughout the whole show, only one person veered from the agreed script, and it was then that Mr. Rayyan intervened. Content analysis of the show reveals that Mr. Rayyan behaved more like a political activist than a professional journalist or even a moderator of a talk-show.

"Palestinians under Israeli Siege" (Episode 60)[27]

On the show, after introducing the topic of discussion, the moderator invites viewers to express their thoughts on American and European peace efforts in the Middle East by telephone and fax.

The first few callers express their displeasure at Arab pressure on Palestinians to give in to Israeli and American demands. Callers were also enraged with U.S. support for Israel and some viewers expressed opposition to any attempt at peace talks, arguing that such talks are simply part of a "conspiracy to stop the *intifada*." Other callers expressed their support for Palestinian fighters and "martyrs." Throughout this series of calls, the moderator's input was limited to short phrases like "Thank you"; "Go ahead," and "May peace be on you as well." This was the case until a viewer from Saudi Arabia spoke against the killing of Israeli civilians:

MODERATOR:	Thank you. Bassam Mohamed from Saudi Arabia. Bassam go ahead.
CALLER:	Good evening brother Jamal.
MODERATOR:	Good evening my brother.
CALLER:	Brother Jamal, I would like to speak about fighting without going on for too long, God willingly.
MODERATOR:	Welcome. Go ahead.
CALLER:	My brother, I would like to send a message to the Palestinian people, the *fida'iyeen* (martyrs) particularly.
MODERATOR:	Yes.
CALLER:	I wish they could direct their martyrdom operations to those who really deserve it, meaning keep away from civilian Jews. I mean every martyrdom operation should be done for the good of the Palestinians and not against them.
MODERATOR:	But there is another side of Palestinians who say that most Israelis are armed fighters who are targeting Palestinian civilians.
CALLER:	I thank you Brother Jamal for this observation, but I would like to call to your attention that what matters is not what Palestinians say, what matters is what the world, or specifically the West, says. The West exploits every negative move by the Palestinian side. Any martyrdom operation against civilian Jews is used against Palestinians. I believe...
MODERATOR:	(interrupting) It is an issue of debate. There are many who say that I am not fighting for the sake of the global media but I am fighting for the sake of the [Palestinian] issue and for the right.
CALLER:	(interrupting) Yes, but our Western media is important, but...
MODERATOR:	(interrupting) And it is the right of the resistance. It is a natural right, and it is justified by all accepted norms.

The above example is part of a broader pattern exhibited by the reporting and analysis practices of Al-Jazeera, whereby the views of the host are presented to the viewers as the mainstream opinion and are defended by the channel's employees against any dissenting view whether from among the audience or from the guests. In the example shown above, we find that the host was reluctant to comment on remarks that condemned Israeli and American policies, praised so-called Palestinian "martyrs," opposed the holding of peace talks, and criticized Arab regimes for not doing enough to support the Palestinian cause. It was only when someone suggested that the targeting of Israeli civilians was hurting the image of the Palestinians and their cause that the host felt compelled to present "the other side of the story." The title of the show was "Palestinians under Israeli siege," but what it reveals to us is not only the Israeli siege of the Palestinians but also the Palestinian siege of Al-Jazeera. Jamal Rayyan and his team of Palestinian producers and aides are but one example of what

Mr. Al-Omer called the "Palestinian settlements," that have a stranglehold on Arab media.

The Arab Media and Coverage of Algerian Affairs

The Arab media's coverage of Algerian affairs vis-à-vis the confrontation between the government and the Islamist opposition exhibits an obvious bias toward the latter. Nadia Mahdeed, a francophone Algerian journalist who covered the war in Iraq for the London-based *Asharq Al-Awsat*, told me "the coverage of Algerian politics at most Arab newspapers including my own was consistently tilted in favor of the Islamic insurgency."[28] One might be tempted to interpret this comment as a predictable complaint from a secular Algerian journalist. Yet, when examining the political background that overshadows this coverage, her observation becomes salient. The origins of the bias are not merely the journalistic partialities at Al-Jazeera, Al-Arabiya, *Asharq al-Awsat*, or *Al-Hayat*. Rather, they can be found in complex political dynamics of the Sahrawi question and a special relationship binding the Gulf monarchies to North African politics.[29]

The Western Sahara question is at the heart of the conflict between Algeria and Morocco. After the end of Spanish rule, Morocco annexed Western Sahara in 1975, instigating a local moved toward independence in the former Spanish colony. The conflict caused tens of thousands of Western Sahrawi people to flee to refugee camps in Algeria. Today, the Moroccan monarchy accuses the Algerian government of supporting the Sahrawi rebels who are trying to secede from the monarchy and establish their own state. Gulf states, particularly Saudi Arabia, were largely supportive of the Moroccan monarchy against the then-socialist Algeria. The Algerian regime was seen by these states as a stronghold of hostile socialist forces that not only went against the principles of Islam, but also against the stability of status-quo monarchies. Thus for Saudi Arabia undermining the Algerian regime achieved two objectives. First, support for the Islamist opposition kept the Algerian government busy with internal turmoil, making it more difficult for it to pursue interventionist regional policies, including giving support to rebel forces in Western Sahara. Second, as Algeria was seen as a Soviet-friendly state, undermining its government was perceived as consistent with coutner balancing against communist forces in the Arab world.

In this regard the struggle between the Gulf media and the Algerian regime was part of the struggle against the spread of communism in the Arab world. This is why the Arab media, heavily financed by Gulf states, provided coverage that favored the Islamists in the early stages of the war until the phenomenon of militant Islam began threatening regimes in the Gulf. Pro-Algerian Islamist media coverage came as a result of three factors. First, it was the result of a confrontation between two camps in the Middle

East: Arab nationalist forces on one side, and status-quo states on the other. Second, it stemmed from an unspoken understanding among Arab monarchies that they would support each other, hence the Gulf royalists were interested in backing a fellow monarch in Morocco against Algeria. And finally on the global level, and up until the end of the Cold War, support for Algerian Islamists in Arab media was part of a broader strategy to use Islamist ideologies to prevent the expansion of the so-called "communist camp," which, in the eyes of Gulf monarchs, included the Algerian regime.

In addition to Al-Jazeera's pro-Islamist coverage, Qatar, the owner of the station, was host to Abbasi Madani, the leader of the Algerian Islamist movement known as the Front Islamique de Salut (FIS), or the Islamic Salvation Front.[30] Algerian journalists also worked in the Gulf states in Kuwait TV and Saudi papers and magazines. The most famous among these are Nadia Mahdeed, who covered the Iraq war for *Asharq Al-Awsat* and Khadija bin Qina of Al-Jazeera who hosts the daily program *al-Sharia wal Hayat*, or "Islamic law and daily life," with Sheikh Yousef Al-Qaradawi, the most famous leader of the Muslim Brotherhood, as her main guest.

In conclusion, the national origin and ideological leanings of Arab journalists shape the way the stories are reported to audiences. Some stories like those about Palestine and Iraq dominate the street because of the relative ease with which these issues can be reported, and because occupying powers do not interfere with Arab media to the same degree as do local Arab regimes. Palestine in particular is an easy story for Palestinian journalists who know all the details about their homeland and the plight of their people. Diaspora journalists feel free to criticize America and European countries because they enjoy the legal protection provided to them by the citizenship they possess. As I have illustrated, most Arab journalists working at Al-Jazeera and Al-Arabiya carry American, French, British, and other European passports. Ironically, anti-Western sentiment in the Arab media is generated by nationals of these Western states. Furthermore, anti-Americanism provides Arab journalists with instant stardom in their local communities. To criticize America is cost-free, while doing the same to an Arab regime might land a journalist or his family in jail. The role of journalists, especially Islamist ones, in shaping the story from a distinct point of view, is very pronounced in a number of Arab media outlets. To focus on the larger agenda of the media owners or media organizations alone and to ignore the role played by journalists is to miss one of the basic elements of the Arab media puzzle.

So it would be wrong to conclude that Arab journalists are mere tools in the hands of those who own the media. As I have shown, some of them may pursue their own agenda, while many others experience great difficulties and personal risks in order to adhere to principles of professionalism and ethical journalism. Unfortunately, it is these journalists that can find themselves unemployed or driven out and many have sacrificed their lives for the sake of integrity and good journalism. These include people like Rida Hilal, Samir Qaseer, and Mai Chediaq. Journalists are part and parcel of the way a story is narrated and studying their movement and the pressures that shape the way they cover a story is an integral part of any study that attempts to draw an accurate picture of the Arab or any media.

CHAPTER 5

PUBLIC DIPLOMACY AND THE ARAB MEDIA

What are the implications of my previous discussion for U.S. public diplomacy in the Arab world? The previous chapters have shown that the Arab media is inherently political. It is either an arm of conflict between states (Qatar against Saudi Arabia or Saudi Arabia against Egypt) or a tool for various factions within the state (Sunnis vs. Maronites or Shia vs. Sunnis in the case of Lebanon). Arab journalists who man pan-Arab media today are socialized within this context and their orientations reflect some of these ideological and sectarian biases. In this regard, Arab journalists are more political actors than professional journalists. In fact they are squatters who pay lip service to the promotion of America while serving their own parochial causes at the Same time. The journalists who work at Al-Hurra and Sawa (the U.S.-sponsored TV and radio stations) are not any different. In fact they are squatters who pay lip service to the promotion of America while serving their own parochial causes at the Same time. They are recruited from the same pool. As they grew up within this highly charged political environment, one should not expect them to be any different. Journalists' orientations certainly influence news selection, reporting, and talk-show items. Like the Voice of America before it, Al-Hurra recruits journalists who have taken leave of absence from their jobs back home. Because these journalists will be going back again to their jobs in the media of whichever country they came from, they are unable to say anything critical of their home countries. If they do, they lose their pension and the job that awaits them when they go back. These are points that I will address in later on in the chapter. The main question here is how are we to understand American public diplomacy in the Arab world in light of these obvious facts. More specifically, how we should understand Radio Sawa and Al-Hurra TV in the context of the Arab media market they compete in.

To begin with, effective public diplomacy, like effective public relations, requires three key components: knowledge of the "product," a clear understanding of the market where the product is going to be sold, and the ability to sell it. In the realm of media, the main tools of American public diplomacy today are Radio Sawa and Al-Hurra TV. If one looks at the current U.S. public diplomacy strategy in the Middle East, it is obvious that the United States has a product that can be sold; that is, American values, culture, and society. So the issue of content might not be the problem. Problems arise when we look at the other two components—understanding the market and employing effective sales people who have a good grasp of American society and culture. The people employed at Al-Hurra TV and Radio Sawa are Lebanese who do not speak English and many of them have just arrived in the United States and have very little knowledge of its culture and society. I was shocked to watch the State Department correspondent for Al-Hurra TV referring to Elizabeth Cheney as the wife of the vice president of the United States. One would expect that journalists recruited to work for Al-Hurra and Sawa would be expected to take an exam on American Politics, society, and culture; something akin to American Politics 101 offered to freshmen in American universities. They should be professional journalists and communicators who are well versed in their subject areas as well as in the ethics of the profession. The reality of the Arab media market is that the best and brightest journalists usually go to Al-Arabiya, Al-Jazeera, or the national TV stations of the various Arab countries. Those who come to Sawa and Al-Hurra are rejects from that market. In fact many of them have never worked in journalism before. For Al-Hurra to compete with Al-Jazeera or Al-Arabiya, it needs to provide a better coverage of America. Unless what is coming from America to Arab and Muslim viewers is better than what Al-Jazeera is offering them, they will tune America out.

Several reports have suggested that United States public diplomacy efforts conducted over the past few years have not been successful in responding to increasing anti-American sentiment in the Middle East.[1] Others claim that a lack of inter-agency coordination has impeded U.S. public diplomacy efforts in the region.[2] As regards the communication of American values to the Arab world, it is obvious that Radio Sawa and Al-Hurra TV, the most recent wide-scale U.S. public diplomacy efforts in the Arab world, have failed to change the hearts and minds of the Arab people. Despite this obvious failure, those who run the stations make exuberant proclamations of success. American public diplomacy officials need a more informed understanding of the Arab media market if they are to have any hope of making an impact in the Arab world through these media. They must take into account the context of the Arab media environment and compare Al-Hurra and Sawa to their competitors in the Arab world. In this section, I will suggest some changes that could transform these stations from their current idle states into powerful platforms for change in the Arab world.

It is my belief that Radio Sawa and Al-Hurra TV have the potential to positively affect the scope of debate in the Arab media. However, this would require a new strategy, new people, even a new name for both stations. Before beginning my discussion of the specific problems that have prevented Al-Hurra and Radio Sawa from succeeding, I will first provide a broad overview of the context that gave rise to these stations. Background information on the key institutions and individuals involved in the designs of these initiatives will provide a framework for the critiques that follow.

International Broadcasting: The BBG, Radio Sawa, and Al-Hurra TV

The U.S. General Accounting Office reports that the approximately $1 billion nonmilitary budget for U.S. public diplomacy is divided almost evenly between the State Department and the Broadcasting Board of Governors (BBG).[3] On October 1, 1999, the BBG became responsible for all U.S. government and government-sponsored nonmilitary, international broadcasting. This was the result of the 1998 Foreign Affairs Reform and Restructuring Act (Public Law 105–277), the most important legislation affecting U.S. international broadcasting since the 1950s.[4] The BBG is a bipartisan group of private citizens with experience in broadcasting and governmental affairs, with the secretary of state as an ex officio member. Each board member is appointed by the president and confirmed by the U.S. Senate.[5] The BBG's mission is to promote "freedom and democracy around the world by providing foreign audiences with accurate and objective news about the United States and the world."[6] BBG broadcasting efforts are required by law to present a balanced picture of American thought and institutions.

The enabling legislation for the BBG is the International Broadcasting Act of 1994 (Public Law 103–236).[7] The Act does not include any provisions against corruption. It placed the BBG under the control of the United States Information Agency (USIA). It also made explicit that nonfederal broadcasting entities such as Radio Free Europe and Radio Free Asia, which were being organized at that time, would report to the Board. In 1998, when USIA was abolished and folded into the State Department, the Broadcasting Act was incorporated with minor language changes in to a new Foreign Affairs Reform and Restructuring Act (Public Law 105–277).[8] The legislations stated that the director of the USIA and, subsequently, the secretary of state, along with the Board, should respect the professional independence and integrity of the International Broadcasting Bureau, its broadcasting services, and grantees.[9]

The Board has long been in violation of this fundamental principle, because it abolished Voice of America (VOA) in Arabic, converted Radio Free Europe/Radio Liberty's Radio Azadi in Persian into a pop music service, and removed the brand names of VOA's Urdu, Dari, and Pashto services from their programming, as Alan Heil, former deputy director of VOA programs, told me.[10] This resulted in VOA's near disappearance around the world. Lately, the Board has endorsed a transfer of VOA's central newsroom to contractors in Hong Kong for seven hours each day, leaving VOA's global news service extremely vulnerable to interdiction by the

People's Republic of China, a government that continues to jam VOA broadcasts in Mandarin and block its website.[11] These actions clearly violate the professional independence and integrity of the VOA.

The BBG representative responsible for the Middle East is Norman Pattiz,[12] founder and chairman of Westwood One, America's largest radio network that owns, manages, and distributes the NBC Radio Network, CBS Radio Network, the Mutual Broadcasting System, CNN Radio, Fox Radio Network, Metro Networks, Metro Traffic, and Shadow Traffic.[13] Mr. Pattiz has an extensive background in American commercial broadcasting, but had no experience in international broadcasting prior to his work with the BBG. The assumption of symmetry between the United States and the Arab world is made in many areas of public diplomacy and has been central to its failure.

For example, in late 2002, the U.S. State Department launched the $15 million "shared values campaign" aimed at winning the hearts and minds of Arabs and Muslims. Through a series of ads, it sought to communicate the idea that the United States is a place where Muslims thrive. Spots featured Muslims in the United States: a firefighter in New York, a basketball player, a Nobel-Prize-winning chemist, and the director of the National Institute of Health. The ads were produced by a New York-based advertising company. Their production was costly and time-consuming. When I saw the spots at the time, I knew that they would not have the desired effect. Indeed, there was no way to measure their reception at all since, with the exception of Kuwait TV, no Arab television channel would agree to run the ads. Thus, failure to take into consideration the political and social context encircling the Arab media led to a fiasco and an absolute waste of money and effort.

The fatal flaw of this campaign was the assumption that it is possible to "win the hearts and minds" of the Arab world according to the commercial dictates of American media standards. The idea that paid ads might be refused based on political considerations simply didn't occur to the people behind the shared values campaign. This was surely due to a combination of ignorance and arrogance on the part of the champions of this type of public diplomacy initiative. Their attempts to propose "culturally sensitive" advertisements showed their ignorance of the very cultural and political setting in which they hoped to become convincing communicators.

Despite the many lessons learned from the variety of media systems[14] and audience responses to media content, the instigators of the campaign mistakenly operated under the assumption that by simply paying for an ad, stations would run it regardless of its content. However, they were soon confronted with the harsh realities of the Middle East where the media, especially television, serves as an extension of the state.

Because of the political nature of the Arab media, it is not surprising that Egyptian TV, Al-Jazeera, and Jordanian TV, to name just a few, refused to run the American public diplomacy ads. Even in Egypt, a country that receives an annual U.S. aid package of $2.1 billion, the American public diplomacy establishment failed to place a single ad on television, radio, or in the newspapers. The truth is that a public diplomacy campaign, tailored by media professionals whose only experience is in the United States and created as though it was talking to a North American audience, could not possibly grasp the complexities of launching a campaign in authoritarian settings in the Middle East. It is also clear that the people who created these ads were taken in by the ecstatic proclamations about freedom and transparency that have often greeted the creation of satellite, privately owned television channels in the region. The Arab and Muslim world is dominated by authoritarian regimes of different stripes. This must be taken into account, even when dealing with the so-called "private" Arab media. The division of private and public in the context of Arab media does not hold, particularly for television. Most media are in fact ultimately controlled by governments, and television is generally directed by the state.

Radio Sawa

In January of 2002, Congress began a new round of public diplomacy initiatives in the Middle East, voting to allot $34.6 million to establish the Middle East Radio Network (MERN), in which Mr. Pattiz played a leading role. On March 23, 2002, MERN began broadcasting in Arabic across the Middle East. The initiative, with its brand name "Radio Sawa" meaning "together" in colloquial Lebanese Arabic, broadcasts around the clock with localized content in several Arab countries. The programming consists of a combination of Arabic (predominantly) and Western pop music, interspersed with brief news segments targeted at young, educated listeners in the region.[15] Radio Sawa replaced the sixty-year tradition of VOA which, according to Norman Pattiz, had attracted only 1 to 2 percent of adult Arab listeners.[16]

Radio Sawa does not resemble VOA in any way. When a veteran director of VOA's Arabic service met with the newly appointed Radio Sawa director to discuss the lessons he had learned from the years he spent in international broadcasting, the new director called him an "interesting man," told him to forget his experience, and sent him on his way.[17] Radio Sawa has a new name, a new strategy, and a new target audience. Therefore, management felt the station could not benefit from the lessons learned through previous American broadcasting initiatives in the Middle East.

According to BBG-sponsored surveys, Radio Sawa has exceeded all expectations. BBG statistics appear to indicate that it has become one of the most popular stations in all areas where it has local FM distribution.[18] The figures increase among the target audience. For example, in Morocco and Qatar, listening rates are said to be among the highest ever recorded for a U.S. international broadcasting service.[19] Armed with these statistics, which are for many reasons deceiving, Pattiz lobbied Congress for a TV counterpart to Radio Sawa. He was soon granted $62 million for the first year of Al-Hurra TV.

Al-Hurra TV

Al-Hurra is operated by a private corporation called The Middle East Television Network, Inc. (MTN). MTN is financed by the American people through Congress and receives its funding from the BBG, which serves as a firewall to protect the professional independence and integrity of its broadcasters.[20] Al-Hurra began broadcasting on February 14, 2004. Reaction from Arab viewers was highly critical. Some said Al-Hurra was a letdown. One columnist in the pan-Arab daily *Asharq al-Awsat* described his disappointment with Al-Hurra by writing, "When we were told about Al-Hurra, America's new Arabic channel, we were expecting something equivalent to CBS and NBC. We were expecting shows like Tim Russert's *Meet the Press* and Bob Shafer's *Face the Nation* or *Sixty Minutes*. Instead America treated us to a second-rate version of the TV channels of the Lebanese civil war. Our bad products seem to have been returned to us."[21] Other viewers insisted the goal of changing hearts and minds required a change in policy, not a new television station. The gap between Arab audiences' high expectation of Al-Hurra as an American-style channel with the standards of NBC and CNN, and what they received, low-quality reporting with a conservative Lebanese slant, undermined the station's credibility as a serious news outfit.[22]

The Al-Hurra initiative has also failed to play well with some American taxpayers. One blogger criticized the station's "rather abysmal" website. Believing Americans ought to have some understanding of the country's newest effort to reach the Arab world, he tried writing to the only email address listed on the website, only to have his emails routinely returned.[23] Another Arab American with several years of international broadcasting experience complained that she never received a response to the several emails she sent inquiring about job opportunities.

One central problem of Radio Sawa and Al-Hurra is the absence of any review process like that which existed at VOA for more than fifty years. The professional staff of the IBB Program Review Office (now called the Office of Performance Review) suggested reviews of Radio Sawa in 2003 and possibly 2004 but were told (presumably by the IBB director): "Now is not the time."[24] The State Department inspector-general auditor's report also noted the absence of a Sawa review during its first thirty-three months on the air. The Board carried out its own review of Sawa, chaired by an outside consultant, late in 2005. The report ignored content, and focused almost entirely on audience research, music playlists, and formats.[25] There has yet to be any review of Al-Hurra.

Below I will describe in detail some of the practices and situations that caused these stations to fail to influence the hearts and minds of Arab audiences. Many of my criticisms are not new. Arab journalists in the region have written about them, but unfortunately, they have yet to reach the decision-makers capable of making necessary changes.

Who Is Promoting America?

As previously stated, effective public diplomacy requires the right people trusted by their target audience to disseminate the messages. In the case of Al-Hurra and Radio Sawa, skilful journalists are needed who are well-versed in American society and values and who also enjoy the trust of Arab audiences. From the top down, the people hired to tell the American story to the Arab world have very little knowledge of America and its story. During the initial hiring, Mr. Muwafac Harb brought in around 400 people from Lebanon who had never lived in the United States and therefore had little, if any, first-hand knowledge of American values. These people could not possibly have been prepared to tell the American story to the Middle East audience. Mr. Harb's hiring process was arbitrary and capricious, with a selection method that followed no set criteria. Employees at the station have said there are no standard test procedures, and no journalism background was required for hiring. One observer from the Middle East Programming Center (MEPC) said people "walked in from the street and were hired."[26] A journalist who moved to Radio Sawa from Al-Jazeera expected the journalistic standards to resemble those of other American media. Upon arrival, he was disappointed. "I was surrounded by people with no experience. I recall carpenters and former security guards."[27]

Some of the problems with the quality of reporting stem from the fact that many of the Lebanese working at these stations grew up speaking French and Arabic. Because of their francophone education, their English skills, particularly in writing and translating, tend to be very weak. In many instances, instead of translating from English sources, they copy their news directly from al-Jazeera.net, reading it on the air without making any alterations to language or content. For example, one Sawa editor told me that Mr. Mohamed Asharqawi, a day shift editor, looked into the work of one Lebanese woman only to discover that her use of terms characteristic of Al- Jazeera such as the "so-called war on terrorism" or "what Bush calls the war on terrorism" was a result of copying and pasting reports from Al-Jazeera.net into her Sawa script.[28] This is not only an example of unethical reporting, but it also undermines the very credibility of the station. Al-Jazeera is the most popular pan-Arab network. Audiences will certainly notice when Al-Jazeera reports are replayed on another station, particularly on an American one.

As the objective of Al-Hurra and Radio Sawa is to provide the Arab public with an alternative to Al-Jazeera, what purpose does it serve to broadcast the same information, in the same language, as that available on countless other Arabic satellite networks? A primary function of Al-Hurra should have been to raise the level of journalistic excellence and force Al-Jazeera into following suit. Al-Hurra should have been ahead of other Arab reporters in reporting America to the Arab world, but unfortunately those working for Al-Hurra do not know America. It is assumed that good reporting on America should not be difficult, especially when Al-Hurra and Radio Sawa have almost unlimited access to both information and events. Instead, they are not taking advantage of their position in America. Al-Hurra reporters rarely travel to events outside Washington, choosing instead to copy information from Al-Jazeera reports. To my knowledge, copying and pasting are not part of the average journalism training. If the stations had hired journalists with editorial, investigative, or at the very least, English language skills, Al-Hurra and Radio Sawa would have a much higher reputation—and greater influence—in the Arab world. The story is that Al-Arabiya reporters like Mona Shaqaqi, a Columbia University graduate, report America far better than those working for Al-Hurra.

The personnel problem began when Norman Pattiz made Harb news director of Al-Hurra and Radio Sawa, giving him full authority with no oversight from native Arabic speakers. "Mr. Harb considers the stations his own, hiring and firing employees as he pleases without supervision."[29] One journalist who eventually left Al-Hurra said the station had become a springboard for people who wanted to try their hand at journalism, leading to a very low level of professionalism among the staff.[30] Favoritism rather than professionalism plays the key role in staffing choices. For example, "Daniel Nassif, hired to be the news director of Sawa, has no background in journalism. His resume shows he is a former president of the American Lebanese Institute, a U.S. Representative of the Council of Lebanese American Organizations, an activist, a consultant, and a spokesperson for General Michel Aoun."[31]

Favoritism can also be seen in Mr. Harb's choices for many on-air positions. For example, the White House correspondent position was given to an Iraqi actress who had very little experience in journalism. A talk-show host position was given to a British Egyptian young woman who could not write in Arabic. She eventually left the station, but when asked how she had obtained the job, she said her friend knew Mouafac Harb, the news director. She said she was hired after a three-hour discussion over drinks at a restaurant in London. The issue of favoritism has resulted in the resignation of three on-air correspondents.[32] None of the three are Lebanese and resigned for reasons of "discrimination."

One employer complained that Mr. Harb had broken labor regulations, giving Lebanese spontaneous salary raises without rhyme or reason. The loose managerial structure he has created allows him to take credit for all successes while avoiding responsibility for all mistakes. Mr. Harb invites his friends to be regular guests, with permanent pay checks. For example, one of Al-Hurra's regular contracted commentators, Mr. Mahmoud Shamam, is at the same time a commentator for Hezbollah's Al-Manar TV and Al-Jazeera. Al-Hurra also put Saad Al-Feqh, a Saudi on the UN list of terrorists, on the air against assistant secretary of state David Sutterfield. When a journalist tried bringing someone new for an interview, Mr. Harb walked by, saw the guest and said, "Why did you bring him? I don't like him. I don't want to see him here."[33] Some of the people on the station's blacklist were so infuriated that they appealed to Congress members to allow them to appear on Al-Hurra and express their opinions.[34]

Another complaint is presented by Magdi Khalil, a former talk-show host on Al-Hurra, who laments that the station has not fulfilled its mission. "Al-Hurra was supposed to achieve two goals, first to introduce quality media to the Arab world, and second present a better image of America in the region. Al-Hurra achieved neither." He also indicates that all his discussions with experts from the Arab world about the television station point to a single conclusion: "Al-Hurra is dead." Khalil also explained his discomfort with Al-Hurra's failure to give Arab reformist elements any voice. Moreover, during his experience at Al-Hurra, he felt uneasy about the channel's reluctance to describe "terrorists" as "terrorists" in news reports—and not *nasheteen* (Arabic for "activists"), as presenters often described them.[35]

Mr. Harb's choices for guests leaves no room for the moderate Arab voices that are also missing from other Arabic network screens. These are the people who could spark debate and raise the bar for other Arab media. Consider this journalist's story. Having moved to the United States from Yemen at a young age, he now carries an American passport and considers himself American. He spent a few years struggling to get an Arabic newspaper off the ground in Michigan. When that didn't work, he moved from state to state trying to make ends meet for his family. He eventually moved to Qatar to take a job working for Al-Jazeera. After being reprimanded by his Al-Jazeera superiors for voicing his opinions and calling for dialogue in an Israeli newspaper, he decided to return to America to work for Radio Sawa. "I made the move because I wanted more freedom. American values. Respect for human rights. It was not long before I realized my situation at Al-Jazeera was better."[36] There, he said, he might not have been able to always report what he wanted, but at least he could write his opinions in other papers and practice journalism. As an employer of Radio Sawa, he couldn't write anywhere else. "They said it was against the law. The law actually says I must have permission to write. I asked for that permission. I asked to write, to defend American values because I am an American citizen. But permission was never granted, so I resigned."[37] These are the voices so often silenced by Arab governments and their media. Instead of providing a platform for these diverse opinions, Mr. Harb shuts them out.

Some of the journalists hired by Al-Hurra were not unknown to Arab audiences. Many had been rejected by stations such as Al-Jazeera and Al-Arabiya and were forced to take jobs at local Lebanese stations, some of which were blatantly anti-American. One reason Al-Hurra is not perceived as a credible news source that supports American values is because audiences are watching the same journalists they saw—in the not too distant past—representing the other side.

Not only is the staff at Al-Hurra and Radio Sawa predominately Lebanese, it is for the most part Maronite Christian, which further jeopardizes the station's credibility in the eyes of a Muslim audience. There are a few Shia Muslims, but there is not a single Sunni Muslim working at Al-Hurra or Sawa.[38] It is shocking that a station created for the Muslim world has failed to employ reporters that represent the largest Muslim community. As one former Sawa reporter put it, "No one is going to trust a station that only puts people named John and Joseph on the air. Where are the Mohamads and the Alis? They have to realize that the majority of the audience in the region is Muslim."[39]

The composition of the staff at Al-Hurra and Radio Sawa has led to serious problems in the language of reports. My research has shown that many of the people recruited to work for Sawa and Al-Hurra do not know the basics about U.S. policies and values. For example, one anchor woman asked a guest whether President Bush was a "Democrat or with the other party." Other Sawa announcers are blatantly anti-U.S. One case in point is anchor woman Waseela Baldi, who cried because the United States captured Saddam Hussein. This is not a surprise, for she is the wife of an Al-Jazeera anchor in Washington. It is almost as if employees of Washington's public diplomacy initiatives are scarcely different from journalists from the region that have referred to Al-Hurra and Sawa as a "media offensive" that "does not differ from the military, political and economic invasion as well as the terror [of the United States]."[40]

Sawa reporters have also been criticized for their lack of Arabic language skills. Newsreaders have trouble reading names of places and people, particularly in Iraq. Sam Hilmy notes in *Radio Sawa: Program Review and Analysis* that Baiji (an important oil town close to Mosul) becomes Beeji, Msayyab (between Baghdad and Najaf) becomes Musayyib, Pachachi (from the Governing Council) becomes Pajaji or even Bajaji, and Rumsfeld becomes Rumsfield.[41] Other Arabic language problems have not gone unnoticed. One BBG representative wrote, "We are deeply concerned about continuing problems with grammar and spelling errors in the scripts for newscasts which are read over the radio... It is no justification to claim that you are too rushed to get the job done accurately and effectively."[42] There have been several instances where language errors were so significant that editors have had to throw stories out as below standard.

The technical situation at Al-Hurra compounds its other problems. The problems that existed during the first few days of broadcasting were excusable, but significant improvements have not been made. A cable from the U.S. embassy in Cairo noted that "several contacts have expressed surprise and frustration with the technical glitches that apparently have not yet been completely ironed out." It cited as an example a news program where the teleprompter apparently malfunctioned briefly, causing the newscasters to appear "utterly nonplussed." The cable continued, "These technical glitches, while not pervasive, contrast poorly to the highly professional and smooth broadcasts on the most watched Arabic news stations such as Al-Jazeera and Al-Arabiya."[43]

Even when Al-Hurra and Radio Sawa attempt to cover events properly, the lack of training and journalism skills cause serious editorial mistakes that damage the station's credibility. For example, Radio Sawa reporters were recently caught in a mistake when they reported a demonstration against the American occupation in Iraq. Sawa reporters on the ground referred to the demonstration as birthday celebrations for Imam Al-Sadr. They might have gotten away with this mischaracterization if it weren't for the fact that other Arab television stations, along with BBC Radio, described the gathering as a Shia demonstration against the American occupation. Viewers could watch the two conflicting reports of the same event almost simultaneously. It was obvious that the Sawa reports were not true. These kinds of mistakes seriously diminish the credibility of the station.

Claude Salhani, international editor at United Press International, was very critical of the editorial decisions of Al-Hurra. "They are programming cooking shows and documentaries on monkeys during the fighting in Fallujah in Iraq and Rafah in Gaza."[44] The editorial decision to play pop music instead of news programming has also sparked criticism. "Pop is a major successful commercial enterprise that targets a wide youthful common denominator. But it is not America, with its rich, multifaceted culture, or its revolutionary ideals, history-making values, ever-renewed vitality, and yes, even America's chronic problems and weaknesses."[45]

Another example of poor reporting was seen in Al-Hurra's coverage of the assassination of former Lebanese prime minister Rafiq Al-Hariri. One journalist noted that, while even the anti-American Al-Jazeera was careful to cover the different sides of the story, Al-Hurra never once aired the Syrian side. On one Al-Hurra talk show, a member of the Lebanese parliament said Arabs should be careful not to put all of the blame on Syria without proof of its responsibility. The Al-Hurra host responded—on the air— with, "Please don't give me the crocodile tears now." Not only was that unprofessional journalism, it also conflicted with the American government's position at the time. Throughout that period, Adam Ereli, deputy spokesman for the State Department's Bureau of Public Affairs, was calling on journalists to wait for everything to pan out before accusing Syria. As one journalist who saw the Al-Hurra show said, "Al-Hurra was acting more royal than the king by overstepping the State Department to blame Syria."

There is a sense among the staff at Al-Hurra that the station is heading in the wrong direction. They are aware of the mistakes being made, and this has led to an atmosphere of panic. One editor attributes this to the journalists' fear of a shutdown of the station before they get their green cards.

"At Voice of America, we had two options. First, we could have our work visas extended every year, with the understanding that we would eventually return to our own countries once the job was complete. Otherwise, we could be reviewed after two years of working and begin the green card process after that." At Al-Hurra, employees begin the green card process the moment they are hired. There is a feeling that they must get it out of the way before the station is shut down. This sense of urgency felt by journalists is also related to money: employees are doing everything they can to make money before their return home. Journalists with no prior relevant experience are being paid $100,000 a year. Preoccupied by the feeling that time is running out, people don't think for a moment about U.S. policies or the American image. "They did not care about America in Lebanon. Why should we assume they care now?"[46]

A final criticism of the people hired to explain American values and policies to the Arab world is that they have failed to support America in the war on terrorism. Mr. Pattiz is quick to boast of a high following of his stations in countries that are friendly with America. However, it has proven to be impossible to measure Sawa's progress in countering support for terrorism in many areas that have been identified as places where Al-Qaeda or affiliated terrorist groups have operated. These areas include: Algeria, Libya, Syria, Yemen, West Bank, and Gaza.[47]

Sawa does not have FM access to Egypt and Saudi Arabia, the most crucial areas in any American public diplomacy campaign. It is for this reason that they are left off of BBG charts that claim Radio Sawa has a high following. Egypt, with a population of 75 million, should be a prime target for any American public diplomacy initiative. BBG statistics seem encouraging, with listenership up to 78 percent in places like Qatar. However, 75 percent of the population of Qatar is still only around 650,000 people. Listenership in Egypt, although static at 7–13 percent, translates into almost 10 million people. Listenership from all of the small Arabic countries combined does not represent half the population of Cairo. Charts that do not take population into account do not provide an accurate picture of how Radio Sawa is being perceived. The strategies of Sawa and Al-Hurra must be changed so that Arabs viewers who need to hear the American message the most are attracted.

The problems with strategy, management, hiring, producing, language, programming, and accurate reporting, along with the inability to help America in the war on terror, make one thing abundantly clear: the right people were not hired to sell the American message to Arab audiences. As I previously stated, effective public diplomacy requires effective sales people who understand the product and the market where it is to be sold. When we look at the staff of Al-Hurra and Radio Sawa, it is clear they are unfamiliar with the product—American values, culture, and society— and they do not accurately understand the market. Of the few who have a journalism background, their pervious focus was always local Lebanese politics. They are unfamiliar with the broader Arab audience. Even if these people were to be familiarized with the product and market, their lack of language skills and journalism training still make them the wrong people for the job.

Understanding the Market—Establishing Credibility

We have to remember that Al-Hurra and Sawa are competing against 170 satellite stations in the Arab world. Effective public diplomacy requires an understanding of the market and the level of competition. It is clear that the people behind Al-Hurra and Radio Sawa did not understand their target audience and have no idea that their voice is drowned out by their competitors.

The predominantly Lebanese make-up of the staff is reflected in the station's programming choices. For example, on April 25, 2005 the most important news story for Arab/American relations was the meeting between U.S. president George W. Bush and Saudi King Abdullah bin Abdel-Aziz in Crawford, Texas. Despite this, the first story Al-Hurra's nightly newscast was the resignation of the head of Lebanon's Sûreté Generale, Major General Jamil Sayyed. When Al-Hurra finally mentioned the Texas visit, their coverage was brief. They did not have a correspondent there. They reported the same information that could be gathered from any other news source. Even the *Daily Star* newspaper, based in Beirut, led with the coverage of the meeting in Texas on that day.

A second example of the Lebanese slant is the coverage of NBA basketball. Across the Arab world, soccer is the most popular sport, with the exception of Lebanon, where it is basketball. On New Year's Eve, when every Arab satellite station had its own party or showed celebrations from around the world, Al-Hurra aired a game of NBA basketball at midnight. Al-Hurra also cut its coverage of a press conference with President Bush to air a game of basketball. To an Arab audience largely uninterested in basketball, these programming choices make little sense. Again, Al-Hurra's credibility is damaged because it is perceived as a Lebanese rather than as an American station.[48]

A recent event that also caused viewers to question Al-Hurra's credibility as a serious news outlet was the station's abrupt withdrawal from Syria. While journalists from CNN, the BBC, and other Arab satellite networks are literally dying while reporting stories from places like Iraq and Palestine, Al-Hurra reporters fled the scene at the first sign of trouble.

The music of Radio Sawa has damaged that station's credibility. Radio Sawa generally airs Arabic music from Lebanon or the Gulf, alienating listeners from North Africa. This is particularly harmful as Egypt has a potential audience of around 50 million. Norman Pattiz has boasted of the diversity at Radio Sawa, saying that "There is a separate stream that reflects local music tastes and language dialects from Iraq, Morocco, the Gulf, Egypt, Jordan and the West Bank, and Sudan and Yemen. This regionalization of format makes Sawa, in effect, six separate radio stations."[49] The different streams do exist, but they have not resulted in music content targeted at local audiences.

The different streams also fail to use broadcasters from their target region. For example, in the Iraqi section, all five of the reporters are Jordanian and the chief editor is Palestinian. When Iraqis work with the team, they are hired on a contractual basis. There is not a single Iraqi actually employed in the Iraqi section. This has caused significant problems because Iraqis do not always get along with Jordanians due to the fact that they have supported Saddam Hussein in the past. The differences in Arabic dialect make it obvious to Iraqi listeners that the broadcasters are not from their own country. According to one Sawa listener, "No one in Iraq is going to want to listen to Jordanian announcers."[50]

The fact that there is not a single interactive program on Radio Sawa is also damaging. One program, *Question of the Day*, does involve audience involvement. A host says something like "Mohamed from Saudi Arabia" asked about a specific topic. Then the host provides an answer. This show is laughed at by Sawa listeners because hosts do not offer a way for people to contact the station. Mohamed who? And from where in Saudi Arabia? And how did he know how to contact the station? This is probably an example of the "news-receiving" phenomenon described earlier. Nothing on Radio Sawa sparks discussion or dialogue. An unclassified cable from the American embassy in Casablanca suggests that listeners are changing the channel when they hear anything but music. The cable quoted one student saying that whenever he listens to Radio Sawa, he tunes into another station as soon as the news starts. News director Mouafac Harb sees no role for audience participation in programming, stressing that Radio Sawa airs policy statements made by the president or other senior officials but it does not discuss issues.[51]

Al-Hurra and Radio Sawa have so little credibility with Arab audiences because the people behind these efforts do not have an accurate understanding of the Arab market. The news director of Al-Hurra dismisses all criticism, saying repeatedly that "his" stations were criticized in the Arab press before broadcasting began.[52] What he leaves out is the fact that, with a name like "Al-Hurra" and offensive promos, potential viewers had plenty to complain about before regular broadcasting started. Any international broadcasting effort is going to be fraught with difficulties and challenges. Understanding the audience, its sensitivities and vulnerabilities, is a crucial step in building an effective public diplomacy strategy. That step was left out in the case of Al-Hurra and Radio Sawa. Their reputations can only be saved through extensive market research and newly designed strategies focused on results. The current BBG approach uses American radio and broadcasting techniques and assumes they will be effective in the Middle East. The opposite is the case. It is time for renewed efforts to be made to understand the diverse audience that exists in the Arab world.

In a complex, and fragile environment like the Middle East, public diplomacy voices should be chosen with great caution. Judging from the lengthy testing processes required for Foreign Service public diplomacy officials, the American government seems to be aware of this important point. One is left wondering why such criteria are not used in the case of Al-Hurra. As they stand now, Al-Hurra and Radio Sawa are embarrassments to the United States. These stations could be very powerful tools if renewed efforts were made to understand the market and employ the right people. What I show in this chapter is that the current management has failed to deliver in these two areas. Had the audience been researched and understood, Al-Hurra would not have offended its potential viewers before getting off the ground. Had the right people been hired, they would have understood American values and devoted everything they could to promoting them in the Arab world. The current situation is in desperate need of change. If nothing is done, Al-Hurra and Radio Sawa will proceed as they are, attracting a tiny audience and making little impact.

Conclusion

Al-Hurra and Radio Sawa can only be saved if they are brought under the control of a serious oversight board committed to both U.S. policies and to setting high standards of professionalism for the Arab media to follow. Thus far, Al-Hurra and Radio Sawa are runaway stations. The only way to keep Al-Hurra in check would be to completely revolutionize the hiring process so that it follows U.S. standards. It needs to have a first-class television manager from the United States paired with a counterpart who is a native speaker of Arabic. Those hired must be recruited from a pool of professional journalists who are well versed in U.S. policies and values. It would prove worthwhile for Al-Hurra to stand for the American value of equal opportunity by advertising its jobs to Arabic-speaking Americans to compete for. These are the people who are familiar with the country and can speak for it. Anything less than a total staff change will not improve the image of Al-Hurra, and the new workforce must reflect the diversity and ethnic distribution of the target audience.

Furthermore, the oversight review board should meet once a month to make sure that Al-Hurra lives up to its mission and that there is congruence between Al-Hurra and the stated U.S. policies for the region. This system of continuous self-evaluation must be established not only within Al-Hurra and Sawa but also throughout all public diplomacy structures. For Al-Hurra to succeed it must follow a two-tiered strategy: (a) promote American values of freedom, human rights, rule of law, and democracy and (b) dig out the dirt on oppressive regimes in the region. Al-Hurra's mission should not be to compete with Al-Jazeera, as Pattiz claimed it would do in the beginning.[53] Its mission should instead be to keep Arab governments and their media on the defensive.

Both Al-Hurra and Radio Sawa have failed to deliver on the two crucial fronts: promoting U.S. values and supporting U.S. policy. For this reason, I recommend the creation of a private foundation for public diplomacy that produces high quality programs to be provided free-of-charge to Arab TV channels, especially for new independent organizations such as Emad Adeeb's Good News Group, that produces the only liberal daily, *Nahdat Masr*, and has many TV programs affiliated with it. There are many Arab television stations that do not have the funding to produce television shows, so they recycle material from Al-Jazeera. If we were to offer them quality programs, we could very easily affect their message.[54] This is especially true about Moroccan TV and the stations of other poor Arab countries.

Reforming Al-Hurra or Working with Natives

For the United States to win the war of ideas, it has to cultivate a community of native supporters of its policies. This network already exists in the spheres of the Arab media. Unfortunately, it is often shunned by U.S. officials who do not have access to the policy-making community or to the U.S.-sponsored Arabic media. Al-Hurra relies instead on the patrimony of the director of news, who pays his guests approximately $1000 per appearance. One of the regular consultants and commentators for Al-Hurra, Mr. Mahmoud Shamam, is a board member of Al-Jazeera and a commentator for Hizbulla's TV station Al-Manar. This largess and even appearance on Al-Hurra is denied to those who are putting themselves in danger on behalf of the United States.

It is easier to cultivate native supporters than to reform Al-Hurra. U.S. public diplomacy officials should hold a meeting with the ten most prominent owners of Arab media and make it clear to them that actively promoting hate of the United States will come at high costs, the least of which will entail a withdrawal of advertisements from American companies. The ten most important owners of the Arab media today include: Al-Waleed Al-Ibrahim, the owner of MBC and Arabiya TV; Sheikh Hamad bin Jasim, the owner of Al-Jazeera; Sheikh Saleh Kamel, the owner of ART and other religious channels; Faisal bin Salman, the chairman of the Saudi publishing Group and the owner of thirteen Arabic publications including the influential daily. *Asharq Al-Awsat*; Dr. Ahmad Bahgat, the owner of Dream 1 and Dream 2 TV; Al-Waleed bin Talal, the owner of Rotana group; Sheikh Abdullah bin Zayed, the owner of Abu Dhabi TV; Khaled bin Sultan, the owner of *Al-Hayat* newspaper and Al-Hayat LBC TV and Egypt's minister of information; and finally the Al-Hariri family who own the *Al-Mustaqbal* newspaper and Al-Mustaqbal TV. There should be rewards for those like *Al-Arabiya* and *Asharq Al-Awsat* who support the United States, and penalties for those who are actively against the United States, such as Al-Jazeera and *Al-Hayat*.

Finally, this strategy will not work unless it is coupled with diplomatic pressure that makes it clear to Arab and Muslim leaders that the United States knows that anti-U.S. media campaigns in the Arab world are undertaken to divert peoples' anger from the failing policies of local regimes. The double talk of Arab regimes should be exposed. The stakes are high and if the United States do not win this war of ideas, U.S. interests in the region are going to suffer for a long time to come.

If the United States looks at its public diplomacy strategy, it can see that it has product it can sell: American values and American society. However, Lebanese who have just set foot in the United States obviously do not know this product well enough to sell it. For anybody to be able to sell America to the Muslim world, he has to have lived in the U.S. for a long time. Unfortunately this is not the case in those who are working at Al-Hurra and Sawa. Instead of pushing for higher objectives in the Middle East like reforming the regime in Syria or Egypt, Washington should opt for the more modest aim of reforming Al-Hurra and Sawa. Thus far, the US has failed in reforming Al-Hurra and this may be symbolic of the larger US failure in the Middle East.

CHAPTER 6

ARAB MEDIA AND POLITICAL CHANGE IN THE MIDDLE EAST

The advent of the internet and the mushrooming of satellite dishes on Arab and rooftops have been heralded in the West as signs of the retreating Arab state, the rise of civil society, the emergence of the public sphere, and maybe the dawn of a new politics. Despite this excitement about modern means of communication and their supposed impact on Arab politics, by the disjunction between these hopes and the realities of Arab politics and societies is striking. The previous chapters demonstrate that the story of the Arab media is the story of the state and its proxies. The Arab media, by implication, is a site for political conflict, be it inter- or intra-state conflict. The many statements describing the Arab media as an agent for political liberalization and openness require serious examination. Such an examination is the purpose of this chapter. I will also try to link the discussion of the Arab media to a broader debate on the impact of information technology on Arab politics.

If one looks at the Arab media, one never fails to notice that they are mostly controlled by Arab governments, whether directly or through proxy owners. This applies to almost all means of mass communication: print, radio, and television. Naturally, as a result, one would expect that the language of those at the helm of the state would dominate the political language in the Arab world. Yet, the dominant language in Arab societies, at least in the past two decades, has been oppositionist and Islamist, or at least dominated by Islamic symbols. Given that states bar these groups from the various media, it is puzzling that their discourse is dominant. We are prompted to ask a variety of questions:

- Why is the Islamist discourse, despite its lack of access to these modern means of communication, still dominant?
- Why is it that state discourse is not taking hold, despite what is available to the elites in terms of means of mass communication and other instruments of social control?
- Why is the Arab state weak?
- What is the relationship between communication and trust?

Before I answer these questions, I would like to contest the assumption that modern media are conneted to sociopolitical change in the Arab world on both theoretical and empirical grounds. Macro-sociologists and economic historians have disputed the relationship between technological change and the openness of the political order or economic growth elsewhere. Contesting the relationship between openness and new technologies from a sociological standpoint, James Beniger argues that the information revolution came as a response to the crisis of control that resulted from the great flows of material and data that accompanied the industrial revolution.[1] This pressing problem of movement of goods, information, and their processing required new means of control. This is why, he argues, we had innovations such as the telegraph, telephone, assembly lines, and scientific management Beniger's conclusions run against the assumption of both medium theory and modernization theory alike. Another argument challenging any direct correlation between technology and economic growth comes from a giant in the field of U.S. economic history. In his book *Railroads and American Economic Growth*, Robert Fogel writes that "despite [their] dramatically rapid and massive growth over a period of half a century...the railroads did not make an overwhelming contribution to the production potential of the economy."[2] Fogel's ideas were very important and generated a great deal of debate among his peers and beyond. His challenge is of particular interest because of the link development theorists make, and still make, between economic growth and political change. Recent data and analyses from China make a similar point. Daniel Lynch suggests that the Chinese case shows that the opening of public space is a result of a combination of administrative fragmentation and forms of property rights, while the role of information technology is very limited.[3] More to the point of this - chapter, he argues for a differentiation between the public sphere in an authoritarian setting and in liberal democracies. In an authoritarian context, the public sphere is not an open place of contestation. It is structured and the rules of the game can be changed by an intrusive state at any time.

Contesting the Theoretical Basis of This Current Debate

Regardless of the variations in conclusions, the current debate on globalization, internet growth, new media, and their implications for Arab polities seems to embrace uncritically the old clichés of modernization and development literature. Some scholars seem to abandon analytical precision in favor of this new hype, claiming a correlation between the new media and the emergence of the public spheres and civil society in the Arab world.[4] The underlying assumption of these studies, with few exceptions, is that the spread of new means of communications, such as the fax machine, the cellular phone, the satellite dish, satellite channels like Al-Jazeera and Al-Arabiya, and finally the internet will crack open the Arab authoritarian order. The intellectual genealogy of these arguments, at least in terms of the communication aspect, can be traced to Marshall McLuhan's medium theory that argues that changes in the means of communication have an impact on the trajectory of social evolution and social change.[5] The intellectual fathers of these arguments in political science in general, and Middle East studies in particular, are Samuel Huntington and Daniel Lerner respectively.[6]

The fact that the study of new media and its impact on the Arab world is in vogue should not dissuade us from seeking greater analytical rigor and a degree of interdisciplinary perspective. Technological determinism is always seductive, in the sense that the history of man is the history of technology. But it can only take us so far. Trying to quantify the communications technology revolution statistically is not enough, nor is focusing on the expansion of communication structures, such as the rate of growth of the internet or the increased number of satellite TV stations available in the Arab world. This may be helpful at the level of data gathering. However, it should not be confused with the whole story. Data need context both for gathering and interpretation, unless we assume that people of the region and their cultures do not matter. Observing rapid transformations in communications, some scholars have gone on to conclude that the communications revolution signifies the expansion of political space. This is partly because they assume that the persistence of authoritarianism is the result of an uninformed citizenry, and that access to information will serve to enlighten the oppressed Arab people. Also, these types of analysis focus exclusively on the structure of communication and do little to explain content, or relate this content to the larger social, economic, and cultural context. Although the Arab world has witnessed an explosion of new media, this transformation has taken place within a specific context that has the capacity to absorb and adapt to these new developments. We have yet to compare social change in Arab countries that went through rapid modernization and technological infusions (the Gulf states) and in those with less technological infusion (Sudan and Yemen).

To understand the role of changing communications in Arab polities, we must analyze institutions of political communication, both new and old. Central to my argument is that the failure of modern and post-modern means of acquiring rootedness in the Arab world is linked to larger issues of communication and trust. Here I would like to argue that new structures, means and processes of modernity, particularly those of the media, are usually absorbed into the local context. Some technologies may remain simply grafted onto the society, and may not take root, at least in certain segments of those societies. There are places where the radio might be the main means of communication, while in other parts of a society television may be dominant, and yet in still other parts non-modern means may be the most efficient means of communication. This is not a problem thus far. The main problem arises when we mistake the means and the processes for mirror images of Western structures accompanied by specific expected functions: in other words, seeing only what is familiar and selecting data on the basis of this familiarity. The main reason that forms fail to take root is because of their foreign bias as modern means of communication. For example, those forms that privilege the domain of the written over that of the oral, or standard Arabic over the vernacular, fail to take root in an Arab world that largely remains within the realm of illiteracy, orality, and vernacular speech.

When studying communication and technology in the Arab world, most scholars have focused on the technology and ignored the Arab world, its histories, cultures, and societies, and human dimensions. Few studies have tried to address the habits of those who are participating, or their interaction with new forms of media. Yet there is a lot to be said about the way in which individuals in the Arab world have engaged with new media forms. For example, when radio was first introduced in the Arab world, whether privately owned or state-owned, many people listened to it in local cafes. Cafes were also the venue where Arabs were introduced to television, video, and satellite television. Now many who study the new information technologies in the Arab world talk about internet cafes, but focus on the access to the technology. Although there is a great deal to be said about access to these new means of communication, very few have addressed the underlying social structure that make cafes the site of mass communication. What is so important about collective viewing in the Arab world, and how does this relate to new communication technologies and the new satellite television phenomenon?

It would be to miss the point of my argument altogether, if one were to classify my critique of the nascent literate that connects new information technologies with the empowerment of civil society and the emergence of public space as part of an anti-globalization discourse. Rather, I argue for a differentiated notion of globalization. Globalization is a consequence of modernity. Placing it in this context will facilitate our understanding of both new and old information technologies and their implications for Arab societies. One of the major consequences of modernity is the distantiation of space and time[7] (as modernity accelerates time, space shrinks), limiting our face-to-face interaction in favor of a faceless interaction and lifting many social relations out of their local context and re-embedding them in a new global context. As we see an event unfold on television, we think we are witnessing it unfold in front of our eyes, and we interpret the event according to our own frame of reference or the frame supplied to us by the cameras and the reporters. We trust that what we are watching is real. But the concept of trust associated with modernity is a different concept from trust in a pre-modern society. As the crux of my argument concerns media and trust in the Arab context, I have to be concerned about the implications of the assumptions of modernization theory and medium theory for the notion of trust.

Communication and Trust and the Arab State

Key to the Arab state's inability to connect with wider society, and its inability to establish hegemony using modern means of mass communications, is the notion of communication and trust. One can point to many examples where trust between Arab societies and state media was broken with no attempt on the part of the state media to win society back. A glaring example took place in 1967, when all Arab newspapers, radio, and television, following the lead of Egyptian radio announcer Ahmed Sa'id, told the Arab people that the Arab armies had crushed the Israeli army and that Israeli planes were falling from the skies like flies. It did not take long for the Arabs to learn the bitter truth from foreign sources such as the BBC. Arabs lost their trust in official announcements whether these came through radio, print, or television.

By trust, I mean people's confidence in and reliance on a person or an institution to be true to their commitments. But the meaning of trust and the accompanying systems of verification vary from one society to the next.[8] Trust in "traditional" societies depends on face-to-face interaction and a specific system of verification.[9] But as relationships become more complicated and people move from one end of the globe to the other, face-to-face verification systems are replaced by institutions and other mechanisms. The bases of modern trust are access points to expert systems where face-to-face encounters meet faceless commitment. This expert system-based trust is what makes us confident that our cars will not break down as long as we are following the maintenance manual. It is the kind of trust that makes even the enemies of the United States believe in the U.S. dollar and the American government's institutional commitment to guaranteeing this token of exchange. Many modernization theorists who believe in clear differences between traditional and Western societies would argue that this kind of trust is "modern" and does not work in a traditional setting, such as the Arab world. However, everyday evidence from various fields show that the Arab world is far more complex than was originally perceived. Arab systems of trust are selective, differentiated, and complex. Arabs trust that their television sets will work, but very rarely trust the messages coming from them. In the case of finance, many Arabs trust financial institutions that exist outside the national boundaries more than they trust the local ones. In the West, a written document enjoys more credibility than an oral source; in the Arab world, the opposite is often true.

Trust, whether one lives in a modern society or a supposedly traditional one, has accompaniments, such as a linguistic environment, a knowledge base, and shared symbols and mutuality. Trusted communication in the Arab world is that which follows something akin to the indigenous model of isnad. This is a method for transmitting the sayings of the prophet orally, a means of transmitting authoritative utterances that references not just the information (the Hadith), but also the name of the person or persons who transmitted it. The reliability of this depends on the unbroken and unimpeachable chain of those who handed down the Prophet's utterances.[10] Although this model is dominant in the religious domain, it shapes the cosmology of the larger society with regard to trust. Information coming from distant places or distant times requires verification. People must acquire a special talent for distinguishing true news from false. Because they have been lied to many times, Arabs seem to be able to select their information with tremendous ease. This is what they do on a daily basis with information they get whether it is printed, or on the radio, television, or the internet.

Information Technology and Political Change: Three Cases from the Arab World

First, with the exception of a few authors, such as William Rugh, who have done extensive surveys of the Arab press, there is very little analysis of radio and television and their impact on the Arab world.[11] Douglas Boyd's book on broadcasting in the Arab world is a very good survey, but short on analysis.[12] Thus, it is still difficult to assess new media when the old media and their impact have not yet been fully investigated. Nonetheless, through a discussion of media examples from three cases from the Arab world; Saudi Arabia, Qatar, Egypt and Lebanon, I would like to raise some warnings concerning the emerging consensus on the role of the new media and their ability to transform Arab societies. Again, central to my argument is the relationship between these means of information and trust.

New Media and the Case of Saudi Arabia

Nowhere in the Arab world has the ability to access the new technology been greater than in the Arabian Gulf. Chief among the countries that invested in the new technology is Saudi Arabia. Most satellite channels that dominate the airwaves in the region are Saudi-owned. For example, Saudi businessman Sheikh Saleh Kamel owns many entertainment channels, such as ART. Saudi-controlled religious channels include Al-Majd and Irqa. In addition to Saleh Kamel, several Saudi royal family members own channels, for instance Al-Waleed bin Talal owns the music channel Rotana and the newly launched religious network Al-Risala. Al-Waleed al-Ibrahim, the brother-in-law of the late King Fahd, owns the MBC group of which the Al-Arabiya news channel and other entertainment networks are a part.

Since the introduction of the fax machine and the internet and their use by the Saudi opposition, predictions about the impending collapse of the Saudi state under the pressure of technology became widespread in the

Western media and among the Western analysts. Many speculated that the political order of the desert kingdom was decaying and was only months away from crumbling at the click of a mouse.[13] This did not prove true for reasons that I will explain later on. Furthermore, due to the state of tension between Saudi Arabia and Qatar many expected that Al-Jazeera would be able to undermine the Saudi system. Although Al-Jazeera has interviewed many Saudi opposition figures, including Sa'd Al-Faqih and Mohsen Al-'Awaji, it has failed to affect change in Saudi Arabia. This is because Saudis see Al-Jazeera's information as suspect. Again this relates to the issues of trust and communication. For one, Al-Jazeera, despite ten years of operation, has failed to break a single Saudi story that the people on the ground can verify and trust. Even the terrorist events in Riyadh from 2003 to 2006 were beyond its grasp. The list of suspected terrorists was reported on the basis of information from the Saudi Ministry of Interior. Without the help of the Saudi government, Al-Jazeera had no access to Saudi society. One can appreciate the difficulty of access to Saudi society. However, it also lacks access to Syria, Egypt, and many of the North African countries. Al-Jazeera has full access only in areas under occupation, such as Iraq and Palestine. It also has access to Western democracies. It can report what it desires about George Bush or Tony Blair, but cannot report one single scandal in the Arab world. While Al-Jazeera, for example, had a free reign in reporting the court case of Michael Jackson; it was not able to report on a case of a pedophile Muslim preacher in Saudi Arabia. Al-Jazeera interviewed the preacher many times but never devoted any coverage to the scandal that is known throughout Saudi Arabia. So much for Al-Jazeera's taboo-breaking coverage.

The Saudi opposition abroad, primarily the London-based Committee for the Defense of Legitimate Rights (CDLR), initially made excellent use of the new media, faxing its communiqués to some 600 numbers inside Saudi Arabia, providing a toll-free telephone link to its London offices, and maintaining a useful web page.[14] But over the past few years, the opposition—the presumed beneficiary of the subversive potential of new communication technology—has suffered a tremendous loss of credibility inside the kingdom.

There are several reasons for this. In 1996, a split occurred between CLR leader Muhammad al-Mas'ari and the head of the London office, Sa'd Al-Faqih. Al-Faqih broke with the CDLR and founded a new rival group, the Movement for Islamic Reform in Arabia (MIRA). This split produced confusion among local supporters back in the kingdom.[15] In addition, nearly all Saudis I interviewed inside the kingdom attested to the popularity of the CDLR faxes when they were still a novelty in the mid-1990s, but indicated that subsequently they had lost their charismatic appeal, becoming routinized and even degenerated into gossip-sheets. In short, there was an accelerated erosion of trust in the information coming from London. The local people's inability to verify some of the news stories through their isnad mechanism (inquiring of relatives and trusted friends who work inside the system about the stories reported) undermined the stories' credibility. In addition, by behaving like a sponsor of Saed Al-Faqih and other opposition figures, Al-Jazeera also lost trust with the Saudi audience. Both Al-Faqih and Al-Mas'ari were seen as international supporters of Al-Qaeda, especially when the United Nations took action against Al-Faqih's finances.[16]

Further eroding the trust, or marginalizing the message, of the Saudi opposition in London are its competitors, addressing almost the same audience, but with more trusted and time-tested media sources at their disposal: i.e. the BBC and other Western media outlets. Consumers of Saudi opposition messages are relatively few. As the London-based opposition uses the written word as its primary means of communicating resistance, its audience is confined to those who read. Information sent over the internet or by e-mail reaches only those who are computer literate and English-speaking. The technologically adept segments of Saudi society are the most unlikely to rebel openly and risk their privileged position. Moreover, this segment of Saudi society has never been deprived of information, previously listening to radio broadcasts of the BBC and VOA inside Saudi Arabia and reading English language newspapers when they were abroad. Now, with the introduction of satellite dishes, the English-speaking segment of Saudi society can get news from the BBC and CNN on television, while logging on to other sources on the web instead of CDLR or MIRA's newsletters and homepages. Thus far Al-Jazeera and Al-Arabiya have been reporting this very information, but in Arabic. So the two channels merely amplified the stories of CNN, the BBC, and Western news agencies like UPI or AFP. From their inauguration to the present, the Arab media have not broken a single story. Even stories like the Abu Ghraib scandal and the Guantanamo were broken by CBS and other Western media. Thus Al-Jazeera and Al-Arabiya merely widened Arab access to Western stories that used to be the privilege of the English-speaking elite in the Arab world.

Chief among the problems of the Saudi opposition in London is information and trust. On March 3, 1998, the opposition in London announced on their websites that King Fahd had died and that the royal family was engaged in covering up the story until it had managed the succession.[17] In addition to the problem of trust the London-based opposition and their messages fail to operate within the dominant domain of orality in the society. This domain is left to the cassette tape, local mosques, and face-to-face communication.

If one looks at the state response to opposition, one sees that it does not take the internet and the fax machine seriously, but focuses its efforts on regulating and cracking down on the opposition using the decidedly old-fashioned methods of cassette tapes and sermons in mosques. This is because many people listen to tapes more frequently than they read a text. Many people have tape players in their cars, whereas very few have faxes. The use of fax machines in Saudi Arabia is extremely limited compared to the use of the phone. Faxes are part of the domain of the written word, and are only used within formal institutions such as state-related organizations and businesses that deal with the state or have international links. Thus, the inherent characteristics of each technology limits its effectiveness and sometimes limits its ability to gain trust.

The failure of website-based opposition comes from its inability to make use of the interface among the various media that cut across the domains of the written and the oral. Furthermore, the access of the Saudi state to these new technologies is greater than that of the opposition. Through its media like the Al-Ikhbariya news channel and Al-Arabiya and media of state proxies such as the internet-based newspaper Elaph, the state has been able to drown out the message of its opponents.

Qatar: The Case of Al-Jazeera

The Qatari Al-Jazeera channel has become the darling of media analysts looking for a transforming Arab media story. Al-Jazeera has almost all the identifiable visuals that we see in the Western media. To be able to see a debate similar to the American show *Crossfire* does not mean that freedom of speech in the Arab world is fully realized, any more than to see voting and ballot boxes means that democracy has taken hold. False cultural cognates can be a serious problem here. Thus, it is important to look at how form and content interplay, and how they connect to the larger socio-cultural terrain of the Arab world. We also need to assess the relationship between these forms, this new channel and trust.

As I explained in Chapter 2, the parent of Al-Jazeera was an offshore station based in London, the Arabic BBC. After this was shut down, the staff of the station were hired to work in Doha for a new station owned by the royal family of Qatar. The chairman of the board of the station is Sheikh Tamir Al-Thani, a member of the ruling family. Although physically in an Arab country, Al-Jazeera continued the tradition of the offshore Arab satellite stations. Most new Arab satellite stations can be conceptualized as offshore in relation to other Arab states. Here the title of Mona Simpson's novel *Anywhere but Here* could work as a perfect slogan to summarise Al-Jazeera's relationship with Qatar and indeed the relationships of all the satellite channels with their host states. The Saudi-owned Al-Arabiya can be critical of any country but Saudi Arabia; the Egyptian satellite channels can be critical of any country but Egypt, and so on.

After ten years of operation, Al-Jazeera remains dependent on financial support from the Qatari government, for it has very little commercial advertising to carry its financial burden. Al-Jazeera's popularity in the Arab world can be traced to its coverage of Operation Desert Fox in 1998. For the first time, the Arabs felt that their news media was not flatly lying to them as the Voice of the Arabs did in 1967. But this trust that Al-Jazeera established with its audience is gradually eroding as the station conforms to the policies of the Qatari government. Because of what has been written about Al-Jazeera and its history elsewhere, I would like to raise a few points that many seem to have forgotten in the midst of the excitement about this station that many predicted would change Arab politics. To begin with, in many respects Al-Jazeera models itself on CNN. It has its *Crossfire*, in Al-Ittijah Al-Mu'akis (The opposite tendency), and its own various Larry Kings. This tendency is not exclusive to Al-Jazeera; most Arab television programs are modeled in one way or another after Western stations, often with literal or near-literal translations of the titles. ABC's *Good Morning America* is all over the Arab world as *Sabah al-Khayr Ya Misr* (Good morning Egypt), *Sabah al-Khayr Ya Kuwayt* (Good morning Kuwait), and so on. The kingdom of Saudi Arabia was a little more liberal with the translation, as the dominant show in Saudi Arabia is called *Al-Mamlaka Hadha al-Sabah* (The Kingdom this morning). Recently, Egyptian television launched a new and attractive show called *Wajih al-Sahafa*, which translates as "Meet the press". Borrowing ready-made molds and fitting them with Arabic is a time-honored tradition in the Arab world. Even radical groups and states resort to translation—when Arab radicals wanted to uplift the nation they adopted the idea of an Arab "renaissance" which translated as al-Ba'th—the Ba'th party dominant in Syria and formerly in Iraq. A song that serves almost as the Egyptian national anthem is modeled on Kennedy's famous "don't ask what your country can do for you," statement: the Egyptian song starts with "don't say what Egypt gave us, but say what we can do for Egypt."

However, at the level of content, Al-Jazeera is modeled on Gamal Abdul Nasser's *Sawt Al-Arab* (Voice of the Arabs) radio station.[18] The Arabic version of *Crossfire* is critical of all Arab countries except Qatar, which owns the station and Syria—the birthplace of the host of the show.

It is easy to confuse Al-Jazeera's call-in shows with their American counterparts. But unlike American call-ins, Al-Jazeera's live shows are extremely managed. The producer of the show usually notifies those whom the station wants to have participate as callers. As the station does not have a toll-free number, the producers usually call the people who will comment. This is because it is very expensive to make an international call from poor countries like Egypt and Morocco, and very few will pay that much money to air their opinions on Al-Jazeera. As the station itself manages the "viewers' calls," the rules of the game are that each guest is also allowed three callers. But this works more in theory than in practice.

If one takes the Arab *Crossfire* (Al-Ittijah al-Mu'akis) as an example, the problems of the station becomes obvious. In this show, the dominant confrontation is between Arab nationalists and Islamists against "pro-Western or Westernized Arabs." The Arab nationalist or Islamist guest represents the view of the station while the other guest usually represents "the defeatist camp," i.e. Arabs who have made their peace with the West and are willing to live in peace with Israel. Usually the host of the show, Mr. Faisal

Al-Qasim, is unabashedly on the Arab nationalist side. No attempt is made to offer even packaged objectivity, such as can be found on U.S. television.

In one show, the station invited a representative of the pro-peace process Copenhagen Group, 'Abd al-Mun'im Sa'id from Cairo, to face off with Amin Iskandar, the head of the Committee of the Struggle Against Normalization with Israel. The host of the show told Dr. Sa'id that he had to let him know the names and phone numbers of three people who would support the objectives of the Copenhagen Group. His opponent would be given the same opportunity. However, in reality those the station called were the Islamist Fahmi Huwaydi, and Ba'thist Mustafa Bakri, plus three other Islamists and nationalists. From the other camp, only one caller supported Sa'id. When Sa'id inquired about this asymmetry, he was told that his people were not available.[19] This was allegedly why the station had to call the Islamists and Ba'thists. This show was aired on August 17, 1999.

To compare the same show over time and see whether or not the picture has changed, let me describe the show of April 26, 2000. In this show broadcast from Cairo, Faisal Al-Qasim invited the station's regular, pro-Saddam Ba'thist Mustafa Bakri, to debate with "defeatist" Egyptian peace activist Nabil Fuda. In addition to the attacks launched by Bakri, show host Al-Qasim weighed in telling Fuda that "Israel is a cancer that should be surgically removed from the Middle East." Then the calls came in from Rif'at Sayyid Ahmad, an Egyptian Islamist supporting Bakri and denouncing "the traitor" Fuda. Unlike 'Abd al-Mun'im Sa'id, Fuda received no calls of support. The station called only those who denounced Israel and the peace process. The show ended with a finely choreographed moment in which Al-Qasim asked Bakri to shake hands with his fellow Egyptian, and Bakri announced that he would not shake the dirty hand that shook hands with Israelis. Of course, in the Cairo journalistic community, it is generally known that Bakri's newspaper Al-'Usbu'a was financed by Saddam and cared more about Saddam's news agenda than about Egyptian stories. After the capture of Saddam, Bakri moved on to another Kafil to support his newspaper. Qatar became Bakri's new Kafil.

With the exception of the half-hour news, any content analysis of Al-Jazeera will reveal that it is a channel that represents the viewpoint of the new alliance in the Middle East, namely the Ba'thists or Arab nationalists and the Islamists. This is an alliance that Arab states have used tactically over the years but never previously granted any voice. Al-Jazeera is the voice of this alliance. As I pointed out in previous chapters, one of the dominant figures in Al-Jazeera is Yousef Al-Qaradawi, a member of the Egyptian Muslim Brotherhood. Another Brotherhood member is one of Al-Jazeera's hosts, Ahmad Mansour. Al-Qasim, Jamil 'Azr, and some of their guests represent the Arab nationalists. I visited Al-Jazeera's headquarters in Doha in 1998 and met some of the producers. In my conversations with them, I identified four ideological camps: Ba'thists, nationalists, Nasserists, and Islamists. These three are various strands of what we call Arab nationalism.

So to what degree is Al-Jazeera different from the Saudi-owned MBC and Al-Arabiya or the Egyptian satellite channels or even the Sudanese channels? For one, Al-Jazeera gained trust through its coverage of Iraq during Desert Fox, which the other stations did not. The difference is rather like that between the London-based *Al-Hayat* newspaper and Egypt's *Al-Ahram*, or between *Asharq Al-Awsat* and *Al-Riyadh*, both Saudi-owned, but the first comes from London, while the other came from Riyadh. It is the difference between the offshore liberal Arab state and its conservative local counterpart. Offshore, Saudi Arabia is represented by the Saudi publishing company headed by Prince Faisal bin Salman bin Abdel 'Aziz and *Al-Hayat* owned by Prince Khaled bin Sultan, which are far more permissive than any locally based Saudi newspapers. It is also represented by the Dubai-based MBC channels and Al-Arabiya.

The new satellite channels may impact on Arab political and cultural language. However, one needs to make two further leap to link that impact to the emergence of a new public space, the rise of a civil society, and political and social change. One must make the case that the general culture of the Arab world is changing due to these new means of communication, and then make the case that the change in political culture will lead to political change. One has to contend with the absence of a mediating institution between the information-loaded Arab citizen and the state. The aggregation and articulation of interest based on the new information is almost impossible without channeling institutions. In addition, the hand of the Arab state is extremely heavy within its local context. It may not be able to shape the discourse, but it can certainly set limits on it and can change the rules of the game any time.

The Egyptian Case

When one looks at Egypt, where a third of the Arab world lives, the figures are startling. To begin with, the literacy rate in Egypt in 2004 was estimated to be 51.4 percent.[20] Second, the number of telephone land-lines in December 2005 was 10.4 million. The number of internet users that year was 5 million. Cellular phone usage was 14 million in December 2005. Thus, the number of cellular phone users is almost triple that of the internet users. This is telling: half of Egypt exists in the domain of orality, while the other half reluctantly exists in the domain of the written word.[21]

In the Egypt of the late 1970s, many activists opposed to Anwar Sadat (president 1970–1981) felt that if the Egyptian government would allow people the use of typewriters and carbon copying, the opposition could topple the regime. The assumption was that Sadat's control of information and the people's lack of knowledge about this regime was what kept it standing. Subsequently, the state has allowed not only the use of typewriters, but fax machines, copying machines, and finally the use of computers and the internet. Despite the differences in the scope of political freedoms between Sadat's and Husni Mubarak's Egypt, very few believe that these changes are the result of increased information and technology diffusion in Egypt.

In fact, any observer of Egyptian political life will say that the newspapers of the opposition parties are the only indications of the existence of these parties. Ordinary Egyptians refer to these parties as Al-Ahzab al-Waraqiyya, or paper parties.[22] It would seem that because of their belief in the power of the media, opposition political parties in Egypt have invested more in their newspapers than in building grassroots support or a power base. Yet these modern media have somehow failed to appeal to a wider public. With the exception of the newspaper and its staff and a few party cadres, one is hard-pressed to find any other influence of Egypt's opposition parties. Thus McLuhan's famous statement "the medium is the message" can be replaced by the "medium is the party" in the case of Egypt's opposition parties. The reasons for this are numerous. But for our purposes here, the point to remember is that opposition newspapers have failed to win the trust of their audience. In addition, there are problems of communication stemming from the disjunction between the language of the newspaper and the language of general society.

Central to the disjunction between the party's newspaper and the larger society may be the absence of trust and the fact that the idiom of the modern opposition in Egypt is that of the written word, standard Arabic, while the target constituency of this opposition operates in the domains of illiteracy, orality, and the vernacular. In the Arab world, communication is conducted primarily through informal institutions, such as interpersonal communication, the mosque, and the souq. These are what Anthony Giddens calls "facework institutions," where the validity of the message and the person delivering the message and their trustworthiness are verifiable.

The main problem of political communication in Egypt, and by extension, in almost all Arab states, is that trust in modern state institutions and the expert system is minimal. This is not because the Arabs exist in a premodern world. Arabs rely on certain access points of modernity, regardless of the distance in space and time. Arabs prefer to keep their money in dollars rather than in local currency, although many of them have never been to the United States. They trust American money because of their experience of it. Even radical Islamists keep their money in dollars while chanting anti-U.S. slogans. Arabs trust that Japanese cars will not break down. Thus, my argument is not that Arabs do not trust the media because it is foreign but that Arabs, like everyone else, are selective about what to trust and what not to trust. Studies of Egyptian television show that villagers prefer entertainment shows and very few of them watch news or public affairs shows. And those who do prefer broadcasting from outside the national boundaries, namely the BBC, Radio Monte Carlo, and Voice of America.[23]

One can identify some basic elements of the failure of modern means of communication and other institutions to gain trust in the Arab social formation. One of these relates to realms of symbolic exchange, the rules that govern them, and the languages and symbols used in this interaction. One of the problems is the absence of an interface between modern standard Arabic, with its links to state authority, and the dialect of the society and the powerless. A number of scholars have already analyzed the relationship between authoritative discourse and media, and the various forms of language used.[24] This problem is compounded by the absence of an interface between the various traditional media institutions on the one hand, and the new grafted-on modern means of communication on the other. The interface between the oral and the written can come about only if the written Arabic integrates the 'ammiya (the local dialects) with what Bourdieu calls "legitimate language," the language of the state and its institutions.[25] The state may in fact have better luck than opposition groups connecting with society, because it relies on means of communication that interface with the realm of orality, though not fully. These means are radio and television, and this interface is apparent most when the messages are communicated through subtle forms like drama and entertainment, rather than through direct speech.

For political communication based on the written word to be effective, the state must increase the levels of literacy. But the issue is complicated by the introduction of audio-visual means of communication, such as the radio and television.[26] These means of communication circumvented the importance of the written word as a means of modern communication. Radio has interfaced better with the domain of the vernacular than the press, at least at the level of entertainment. However, the worldview of the villages and that of the urban-based state remains far apart. It is only when the state talks about defending the honor of the nation or defending Islam that people listen and share its language. Complications raised by the co-existence of the written word in the press with vernacular expression in audio-visual forms of communication are very likely to be carried over into the internet, especially when it comes to text-based messages. It is also important to note that English dominates the internet. The internet may allow for greater use of vernacular in one-to-one communication, but mass mailing or posting intended for a mass audience may not be in standard Arabic, but rather in some form of formal Arabic. The function of this formal Arabic is not the preservation of the language of the Quran, but linking the state and its institutions to past continuities.

General Conclusions and Implications

As we have seen, trust between Arab society and its media was broken when Ahmad Sa'id, the beloved announcer on Sawt Al-Arab, told the Arabs in 1967 that they were winning a war that in fact they were losing. Since then trust was broken between the public and these media institutions, Arab states have done very little to restore public confidence in the media. Thus, the majority of the Arab world relies either on expert systems of modernity outside the national boundaries, such as the BBC or CNN, or on face-to-face communication, or on a verifiable source of local information, something akin to the isnad model.

Our inability to conceptualize the flexibility of the Arab public in dealing with information technologies comes from our uncritical commitment to our theories about the Arab world. It is wrong to categorize the Arab man or woman as either Westernized, modern, or a traditional Islamist. No one exists exclusively in the realm of tradition or in the realm of modernity. Arab individuals engage tradition at times and modernity at others. This is not the image of the camel, the tent, and the cellular phone. It is much more complex than that. The complexity of the Arab world comes from its cultural specificity, its encounters with modernity and postmodernity, and the notion of trust associated with each of them. It is not a blind trust; it is a differentiated trust. For example, when a Syrian women was asked in an interview whether she liked Al-Jazeera and whether she trusted the station and the show of her countryman Faisal Al-Qasim in particular, her answer made this point about differentiated trust very clear. "Sometimes I trust him but most of the time I don't. For he is a Ba'thist and also a minority Druze. When he sings the praise of the Ba'th of Syria, I know he is lying, when he is critical of some Syrian practices, I also know he is lying," she said. "This is because you don't know when he becomes a minority Druze or a Ba'thist and on what issue." Her views are typical of young Arab audiences watching Al-Jazeera today.

It is obvious from the above discussion that the arguments that connect new information technologies with the rise of civil society or the public sphere, let alone political change, are not warranted. There are many problems associated with our approach to these issues, and many others related to the specific relations between these new modern media and the local setting. At the core of these problems are the issues of communication and trust and their correlates. Some of the accompanying issues of trust that we should take very seriously are those of language, format, and methods of verification and authentication of the data transmitted. In the case of the internet, it is obvious that thus far English remains its lingua franca. The language used is as important as the medium. Muslim chat groups may form as many imagined communities as they can, but they are mostly English language-based imagined communities. The shift in language has positive and negative implications for the elaboration of Muslim discourse. English allows the use of the vernacular as opposed to standard, as is the case for Muslims using Arabic for communicating Islamic ideas. It has the potential to bring the world of daily life and the formal world together. But the use of English in the formal sphere of state institutions and business, while advantageous to a segment of the society, is a complicating factor for others. For the average Arab, the option of using English adds a new demand of literacy that disadvantages his/her economic opportunities. When English became standard in India, the Muslims saw it as another impediment to their struggle for economic and political parity with the Hindus. The Indian case may be not replicated in the Arab world, but it makes us aware of the complexity of the issue of literacy. One has to compare this with the situation in North Africa where other languages compete for central position: Arabic, French, and the local Berber dialects. At least in the Arab world, people do not use standard Arabic to communicate with each other. And moreover there is the cost associated with the use of the internet in the Arab world in terms of hardware as well as software. Many internet advocates understate the magnitude of startup costs. But even those who assume that software and hardware costs will become less burdensome allow that educational costs will rise the more the medium is used. This is particularly significant in an era in which there is tremendous pressures (from the United States, World Bank, etc.) to reduce public expenditures. The Arabs are consumers rather than producers of computers. Thus, questions of dependency are also relevant here.

For social scientists interested in gathering data from Arab newspapers, Arab radio, and Arab satellite television, it is very important to take the issue of socio-linguistics and social epistemology seriously. To understand Islamism for instance, one has to see why the discourse of Egyptian television preacher Sheikh Mutawalli Al-Sha'rawi (1911–1998) and the late blind opposition preacher Sheikh 'Abd al-Hamid Kishk (1933–1996)[27] are popular, while the discourse of other Islamists and nationalists are not. The popularity of these two sheikhs among mainstream Egyptians stems from the fact that unlike many other preachers, both of them used dialect when explaining the standard Arabic of the Hadith and the Quran. The official Islam of the state through the institution of Al-Azhar has failed to create this interface between the standard and the dialect, the oral and the written, and this is why it has not made any inroads into wider society. It is no accident that the Islamists employed cassette tapes rather than written tracts to propagate their message in working-class quarters of Cairo and in the rural areas.

Looking at the question of language may help social scientists understand why Marxist intellectuals move to the Islamic camp with ease. If one examines the language of state nationalism and that of "high" or official Islamism, one would recognize immediately that both camps use formal Arabic as a medium. They also rely heavily on standard Arabic as a means of modernizing the domain of the vernacular. Both the Islamists and the state see the world of the vernacular and orality as one of backwardness. Because both state nationalism and high Islamism are part of the regime of modernity, they fail to connect with the lager realm of orality. If one looks at the issue this way, one will not be surprised to see a modernizing Marxist like the late 'Adil Husayn becoming an Islamist. It is not a difficult transition at all, as Islamists, Marxists and nationalists all use the same language. It is therefore not surprising that Marxists, Islamists, and state nationalists move between these ideological camps with great ease. Perhaps the Ba'thists, Nasserists, and Arab nationalists coexist in Al-Jazeera, simply because they speak the same language.

Because of the intrusiveness of the state and its heavy-handedness, in the Arab world as in many authoritarian settings, journalists and creative writers exchange positions. Fear of retaliation makes social commentators and social historians adopt creative forms of writing as a way of protecting themselves. In this formula the main job of journalists, television announcers, and to some degree intellectuals of the regime is to socialize the citizens into the status quo. Journalists critical of the regime pay dearly for their candor. Thus, to understand the political dynamics of these societies one is well advised to read fiction or to listen to off-stage discourse. Since the second is not easily accessible, fictionalized accounts may be the best alternative. Fiction writers can avoid the intrusiveness of power by claiming that the work is fictional and that any correspondence to reality is a mere accident. Even with this alibi, some fiction writers are persecuted in the Arab world.

Another way of getting access to data in the Arab world that may accurately describe the political dynamic of a regime like say, Saddam's Iraq, is to wait until the regime collapses. Only then one may have access to some accurate data concerning what went on during that political period. Thus, ex post facto and historical data may be the best way to gain insights into Arab political dynamics.

If one is desperate to write about the contemporary state of the Arab world, the principle of "anywhere but here" is a good beginning. Thus if one wants to know about Egypt, one should watch Al-Jazeera and read the Arab press, except that coming from Egypt. If one wants to know about Qatar, one should examine all Arab press except that of Qatar. Only through such methods can one understand Arab politics. If one is to read the Arab press or watch Arab television without observing this rule, ones enterprise is destined for failure.

Thus, the main issue in the Arab world is not the diffusion of new information technologies or the rise of many satellite television channels. The main question is one of trust. State-owned media in the Arab world have failed to win back the trust of the Arab populace that was lost in 1967. Al-Jazeera won trust on the basis of its coverage of Desert Fox from inside Iraq, but now has begun squandering this trust, as people have started noticing the absence of any Qatar-critical stories and the influence of Qatari government on the station. The internet is a different story. Amazon.com is not doing well in the Arab world, but not because of Arab lack of access to the internet. The reason is that the threshold of trust associated with buying and selling on the internet is higher. While consuming news from a television channel requires trust in that channel, selling and buying on the internet requires trust in the whole system. One needs a credit card to buy from Amazon.com. Thus one needs to establish trust in what is being sold and the financial institutions issuing the cards. It is not enough to trust the medium or the message, one must also be able to trust the whole social, economic, and political system.

Finally, the Arab media remains an expensive political tool that is not expected to be ceded by states to their respective civil societies any time soon. Most media outlets remain status-quo institutions, at least in relation to their host countries. While access to new forms of information technology is constantly growing, the political context precluding the interaction between the individual and those technologies, as well as the broader relationship between the society and the state, is largely static. The Arab media reflect the political, social, and legal changes on the ground more than they shape it.

CONCLUSIONS

The Arab media are inherently political. This has been shown to be true in the case of Al-Jazeera and Al-Arabiya. These channels were created for political purposes and in response to security concerns of Saudi Arabia and Qatar, both in relation to each other and vis-à-vis other regional powers. In the case of Lebanon, the networks of political, ethnic, and religious groups that govern its media were apparent in my analysis of the coverage of Hariri's assassination. Although these analyses do not include a full account of all audio-visual and print media in the Arab world, they still allow us to identify a number of important traits of the Arab media from the case studies I examined in this book. One such trait is that media in the Arab world do not function in accordance with the Western conceptions of "private" media. In authoritarian settings of the Arab and by extension, the Muslim world, the private/public model does not hold. The owner and the person-in-charge are not synonymous in the context of Arab media. Moreover, to understand the motivations driving the creation of media outlets in the region, particularly news media, one must take into consideration the political context that governs these societies. Six years ago, in *Saudi Arabia and the Politics of Dissent*, I wrote about how the advent of information technology and the internet has allowed opposition groups in Saudi Arabia to amplify their message and impact audiences at home. However, those very technological advancements and new media are not exclusively oppositionist. In fact, states are more adept at using these new technologies and new media to consolidate their power and intimidate their enemies. Put differently, civil society and political opposition are not the only actors who have taken advantage of the opportunities and influence that the realm of technology has to offer. States and ruling elites have seized on new technologies to reinforce the status quo and to advance their own political agendas. The state's ability to use media more effectively than the various segments of civil society contradicts the nostrums of globalization discourse and those who argue for the declining role of the state.

The Arab satellite media is in particular a world that remains highly controlled by rulers and states through both direct and indirect links. This characteristic of the Arab media cannot be fully discerned unless we fine-tune the way we think about the relationship between private and public, the state and kinship and ethnic ties. Such relationships have been closely studied by scholars of the Arab and Muslim world, but have not been generally linked to the study of contemporary mass media because of the continued dominance of theories about the media drawn from ideal types of neo-liberal societies.

The larger point that I seek to convey in this book is that we cannot understand the Arab media in isolation from the web of social and political relations that determine what is reported or talked about in the newspaper and on the television screen. In the social webs and networks that make up the media, I have identified a number of critical parameters that determine the nature of programming and coverage we find on Arab media. *Ownership of media* is one such parameter. Al-Jazeera, for example, can criticize any country or government in the Arab world, but cannot make even the mildest comment about its owners. The same thing applies to the Saudi-owned Al-Arabiya. It can comment on news and air views about any country in the Arab world with the exception of Saudi Arabia (Chapter 2). Even channels that appear private, operating in semi-democratic settings like Lebanon, such as Future TV, owned by the Hariri family, can be critical of all political forces in Lebanon except the practices of their proprietors. The relationship between loyalty to owner, be it a person, a government, or a political group, and programming, is vividly illustrated with many examples in Chapter 3. The ownership of a given media outlet determines its coverage and the type of commentaries it airs.

Paradoxically, the Arab media are freer under occupation than they are in lands controlled by Arab regimes. Notwithstanding the hardships and the pressure faced by journalists in such areas, reports from the occupied territories in West Bank, Gaza, and Iraq are more vigorous than those coming from bureaus in Damascus or Cairo. This is because Israeli and American forces do not enjoy the same privileges that Arab autocrats have in their own countries: jailing, kidnapping, or killing reporters. The threat of revenge from authoritarian regimes causes many journalists and media organizations to shy away from balanced reporting. Thus the authoritarian setting encircling the Arab media continues to be a very important factor in shaping news coverage and programming (Chapter 1).

Furthermore, the journalists themselves as a transnational force affect the kind of reporting we see in the Arab media. Their respective ideological and nationalist loyalties and ethnicities affect how they report issues. As I have shown in Chapter 4, Islamists have managed to penetrate the realm of Arab media in their capacities as journalists, commentators, or regular guests on talk-shows. The Muslim Brotherhood, for instance, was able to secure a solid forum for its members on Al-Jazeera through reporters and commentators sympathetic to, if not members of, the Brotherhood. There is little doubt that the Islamist presence in the Arab media is directly related to the prioritization of Islamic causes and issues on the news agendas of stations like Al-Jazeera. The Islamist perspective is also apparent in the way such stations report Iraq, Palestine, Algeria, and Egypt. It is anything but a coincidence that Al-Jazeera usually gives personalities like Mahmoud Al-Zahar and Ramadan Salah, of Hamas and Islamic Jihad respectively, more airtime and more favorable coverage than Mahmoud Abbas and the Palestinian Authority. Additionally, atrocities committed by governments and groups that embrace an Islamist identity are rarely criticized. One rarely hears journalists speaking against the tactics employed by the Palestinian Islamic Jihad or Al-Aqsa Brigade on any Arab news channel. The atrocities of the Islamic government in Darfur were either reported to justify government actions or to minimize the magnitude of this human disaster caused by Islamists. In the case of the Arab media's coverage of the Algerian government's standoff against local Islamists, we find a clear bias in favor of the latter. The influence of Islamist journalism in Al-Jazeera has also given airtime to the taped messages of Osama bin Laden, Ayman Al-Zawahiri, and Abu Musab Al-Zarqawi.

The modus operandi of Al-Jazeera and Al-Arabiya cannot be understood without investigating the politics that produced them as well as the history of media wars in the region. As explained in Chapter 1, Al-Jazeera and Al-Arabiya are close to being visual versions of Nasser's Sawt Al-Arab radio. Like Sawt Al-Arab, both channels are used by their respective governments as part of their bid for regional hegemony. The Saudi media empire from *Asharq Al-Awsat* to *Al-Hayat* in print to MBC, Al-Ikhbariya, Al-Arabiya, and the many religious channels like ART's Iqra were all launched as counterweights to Arab nationalist media and its post-Cold War remnants. The Islamic or quasi-Islamic tinge of this new media was designed to draw audiences away from secular Arab nationalism. The strategy was successful partly because of the huge amount of money invested, but also because the revived Islamist discourse appeared indigenous compared to the "alien" discourse of Arab nationalism. Marx and Lenin hold little value in the sands of Arabia compared to the rallying cries of "Allahu Akbar" and other Islamic slogans that drive the passion of the Arab street. By the end of the Cold War, secular Arab nationalists like Saddam Hussein seemed to have learned that lesson. Saddam decided to add the words "Allahu Akbar" (Allah is Great) on the Iraqi flag during the second Gulf War. At that time the earliest episodes of media battles between Arab nationalism and Pan-Islamism took place on television.

The rise of Al-Jazeera in 1996 was in a way a response to Saudi dominance of Arab media. As explained in Chapter 2, Saudi Arabia represented a threat to Qatar in the same way Saddam's Iraq represented a threat to Kuwait. Qatar resorted to a three-tier strategy to preclude potential Saudi threats. First, they secured American protection by hosting U.S. military bases. The headquarters of the U.S. Central Command was moved from Tampa, Florida to Qatar. Secondly, Qatar was successful in soliciting partnerships with big American oil companies like Chevron to develop its growing natural gas production industry. Al-Jazeera was the third component of this strategy. It was designed to execute Doha's plan to silence the Saudis. While giving the airstrip to the Americans, Qatar gave the airwaves to Bin Laden and Saudi opposition forces. Bin Laden became Qatar's super-gun against Saudi Arabia.

Understanding this history helps us to avoid the traps of media analysis models imported from Western experiences and applied to the Arab media. The Arab media is a special case in the same way that the Arab world is a special context. This analysis of the Arab media holds important implications for the larger debate about political and social change in the Arab world. This book has shown that the Arab media are anything but independent social institutions, and by implication, they are not part of Arab civil society. In fact, one can make the case that these media outlets are state constructions superimposed on the societies over which they rule. To take it a step further, it is quite possible to view the growth of Arab transnational television as a constraint on the development of a healthy civil society. These media are extra-territorial spaces or virtual spaces that allow various social groups to air their grievances in a controlled environment. The discourse of Arab media through these satellite channels has been emptied of its elements of danger. It is a tamed and dull discourse. It is a safety valve for these authoritarian regimes.

As we all know, authoritarian systems need some space to breath if they are to survive. In the same way that Hong Kong functions as the lungs of the Chinese communist system and Lebanon served as the lung for the totalitarian system of Asad of Syria, the Arab media serve as a non-territorial lung for all these autocracies and semi-autocracies. To confuse this with democratic public spaces is to fall into the trap laid down by the authoritarian regimes. The Arab media in its current state is an impediment to genuine political reform rather than its catalyst. It functions as a tool of governments against both internal and external enemies. This feature was obvious in the Egyptian context when the local media conducted an intense campaign against Saad El Din Ibrahim and against Ayman Nour because they challenged the sitting president of Egypt; they dared to cross the red-lines. This is only one example among thousands that could be used to illustrate the continued use of media to vilify the internal enemies of regimes. In terms of the use of media to intimidate another state one can point to how Qatar used Al-Jazeera in an attempt to silence Saudi Arabia and how Nasser used Sawt Al-Arab against King Faisal and other monarchs in the Middle East. The media is an extension of the authoritarian order it serves. For media to act as an agent of political change, they must be integrated into the institutions of civil society, and must be part of the flow of blood within the body politic. Superimposed media institutions are simply agents and instruments of status-quo forces.

To understand anti-Americanism, one has to comprehend five factors that shaped this phenomenon. The first is the residue of Soviet propaganda adopted by Arab nationalist regimes like that of Nasser. Throughout the 1960s and 1970s Nasser and his radio station Sawt al-Arab filled the airwaves with anti-American and anti-colonial rhetoric. As we have seen in the case of the news coverage of the American occupation of Iraq, Arab journalists opted the easy way out. They did not want to disturb their audience with new facts or new clues and frames of reference that differentiate the American occupation of Iraq from the Israeli occupation of the West Bank and Gaza. Instead they resorted to substituting the Americans for the Israelis and the Iraqis for the Palestinian and used the same discourse to describe the totally different turmoil in Iraq. The same goes for anti-Americanism today. Arab journalists dug out the discourse that their predecessors were using against the British and the French and tagged it to the Americans. These two factors of pro-soviet propaganda of the cold war and the colonial legacy provided the intellectual underpinning of anti-Americanism today.

Other factors are related to the local regimes and local movements and their view of U.S. policies. Yet another is related to the U.S. democratization initiative. It is an easier strategy for some of the authoritarian Arab regimes to use anti-U.S. rhetoric to deflect criticism from the failed policies of Arab regimes and blame it on the outside world, namely the imperialist West or Zionist conspiracies. Anti-Americanism also emanates from the consequences of American policies in the region and the kind of enemies they create. Here I do not mean America's policy toward the Arab–Israeli conflict, though this is a contributing factor. This particular brand of Anti-Americanism we see today is a direct result of actions by the American administration that earned the animosity of Arab nationalists, the radical Islamists, and the ruling elite all at the same time. By attacking Iraq and undermining the Ba'ath regime of Saddam Hussein, Americans anger the Arab nationalists. By attacking the Taliban and Bin Laden, the administration angers the Islamists. By adopting reform as the only way to change the political environment in the Middle East, the United States angers the ruling elite. Thus, America is hated by the Islamists, Arab nationalists, and regimes at the same time. Who is left to support the United States? Only genuine liberals who care about reforming their societies. But these are the people the U.S. administration does not talk to. These are not cheerleaders for America but potential allies who seek to reform the Middle East and transform it into a democratic or at least semi-democratic order. When we think about addressing the issue of anti-Americanism in the Middle East, we have to be fully cognizant of these factors and have the ability to disentangle them instead of lumping them together.

Many in the world counted on the transforming power of the Arab media with respect to political regimes and societies. The reality is that the Arab media's impact on transforming Middle Eastern societies is at best minimal. The discourse may change on the screen, but on the ground the states and security apparatus are very entrenched. TV screens become like a virtual space where criticism of government might be permissible, but actual gatherings of people on the streets are very costly for those who participate in them. One has to look to Egypt's Kifaya movement and the number of them who went to jail for "illegal" public gatherings to comprehend this point.

As I indicated in Chapter 6, the fact that there has been a breach of trust between the media and its audience due to accumulation of historical experiences means that the media's impact minimal. The Arab media told the Arab world in 1967 that Arab armies were crushing the Israelis and then the Arabs woke up to the shock of horrible defeat. The absence of trust persists. Very few Arabs trust newspapers or television to tell them the facts. For these they go to foreign media like the BBC. Trust in the Arab world is based on interpersonal communication. Even if someone hears on radio or TV or reads in a newspaper that the exchange rate of local money against the dollar has changed, usually he picks up the phone and calls his relative working at the newspaper or at the ministry of finance to verify the information. The point here is that those who count on the Arab media to expand public space create a false symmetry between the Arab world and democratic systems in the same way that a false symmetry between Al-Jazeera and BBC is created.

This does not mean that the Arab media is a hopeless case. What it means is that you cannot make changes in what is being said on the airwaves and expect it to correspond with what is happening in any lived reality. Laws have to change and the space of freedom has to expand, and the role of the police state in society has to shrink before we can talk about any kind of genuine transformation. Change starts in a particular place, among people. Only then does the media change. As I have tried to show throughout this book, this is because the entrenched interests that have a stranglehold on Arab societies are those that control the media. A larger theoretical point is that political scientists and media theorists who adopted the discourse of globalization and argued for the declining role of the state should take stock of these cases to revise their theoretical positions and refine their empirical findings.

Notes

Introduction: The Politics of the Arab Media

1. Daniel C. Hallin and Paolo Mancini, *Comparing Media Systems: Three Models of Media and Politics* (London: Cambridge University Press, 2004).

2. Very few media studies have attempted to de-Westernize the debate. For a good critique of the dominance of the Western model in media studies, see James Curran and Myung-Jin Park (eds), *De-Westernizing Media Studies* (New York: Routledge, 2000).

3. See Kamal Qubaisi, "The return to killing journalists," *Asharq Al-Awsat* June 3, 2005; *Al-Hayat* had a front page picture of Qaseer, testimonials by some ten authors, including the editor-in-chief of the newspaper, Mr. Ghasan Sherbal. See *Al-Hayat*, June 3, 2005. Qaseer's own newspaper *Al-Nahar* ran two pictures of him. On the left it had a picture of his car and his body inside leaning against the steering wheel and on the right one of him as the smiling author. These were followed by testimonials about his harassment by Lebanese security officials and the Syrians. Al-Arabiya TV had similar coverage to *Al-Nahar*. Mr. Qaseer's wife Jazeel Khoury works as a host of a political talk show called *bil Araby*.

4. For more on Samir Qaseer's anti-Syrian writings, see Samir Qaseer, *Syrian Democracy and Lebanon's Independence: The Search for a Damascus Spring* (Arabic) (Beirut: Dar Al-Nahar, 2004) and *Soldiers against whom? Lebanon, the Lost Republic* (Beirut: Dar Al-Nahar, 2004).

5. Many vocal journalists such as Sayid Al-Qimini in Egypt, Meshari Al-Zaidi, and Mansour Nuqidan have received threats from jihadist movement on the basis of a fatwa.

6. Based on author's conversation with Nasr Hamid Abu Zeid, Washington, DC, 1998.

7. The Egyptian weekly *Al-Osbou'* plays this role on behalf of state security. The newspaper would engage in any targeted campaign against Saad Al-Din Ibrahim, Ayman Nour, and Rida Hilal.

8. "Fadihat cubonat Saddam" (The Scandal of Saddam's Vouchers), *Al-Hayat*, January 26, 2004.

9. Ahmed Rubai, "The Egyptian press crisis," *Asharq Al-Awsat*, June 20, 2005.

10. For more on these novels see Mamoun Fandy, "Political silence without clothes: the politics of dress or contesting the spatiality of the state in Egypt," *Arab Studies Quarterly*, Vol. 20, No. 2 (Spring 1998).

11. For more on this topic see James C. Scott, *Domination and Arts of Resistance* (New Haven: Yale University Press, 1990).

12. http://www.guardian.co.uk/armstrade/story/0,10674,726395,00.html1.

13. Ibid.

14. Twice Nabil Sharaf Al-Deen and Rida Hilal told me to expect a call from *Al-Ittijah al-Muakis* because they had selected me to support their point of view.

Other journalists report the same thing. Author interview with Talha Jibreel, Washington, DC, January 18, 2006.

15. Interview with Abu Addas's sister on Future TV, May 12, 2005.

16. Author interview with advertising mogul in Lebanon, Antoine Chauri, February 12, 2005.

17. Tareq Abdul Hameed, "Private Saudi media between viability of investment and the understanding of the message of the media," *Al-Ilam wa al-Itissal*, March 11, 2005, p. 14.

18. See Hugh Miles, *Al-Jazeera: The Inside Story of the Arab News Channel that is Challenging the West* (New York: Grove Press, 2005); Mohamed Zayani (ed.), *The Al-Jazeera Phenomenon: Critical Perspectives on New Arab Media* (Boulder, CO: Paradigm Publishers, 2005); and Mohammed el-Nawawy and Adel Iskandar, *Al-Jazeera: The Story of the Network that is Rattling Governments and Redefining Modern Journalism* (Cambridge, MA: Westview Press, 2003).

19. In five separate interviews with leading journalists including two former heads of the Egypt press syndicate I was told that *Al-Osbou'* is the state security newspaper. Its vilification of dissidents like Saad al-Din Ibrahim and Ayman Nour on behalf of the security chiefs was cited as evidence. The interviewees also cited the newspaper's special status as the first "private" newspaper to be given a license to publish in Egypt. This is yet another indication of its strong ties with the security services.

Chapter 1: National Press on the Eve of the Satellite Era

1. For more on Umm Kulthum and her influence in Egypt and beyond, see Virginia Danielson, *The Voice of Egypt: Umm Kulthum, Arabic Songs, and Egyptian Society in the Twentieth Century* (Chicago, IL: University of Chicago Press, 1997).

2. Munir K. Nassar, "Egyptian Mass Media under Nasser and Sadat: Two Models of Press Management and Control," *Journalism Monographs*, No. 124 (December 1990), p. 4.

3. *Akhbar Al-Youm* is the Saturday edition of the daily newspaper *Al-Akhbar*. Prior to his resignation Saeda was the chair of the Al-Akhbar publishing house and the editor-in-chief of the Saturday edition.

4. *Akhbar Al Youm*, June 18, 2005.

5. This view was supported by a prominent opposition leader, Nabil Zaki, in an interview with *Al-Ahram Weekly*. See *Al-Ahram Weekly*, June 23–29, 2005.

6. Examples of such journalists include Mohamed Al-Shinawy, Mohamed Abdul Kereem, Fayza Al-Masry, and Abbas Metwally.

7. TBS interview with Hala Sirhan, "A Dream TV Come True," *Transnational Broadcasting Journal*, No. 8 (Spring/Summer 2002) <http://www.tbsjournal.com/Archives/Spring02/sirhan.html> visited: November 7, 2005.

8. Ibid.

9. *Al-Ahram Weekly*, November 7–13, 2002.

10. Ibid.

11. Ahmed Osman, "Rude awakening: dream drops top talkers," *Transnational Broadcasting Journal*, No. 12 (Spring/Summer 2004), <http://www.tbsjournal.com/dream.htm> visited: November 7, 2005.

12. Quoted in Ibid.

13. Ibid.

14. "A Mideast Media Revolution," *Business Week*, December 23, 2002, <http://www.businessweek.com/magazine/content/02_51/b3813026.htm> visited: November 7, 2005.

15. See Egyptian Media Production City website <http://www.empc.com.eg/ English/Home/home.htm> visited: January 17, 2006.

16. *Al-Ahram Weekly*, November 7–13, 2002.

17. Osman, "Rude Awakening: Dream Drops Top Talkers."

18. Timothy Mitchell, "Dreamland: the Neoliberalism of Your Desires," *Middle East Report Online*, No. 210 (Spring 1999), <http://www.merip.org/mer/mer210/ mitchell.html> visited: November 7, 2005.

19. Osman, "Rude Awakening."

20. *Al-Ahram Weekly*, November 7–13, 2002.

21. Author interview with Dream TV CEO Amr Khafajie, Cairo, December 21, 2005.

22. Ibid.

23. Naila Hamdy, "El Mehwar the Mercurial," *Transnational Broadcasting Journal*, No. 9 (Fall/Winter 2002), <http://www.tbsjournal.com/Archives/Fall02/ Mehwar.html> visited: November 9, 2005.

24. Al-Mehwar website <http://www.elmehwar.tv/about/board1.html> visited: November 9, 2005.

25. Interview with Gamal Enayet, Cairo, December 20, 2005.

26. *Al-Ahram Weekly*, May 12–18, 2005.

27. Cairo Institute for Human Rights Studies, "Monitoring the Media Coverage of Egypt's Presidential Campaigns 2005," September 6, 2005, <http://www.cihrs.org/ pdf/pre_report17Aug%20_4Sep_EN.pdf> visited: November 9, 2005.

28. The capital of Al-Mehwar is $14 million, and writing in 2001, Naomi Sakr deduced that one would need at least $60–70 million to run a satellite channel in the Arab world in the late 1990s. Clearly, the use of government facilities at the Media Production City has reduced much of the costs of operating satellite channels in Egypt. See Naomi Sakr, *Satellite Realms: Transnational Television, Globalization and the Middle East* (London: IB Tauris, 2001), p. 116.

29. John Waterbury, "Whence will Come Egypt's Future Leadership," in Phebe Marr (ed.), *Egypt at the Crossroads: Domestic Stability and Regional Role* (Washington, DC: National Defense University Press, 1999), p. 23.

30. Ibid., p. 23.

31. See Nassar, "Egyptian Mass Media under Nasser and Sadat."

32. Manabir (singular minbar) is the Arabic word for the place in the mosque where a preacher delivers a sermon (the equivalent of pulpit), and its use here suggests that these groups were not to be political parties but rather forums for expressing particular political opinions. The three manabir; Al-Yameen, Al-Yassar, and Al-Wasat, were based upon the existing left, center, and right platforms of the ASU. The word manabir suggests that Sadat was not fully prepared to deal with the idea of a multi-party system in Egypt. In fact present-day Egyptian political parties remain manabir with newspapers but there is very little opportunity for organizing social forces on the ground. Even the limited space given to them through the party newspaper is constantly under siege.

33. Nassar, "Egyptian Mass Media under Nasser and Sadat," pp. 14–15.

34. For more on Egyptian politics during Mubarak's early reign see Robert Springborg, *Mubarak's Egypt: Fragmentation of the Political Order* (Boulder: Westview Press, 1989).

35. Ministry of Information, *Press in Egypt* (State Information Service), p. 83.

36. Law 148 of 1980.

37. Specifically, in addition to the personalities appointed by the Shura Council, the Supreme Press Council consists of: the president of the Shura Council; board of chairs of national newspapers; editors of party newspapers established according to the Parties Act; the president of the Egyptian Press Syndicate; the board chairman of the SIS; the board chair of MENA (Middle East News Agency), the

official state news agency; the president of the board of trustees for broadcasting and television; the president of the printers' union; the board chair of the National Company for Distribution; a circulation expert; and the head of the writers' union. Members serve renewable four-year terms.

38. Abdalla Khalil, *al-Qawaneen al-muqaida lil huquq al-madania wal siyasia fi al-tashre'a al-misri* (Laws Restricting Political and Civil Rights in Egyptian Legislation) (Cairo: EOHR Publications, 1993), p. 119.

39. Article 14 states: Any person wishing to publish a newspaper must submit a written request to the HPC signed by the newspaper's legal representative, giving the name of the newspaper and the language in which it is to be published, the manner of publishing, the address of the editor and the printing house where it is going to be printed.

In case of any planned changes after authorization, the HPC has to be notified at least eight days before such changes are to be put into effect, except in case such changes are introduced in a manner not anticipated. In this case notification has to be made eight days at maximum after the changes were made.

The legal representative is subject to a penalty of at least three months in jail; and a minimum sum of L.E. 500 and not exceeding L.E. 1000, or both in addition to a three months suspension of the newspaper, if he fails to make the notification in time.

Article 15: The HPC shall decide on the notification to publish a newspaper within a period not exceeding 40 days from date of notification. If no decision is published during this period, it shall be taken the HPC has no objection to the publication.

In case a decision is made refusing authorization, the party concerned may appeal to the Ethics Court within a period of thirty days after the refusal of the decision.

Article 16: If the newspaper is not published during the three months following authorization, or if it is not published regularly for six months, the authorization becomes null and void. The HPC shall decide whether a newspaper has or has not been published regularly and notify the party concerned.

40. See *Al-Ahram Weekly*, November 4–10, 2004. The three political parties that were licensed by the committee with no litigation were Al Wefaq Al-Watani (National Accord) in 2000, Al Geel Al Democrati (Democratic Generation) in 2001, and Al-Ghad (Tomorrow) in 2004.

41. Khalil, *Laws Restricting Political and Civil Rights in Egyptian Legislation*, p. 119.

42. For more on the Higher Press Council, see Ministry of Information, *Press in Egypt*, pp. 75–76.

43. Khalil, *Laws Restricting Political and Civil Rights in Egyptian Legislation*.

44. Author interview, Cairo, February 2, 2003.

45. Khalil, *Laws Restricting Political and Civil Rights in Egyptian Legislation*.

46. For more on the concept of semi-authoritarianism, see Daniel Brumberg, "Liberalization versus Democracy: Understanding Arab Political Reform," *Carnegie Endowment Working Papers*, No. 35 (March 2003) and Marina Ottaway, *Democracy Challenged: The Rise of Semi-authoritarianism* (Washington, DC: Carnegie Endowment for International Peace, 2003).

47. Mona El-Ghobashy, "Egypt Looks Ahead to Portentous Year," *Middle East Report Online*, February 2, 2005, <http://www.merip.org/mero/mero020205.html> visited: August 11, 2005.

48. *Al-Arabi*, October 17, 2004.

49. *Al-Arabi*, October 31, 2004.

50. *Al-Arabi*, November 6, 2004.

51. Author interview with Mahmoud al-Maraghi, Cairo, July 28, 1994.

52. *Al-Ahram Weekly*, April 20–26, 2000.

53. *Al-Sha'ab* has been banned since 2000, but continues to produce an online edition.

54. Telephone interview with Abdel Sattar Abu Hussein, September 29, 1994.

55. Ibid.

Chapter 2: Arab Media and Interstate Conflict: Qatar vs. Saudi Arabia

1. The best summaries of the history of Arab media are in William Rugh, *Arab Mass Media* (New York: Praeger, 2004) and Douglas A. Boyd, *Broadcasting in the Arab World: A Survey of the Electronic Media in the Middle East* (Ames: Iowa State University Press, 1999).

2. See Michael N. Barnett, *Dialogues in Arab Politics: Negotiations in Regional Order* (New York: Columbia University Press, 1998), and Barnett and Shibley Telhami (eds.), *Identity and Foreign Policy in the Middle East* (Ithaca: Cornell University Press, 2002).

3. I discuss the role of history and its impact on contemporary Arab media in "Perceptions: Where Al-Jazeera & Co. are Coming From," *The Washington Post*, March 30, 2003, B-01.

4. Even today adult literacy rates in Arab countries remain below the world average. UNESCO statistics show that the average adult literacy in Arab countries between 2000 and 2004 was 62 percent, compared to a world average of 82 percent. See UNESCO, *Education For All Global Monitoring Report: 2005.*

5. Nassar, "Egyptian Mass Media under Nasser and Sadat."

6. See Danielson, *The Voice of Egypt.*

7. Today, many observers draw parallels between Sawt Al-Arab and the false statements of the Iraqi government, particularly those of former Iraqi minister of information Mohammed Saeed Al-Sahaf during the early phases of the American invasion of the country in 2003. See: Ahmed Al-Rabei, "Catastrophe or Joke?" *Asharq Al-Awsat*, June 6, 2005.

8. For more on the change in dress in Egypt, see Fandy "Political science without clothes."

9. For more on the relationship between media and migration see Susan Ossman, *Picturing Casablanca: Portraits of Power in a Modern City* (Berkeley: University of California Press, 1994) and David Morley, *Home Territories: Media, Mobility and Identity* (New York: Routledge, 2000).

10. See David E. Long, *The Kingdom of Saudi Arabia* (Gainesville: University of Florida Press, 1997).

11. The term "victory" here refers to the political victory attained by Arabs from the 1973 war, despite the fact that the war did not result in the recovery of lost territories after Arab armies were subdued by Israel's counteroffensive.

12. Mamoun Fandy, *Saudi Arabia and the Politics of Dissent* (New York: St. Martin's Press, 1999), p. ii.

13. Prince Al-Waleed bin Talal is the son of Prince Talal bin Abdel Aziz, half-brother of King Fahd, a member of the liberal "Free Princes" movement, and an obvious rival to the "Sudairi Seven." He is also the grandson of Lebanon's first prime minister, Riad Al-Solh. After receiving his master's degree from Syracuse University, al-Waleed sreturned to Saudi Arabia, launched one investment after an other and, by the end of the 1980s, held shares in Chase Manhattan, Citicorp, Manufactures Hanover, and Chemical Bank. He is also known to have had investments in Disneyland Paris, News Corporation, Time Warner, Four Seasons Hotels and Resorts, and Mövenpick Hotels and Resorts.

14. "TBS Feature Interview: Sheikh Saleh Kamel, Chairman of the Board, ART," *Transnational Broadcasting Journal*, No. 1 (Fall 1998).

15. Sakr, *Satellite Realms*, p. 34.

16. Abdul Qader Tash, "Islamic Satellite Channels and their Impact on Arab Societies: Iqra Channel—A Case Study," *Transnational Broadcasting Journal*, No. 13 (Fall 2004).

17. Khaled Montasser, "Ikrah satellite Channel," (Arabic) *Elaph* December 4, 2006. <http://www.elaph.com/ElaphWeb/ElaphWriter/2005/12/110548.htm> visited: February 2, 2006.

18. Author interview with Tarik Al-Ajmi, director of Kuwait TV, Kuwait City, May 15, 2005.

19. Interview with Sheikh Abdul Rahman Al-Thani, Doha, March 15, 1997.

20. Kohei Hashimoto, Jareer Elass and Stacy Eller, "Liquified Natural Gas From Qatar: the Qatar Gas Project," *James A. Baker III Institute for Public Policy Energy Forum Working Papers* (December, 2004), p. 33. <http://www.rice.edu/energy/publications/docs/GAS_QatarGasProject.pdf> visited: October 26, 2005.

21. For a glance at the Egyptian response to Al-Jazeera see S. Abdallah Schleifer, "Egyptian media waxes and wanes in its attacks against Al-Jazeera," *Transnational Broadcasting Journal*, No. 5 (Fall/Winter 2000).

22. Author interview with a foreign ministry official, Cairo, April 5, 2004.

23. I was in Doha during Omar Sulaiman's visit, and I discussed the issue with Qatari Sheikh Abdul Rahman Al-Thani, chief of staff of the emir, and Patrick Theros, former U.S. ambassador to Qatar.

24. This number was calculated on the basis of several interviews I conducted in Washington, London, Dubai, Cairo, and Riyadh.

25. See Edmond Ghareeb, "New Media and the Information Revolution in the Arab World: An Assessment," *Middle East Journal*, Vol. 54, No. 3 (Summer 2000), pp. 405–412.

26. Ibid. pp. 407–408.

27. When I asked a senior producer at Al-Jazeera about people who are blacklisted, he told me that sometimes these blacklists are not official. "Sometimes it is done through producers and managers at the station without the knowledge of the Qatari government," he says. He also told me, "Once I told a guest booker not to invite so-and-so for he appeared many times before. The booker thought that I meant this guest is banned or blacklisted and thus he did not invite that guest at all." Interview with a former senior news producer at Al-Jazeera, London, June 16, 2006.

28. See Al-Bannah, two-part documentary aired on Al-Jazeera January 27–February 3, 2006.

29. *Al-Siyasa*, November 28, 2002.

30. This report is based on two interviews I had with Ahmad Mansour in Kuwait in 1997, another interview in Doha, Qatar in 1998 and three telephone conversations in 1999.

31. See Andrea Rugh, *Reveal and Conceal: Dress in Contemporary Egypt* (Cairo: AUC Press, 1986).

32. "Iran Cleric Accuses Qatar of Treason," *Associated Press*, September 20, 2002.

33. "U.S.—Qatari Relations," *Embassy of Qatar in Washington DC Website*, <http://.qatarembassy.net/foreign_policy.asp> visited: June 2, 2005.

34. Jeremy M. Sharp, "Qatar: Background and U.S. Relations," *Congressional Research Service of the Library of Congress* (March 2004), p. 3.

35. Ibid., p. 3.

36. Hashimoto, Elass, and Eller, "Liquified Natural Gas From Qatar," p. 42.

37. Comment made at a lecture at the James Baker III Institute for Public Policy, Houston, TX, June 21, 2002.

38. One has to see how Al-Jazeera has been covering the various energy conferences hosted in Doha. The latest of three conferences that enjoyed coverage on special economic programs and in every news bulletin was the one held in Doha January 30–31, 2006.

39. "Bin Laden tape: text," BBC News, February 12, 2003, <http://news.bbc.co.uk/2/hi/middle_east/2751019.stm> visited: March 2, 2005.

40. "Arab Media Moguls," (Arabic) *Forbes Arabiya* (Jan 2005), p. 25.

41. According to Al-Jazeera producer Khalid al-Mahmoud, advertising revenue only covers 35–40 percent of Al-Jazeera's operating expenses. See Sharp, "Qatar,"p. 4.

42. "Interview: Mohamed Jasim Al-Ali, Al-Jazeera Managing Director," *Transnational Broadcasting Journal*, No. 5 (Fall/Winter 2000). I also interviewed Mr. Al-Ali both in Qatar in 1998 and in Cairo in 2004, and he made clear that the Qatari government controls Al-Jazeera.

43. *Al-Mada*, January 25, 2004.

44. Mohamed I. Ayishy "American-style journalism and Arab world television: an exploratory study of news selection at six Arab world satellite television channels," *Transnational Broadcasting Journal*, No. 6 (Spring/Summer 2001). Also, MBC moved its headquarters from London to Dubai in 2002.

45. "Arab media moguls," p. 20.

46. Author's interview with Al-Rashed, Washington, DC, May 1, 2005.

47. "Profile: Al-Arabiya TV," *BBC News*, November 25, 2003, <http://news.bbc.co.uk/1/hi/world/middle_east/3236654.stm> visited: February 22, 2005.

48. Samantha M. Shapiro, "The War Inside the Arab Newsroom," *New York Times Magazine* (January 2, 2005).

49. Hameed, "Private Saudi media between viability of investment and the understanding of the message of the media," p. 9.

50. This report was prepared and delivered by Al-Jazeera Washington correspondent Mohammed Al-Alami. I talked to Mohammed about the report and asked him about reducing the global report to being about Saudi Arabia alone. He said with laughter, "Do not forget that I said the State Department report was also critical of China. It is one billion people. Isn't this enough for you?" It was obvious that Mohammed was embarrassed by my question. He also told me that he works for Qatar and not Sweden.

51. Author telephone interview with Abdul Rahman Al-Rashed, March 18, 2005.

52. The segments were aired on Al-Jazeera TV and Al-Arabiya TV between 9:00 a.m. and 1:00 p.m. Central Time on April 25, 2005.

53. "A rights group demands that Bush intervene for the release of Saudi oppositionists," (Arabic) *aljazeera.net*, April 25, 2005.

54. "The Qatari Prince faces 8 years of prison in the event of his conviction," (Arabic) *alarabiya.net* (April 25, 2005). <www.alaribya.net/Articlep.aspx?P=12515> visited: April 25, 2005.

55. Ibid.

56. "Bila Hudoud: The Demands of Reform Advocates in Saudi Arabia," (Arabic) *aljazeera.net*, November 5, 2003.

57. "Bila Hudoud: The Popular Position on Anti-Saudi American Campaigns," (Arabic) *aljazeera.net*, July 10, 2002.

58. "Dimensions and Backgrounds of Violence in the Arab Region," (Arabic) *aljazeera.net*, June 5, 2004.

59. "Bila Hudoud: The Reasons Behind the Spread of Violence, Extremism, and Takfir," *aljazeera.net*, January 1, 2004.

60. For examples see "Al-Faqih Delays a Saudi plane," (Arabic) *aljazeera.net*, February 2, 2005; "Security Council Adds Al-Faqih to the Terrorist List," (Arabic)

aljazeera.net, November 13, 2004; "Al-Faqih rebuffs Saudi pardon and Bin Za'er thankful but will not be silent," (Arabic) *aljazeera.net*, August 9, 2005.

61. See for example "Sa'd Al-Faqih accuses Saudi Arabia of trying to kidnap him," (Arabic) *aljazeera.net*, April 23, 2003.

62. "Yemeni–Saudi Border Problems," *aljazeera.net*, February 9, 2006.

63. "Al-Rashed: We did not come up with the Qatari events . . . My rivals resort to 'religious defamation'," (Arabic) *alarabiya.net*, May 1, 2005.

64. "Ma'aref: Israeli Education Minister visited Qatar secretly with an official invitation,"(Arabic) *alarabiya.net*, February 24, 2005.

65. "Arab inquiries about Doha," (Arabic) *alarabiya.net*, February 26, 2005.

66. "Disagreement between Al-Arabiya and Qatar regarding the invitation of an Israeli official," (Arabic) *alarabiya.net*, February 28, 2005.

67. "Israel affirms that Qatar asked it to support its nomination to the Security Council," (Arabic) *alarabiya.net*, May 17, 2005.

68. "Qatar donates 10 million dollars to an Israeli soccer team," (Arabic) *alarabiya.net*, August 4, 2005.

69. "Qatar presents financial aid to the building of a sports stadium in the Israeli city of Sakhneem," (Arabic) *alarabiya.net*, October 11, 2005.

70. "Qatari foreign minister meets with his Israeli counterpart in New York," (Arabic) *alarabiya.net*, September 15, 2005.

71. "Qatari foreign minister wants 'partnership' in return for 'reform'," (Arabic) *alarabiya.net*, March 16, 2004.

72. "Saddam Hussein imprisoned in Qatar without the knowledge of its leaders," (Arabic) *alarabiya.net*, April 7, 2004.

73. See for example the *Taht al-dou'* (Under the light) show about the future of American military bases in the region. "Taht al-dou': the presence and the future of American bases in the Middle East region," (Arabic) *alarabiya.net*, October 6, 2005. See also "Washington develops its air bases in the Middle East with support from Gulf countries," (Arabic) *alarabiya.net*, September 18, 2005.

74. "Qatari tribe loses its citizenship en masse for supporting the father of the Qatari emir," (Arabic) *alarabiya.net*, March 30, 2005.

75. See for example "An Al-Murrah family tells the story of the gradual murder it faced in Qatar," (Arabic) *alarabiya.net*, April 16, 2005.

76. See for example an episode of *Al-tab'a al-akheerah* (Last Edition) "Al-Tabha al-akheerah: the deterioration of the Qatari tribe Crisis," (Arabic) *alarabiya.net*, April 16, 2005. An entire episode of *taht al-dou'* ("Under the light") was devoted to the topic: "Taht al-dou': The revoking of Qatari citizenship of Al-Ghufran," (Arabic) *alarabiya.net*, June 23, 2005.

77. See "3500 people resort to Saudi Arabia after the revoking of their Qatari citizenship," (Arabic) *alarabiya.net*, April 20, 2005; "A Qatari human rights report documents the revoking of the citizenship of nine individuals and ignores the revoking of the citizenship of a tribe," (Arabic) *alarabiya.net*, May 10, 2005; "A Qatari governmental human rights group follows the revoking of the citinzenship of a tribe," (Arabic) *alarabiya.net*, June 13, 2005; "Qatari migrants affirm their continued suffering.," (Arabic) *alarabiya.net*, June 26, 2005.

78. "Ten thousand pounds fine for an Iraqi newspaper in the court case of the Qatari emir's wife," (Arabic) *alarabiya.net*, January 26, 2005.

79. "Qatari print and visual media ignored the incident of 'Antiquities Sheikh'," (Arabic) *alarabiya.net*, March 14, 2005. Another report ran a few days later alleging that many of the antiques purchased by Sheikh Saud bin Mohamed Al-Thani were unaccounted for.

80. This article appeared on alarabiya.net. <http//www.alarabiya.tv/articlep. aspx?P = 9837> visited: March 29, 2005.

81. See "Member of the Qatari Royal family who had sex with underage girls put on trial in Prague," (Arabic) *alarabiya.net*, March 29, 2005; "Czech police receives bribes to free Qatari prince," (Arabic) *alarabiya.net*, April 20, 2005; "Qatari sheikh faces Czech court for accusations of having sex with underage girls," (Arabic) *alarabiya.net*, April 25, 2005; "Czech courts refuses to hand in Qatari sheikh to receive trial in his country," (Arabic) *alarabiya.net*, August 10, 2005.

82. "A leader in the Qatari ruling family had sexual relations with young girls in Prague," (Arabic) *alarabiya.net*, March 29, 2005, <http://www.alarabiya.net/articles/2005/03/29/11714.htm> visited: March 17, 2006.

83. Khaled Taha, "Rise in Syrian Exports to Qatar," Elaph, February 10, 2006, <http://www.elaph.com/ElaphWeb/Economics/2006/2/127263.htm> visited: February 10, 2006.

84. The report is available online. See "Assassination of Lebanese parliamentarian Jibran Tueini," (Arabic) *aljazeera.net*, December 13, 2005, <http://www.aljazeera.net/NR/exeres/C6259861–4B68–4DFE-A961-BCDAEDCFFB2D.htm> visited: February 8, 2005.

85. "Saniora: Lebanon will ask the United Nations to investigate the assassination of Tueini," (Arabic) *alarabiya.net*, December 12, 2005, <http://www.alarabiya.net/Articles/2005/12/12/19408.htm> visited: February 8, 2006.

86. Ibid.

87. "Damascus assures the possibility of Mehlis meeting with Farouk al-Shar'a," (Arabic) *alarabiya.net*, December 13, 2005, <http://www.alarabiya.net/Articles/2005/12/13/19458.htm> visited: February 8, 2006; "Jumblatt calls for the fall of the 'Syrian regime' and compares Asad to 'a sick man'," (Arabic) *alarabiya.net*, December 14, 2005, <http://www.alarabiya.net/Articles/2005/12/14/19465.htm> visited: February 8, 2006; "Shia ministers continue the boycott and Mehlis links all the explosions in Lebanon," (Arabic) *alarabiya.net*, December 15, 2005, <http://www.alarabiya.net/Articles/2005/12/15/19502.htm> visited: February 8, 2006; Al-Arabiya also ran a segment about allegations that the Syrian permanent representative to the UN had compared Tueini to a dog, see "American newspaper: Syria's Permanent Representative to the UN compares Jibran Tueini to a 'dog'," (Arabic) *alarabiya.net*, December 16, 2005 <http://www.alarabiya.net/Articles/2005/12/16/19532.htm>; "Mehlis assures that Syria is behind the assassination of Hariri," (Arabic) *alarabiya.net*, December 17, 2005, <http://www.alarabiya.net/Articles/2005/12/17/19547.htm> visited: February 8, 2006; "Waleed Jumblatt warns of a plan to bring back Syrian rule over Lebanon," (Arabic) *alarabiya.net*, December 19, 2005, <http://www.alarabiya.net/Articles/2005/12/19/19610.htm> visited: February 8, 2006; "Lebanese court sets Syria as suspect in assassination of Jibran Tueini," (Arabic) *alarabiya.net*, December 27, 2005, <http://www.alarabiya.net/Articles/2005/12/27/19854.htm> visited: February 8, 2006.

88. "Khaddam denies the repetition of the Iraqi scenario in Syria," (Arabic) *alarabiya.net*, January 1, 2006, <http://www.alarabiya.net/Articles/2006/01/01/19959.htm> visited: February 8, 2006.

89. "Damascus releases opposition and Khaddam will form an exile government," (Arabic) *aljazeera.net*, January 14, 2006, <http://www.aljazeera.net/NR/exeres/3FA26C49–2FD0–4A23-B99D-AD3202EEEDA9.htm> visited: February 8, 2006.

90. See for example *Minbar Al-Jazeera* on January 8, 2005. Transcripts are available online: "Arab prospects for the year 2006," (Arabic) *aljazeera.net*, January 8, 2006. <http://www.aljazeera.net/NR/exeres/E34A8091–89F9–4D9B-8CCF-8BDE770363EF.htm> visited: February 9, 2006.

91. "Al-Jazeera this morning 1/1/2006," (Arabic) *aljazeera.net*, January 1, 2006, <http://www.aljazeera.net/NR/exeres/476E3458–88A3–440F-8E38–3042DBB505DB.htm> visited: February 9, 2006.

92. *Asharq Al-Awsat*, January 6, 2006.

93. Waeed Choucair, "Saudi Arabia, Egypt work hard to soothe Syria," *The Daily Star*, January 14, 2006, <http://www.dailystar.com.lb/article.asp?edition_id = 1&categ_id = 2&article_id = 21432> visited: February 9, 2006.

94. *Asharq al-Awsat*, August 22, 2006.

95. See the text of the show on *aljazeera.net* in which Faisal Al-Qasim interviews Ibrahim Alloush and Ali Salim, *aljazeera.net* August 8, 2006. http://www.aljazeera.net/NR/exeres/81E89477-FD0C-476F-A1E6–63D2B72A122E.htm

Chapter 3: Arab Media and Intra-State Conflict: The Case of Lebanon

1. Marwan Kraidy, "Arab satellite television between regionalization and globalization," *Global Media Journal*, Vol. 1, No. 1 (Fall 2002), p. 2.

2. Nabil H. Dajani, "The changing scene of Lebanese television," *Transnational Broadcasting Journal*, No. 7 (Fall/Winter 2001).

3. Sakr, *Satellite Realms*, p. 53.

4. Kamel was quoted saying "Our investment in LBC involves the delivery system; we are not responsible for content. Whoever subscribes to it does so of his own free will. We have, nevertheless, been able to influence the choice of programming at LBC, especially that having to do with their aims concerning the Islamic faith." See "TBS Feature Interview: Sheikh Saleh Kamel, Chairman of the Board, ART."

5. TBS interview with Jihad Al-Khazen, "Super news center setting up in London for Al-Hayat and LBC: an interview with Jihad Khazen and Salmeh Niematt" *Transnational Broadcasting Journal*, No. 9 (Fall/Winter 2002).

6. See: Audio-Visual Law, Law No. 382–94 of November 4, 1994.

7. "Arab Media Moguls," p. 26.

8. Interview with Future TV's managing director, Ali Jaber, in *Gulf Marketing Review* (Dec. 1997), p. 31.

9. Quoted in Sakr, *Satellite Realms*, p. 116.

10. Ibid., p. 55.

11. *The Washington Post*, June 19, 1995.

12. Quote taken from an interview held in Beirut between Nayef Krayem and Avi Jorisch, author of "Al-Manar: Hezbollah TH, 24/7." Interview held: June 27, 2002.

13. See Avi Jorisch, "Al-Manar: Hezbollah TH, 24/7," *Middle East Quarterly* (Winter 2004).

14. Ibid.

15. *Ar-Ra'y*, May 31, 2000.

16. Jorisch, "Al-Manar: Hezbollah TH, 24/7."

17. Sawsan Al-Abtah, "Ma'rakat fada'yatay al-manar wa al-mostaqbal lekasm qeloub al-lebnaneyin" (The battle between Al-Manar and Future Television to win the hearts of the Lebanese), *Qadaya 'Alamiyya*, No. 2 (May–June 2005), p. 135.

18. Ibid., p. 135.

19. "Arab Media Moguls."

20. Daniel Nassif, "Nabih Berri Dossier," *Middle East Intelligence Bulletin*, Vol. 2, No. 11 (December 2000).

21. Ibid.

22. Augustus Richard Norton, *Amal and the Shia: Struggle for the Soul of Lebanon* (Austin: University of Texas Press, 1987), p. 68.

23. Nassif, "Nabih Berri Dossier." According to a 1996 study by Judith Palmer Harik of the American University of Beirut, Aoun ranked higher than Berri and all other politicians among Shi'ite respondents asked to name their most preferred

Lebanese leader in an open-ended survey. See Judith Palmer Harik, "Between Islam and the System: Popular Support for Lebanon's Hezbollah," *The Journal of Conflict Resolution*, Vol. 40, No. 1 (March 1996), p. 52.

24. C. Jacob, "Reactions to Former Lebanese Prime Minister Al-Hariri's Assassination", *MEMRI—The Middle East Media Research Institute*, February 24, 2005.

25. Al-Abtah, "The battle between Al-Manar and Future Television to win the hearts of the Lebanese," p. 135.

26. Ibid., p. 131.

27. Magda Abu-Fadil, "Live from the martyrs' square: Lebanon's 'reality TV' turns coverage of peaceful protest into a media battle," *Transnational Broadcasting Journal*, No. 14 (Spring 2005), <http://www.tbsjournal.com/abufadil.html> visited: June 6, 2005.

28. Ibid.

29. Ibid.

30. Sanaa Al-Jacques, "Al qabd I'elamiyyan 'ala al lahza..doon al dekhool fi 'omq tahawolat al shari' al lobnani" (Catching the moment through the media without dealing with the deep changes on the Lebanese street) *Qadaya 'Alamiyya*, No. 2 (May–June 2005), p. 142.

31. Abu-Fadil, "Live from the martyrs' square."

32. "The number of protesters on Monday was estimated to have reached a million, according to the Lebanese LBC TV. Others have put the figure at about 800,000." See: "Lebanese Rally Biggest Yet" *english.aljazeera.net*, March 15, 2005, <http://english.aljazeera.net/NR/exeres/29BC1F0B-A63D-4C72-9635-75C854A28168.htm> visited: March 16, 2006.

33. "Opposition blames Syrian and Lebanese governments for Hariri's assassination," *Press Corner*, February, 15 2005, <http://www.freemuslims.org/news/article.php?article = 416> visited: April 1, 2005.

34. Nadeem Al-Munla in a two-hour interview on Zahi Wahbi's show, *Khaleik bil Bayt*, Future TV (March 29, 2005).

35. Ali Hamada, "Where are Your Terrorists Going?" *Al-Nahar*, February 15, 2005.

36. Ibid.

37. Mohalhel Fakih, "Voices of Dissent," *Al-Ahram Weekly*, February 24–March 2, 2005.

38. Hazim Al-Amin, "Future TV and Al-Manar . . . The Two Shores of TV Confrontation in Lebanon" *Al-Hayat*, March 14, 2005.

39. "Hezbollah Challenges 1559 Resolution" *al jazeera.com*, March 17, 2005, <http://aljazeera.com/cgi-bin/news_service/middle_east_full_story.asp?service_id = 7403> visited: March 16, 2006.

40. Al-Jacques, "Catching the moment through the media without dealing with the deep changes on the Lebanese street," pp. 142–143.

41. Abu-Fadil, "Live from the martyrs' square."

42. Donna Abu Naser, "Anti-Syria coalition is a fractious group," *AP News Wire*, March 15, 2005.

43. Gary Gambill, "With Syrian Backing, Saudi Prince Challenges Hariri," *Middle East Intelligence Bulletin* (September 2002).

44. Samir Atallah, "The square and the Newspaper," *Asharq Al-Awsat*, March 15, 2005.

Chapter 4: Arab Journalists as Transnational Actors

1. Telephone interview with Nadia Mahdeed, October 15, 2005.

2. Author interview with Salameh Neimatt, Washington, DC, October 20, 2005.

3. Author interview with Qasem Ja'far, board member of Al-Jazeera, Washington, DC, October 4, 2005.

4. "27 Years for Al-Qaeda Cell Leaders," *CNN.com*, September 26, 2005, <http://www.cnn.com/2005/WORLD/europe/09/26/spain.terror.trial/index.html> visited: October 19, 2005.

5. Interview is available online. See "The situation with Tucker Carlson for July 8," *MSNBC.com*, July 11, 2005, <http://www.msnbc.msn.com/id/8541694> visited: October 15, 2005.

6. This is clear in Howeidi's columns published in 2005. See for example Fahmi Howeidi, "Ayn al-Maslaha fi al-tadbee' al'aan" (Where is the interest in normalization with Israel now?) *Asharq Al-Awsat*, September 28, 2005; "Hal takhrog ghazah min da 'erat al-sera' " (Will Gaza get out of the cycle of conflict?), *Asharq Al-Awsat*, October 5, 2005; "Al-Tadbee' al-bakistani ma'a isra'eel: wekou' fi al-haraam al-siyasi" (Pakistani normalization with Israel: falling into prohibited politics) *Asharq Al-Awsat*, September 7, 2005; "Ma qabl al-tawarot fi al-tandeed bil moqawama al-filistiniyya" (Before engaging in condemnations against the Palestinian resistance), *Asharq Al-Awsat*, July 20, 2005; "Al-tadakhol al-khariji..heen yashom fi ta'jeeh al-irhab" (Outside intervention . . . When it helps spread terrorism), *Asharq Al-Awsat*, February 16, 2005; "Intatheroo al-mazeed . . . inaho tsunami siyasi" (Wait for more . . . it is a political tsunami), *Asharq Al-Awsat*, February 23, 2005; "Risalat Al-Zilzal wa tahthiratoh lil 'alam al-'arabi wa al-'islami" (The message of the earthquake and its warnings to the Arab and Islamic worlds), *Asharq Al-Awsat*, January 12, 2005.

7. *Asharq Al-Awsat*, August 29, 2005.

8. See Gilles Kepel, *Muslim Extremism in Egypt: The Prophet and the Pharaoh* (Berkeley and Los Angeles: University of California Press, 1985), pp. 40–41. For a good discussion of the links between religious extremism among the Muslim diaspora in Europe, see Khaled Hroub, "Al-Binladinyya wa 'arab ourobba" (Binladenism and European Arabs) *Qadaya 'Alamiyya*, No. 3 (August–September 2005).

9. Mohammed El-Oifi, "Influence Without Power: Al-Jazeera and the Arab Public Sphere," in Zayani (ed.), *The Al-Jazeera Phenomenon*, p. 70.

10. Ghassan Sherbel (Lebanese) is the editor-in-chief, Abdul Wahhab Badrakhan (Lebanese) the deputy editor-in-chief. The managing editor in the UK, Zuhair Qysbati, and managing editor in Lebanon, Mohamed Farahat, are also Lebanese.

11. Al-Jacques, "Catching the moment through the media without dealing with the deep changes on the Lebanese street," pp. 143–144.

12. The Al-Jazeera website identifies only four Lebanese presenters, and they are Lina Zahr Al-Din, Jimanah Nemour, Julnar Mousa, and Bassam Al-Qadri.

13. Abu-Fadil, "Live from the martyrs' square."

14. El-Oifi, "Influence without power," p. 72.

15. Faisal Al Qasim, "The Opposite Direction: A Program Which Changed the Face of Arab Television," in Zayani (ed.), *The Al-Jazeera Phenomenon*, p. 103.

16. Author interview, Washington, DC, October 4, 2005, 11:00 p.m.

17. Khartoum accuses Darfur rebels of attacking a town north of the region," *aljazeera.net*, October 17, 2005, <http://www.aljazeera.net/news/archive/archive?ArchiveId = 130579> visited: March 17, 2006.

18. "Seven dead in Darfur and the African Union criticizes the rebels," *aljazeera.net*, October 18, 2005, <http://www.aljazeera.net/news/archive/archive?ArchiveId = 130626> visited: March 17, 2006.

19. Quoted on BBC news: see "Sudanese media defiant on Darfur," BBC News, July 28, 2004, http://news.bbc.co.uk/go/pr/fr/-/1/hi/world/africa/3933825.stm. visited: October, 12, 2005.

20. "Itihad al-sahafiyeen and 'arab yodeen qatl al sahafiyeen bi al-'eraq wa yo'ed taqrir 'an 'Darfur'" (Arab Union of Journalists condemns the killing of

journalists in Iraq and prepares a report on Darfur) *elsohof.com*, January 1, 2005, <http://www.elsohof.com/horiyat.html> visited: October 20, 2005.

21. Ali Fardan, "Qanat Al-Jazeera: Limdha fi Baghdad wa lays fi Darfur?" (Al-Jazeera Channel: Why in Baghdad and Not in Darfur?), *Middle East Transparent*, August 8, 2004, <http://www.metransparent.com/texts/ali_fardan_jazeera_iraq_darfour.htm> visited: October 20, 2005

22. Ibid.

23. For example, see "They chanted for the fall of the Sudanese government: people fleeing Darfur meet Anan with stories about rape and murder," (Arabic) *alarabiya.net*, May 29, 2005; and "Security Council delays Sudan sanctions for three months," (Arabic) *alarabiya.net*, July 6, 2005.

24. Othman Al-Omer, former editor of the *Asharq Al-Awsat* newspaper and the current owner of influential online news service Elaph.

25. See UNDP, *Human Development Report: 2004*.

26. Author interview with Qassem Ja'fer, Washington, DC, October 4, 2004.

27. "Al-Sha'b Al-Filistiny that Al-Hisar and Isra'ely: 60" (The Palestinian people under Israeli siege) *aljazeera.net*, May 31, 2002, <http://www.aljazeera.net/NR/exeres/4D5CC5AA-329E-4A53–9B10–161689D87B6C.htm> visited: October 10, 2005.

28. Two telephone interviews with Nadia Mahdeed, October 15 and 18, 2005.

29. Ibid.

30. For the past two years Abbasi Madani has been living in Qatar.

Chapter 5: Public Diplomacy and the Arab Media

1. See GAO reports *US Public Diplomacy: State Department Expands Efforts but Faces Significant Challenges, GAO-03–951* (Washington DC: September 4, 2003) and *US International Broadcasting: New Strategic Approach Focuses on Reaching Large Audiences but Lacks Measurable Program Objectives, GAO-03–772* (Washington DC: July 15, 2003).

2. See: US Advisory Commission on Public Diplomacy, *2004 Report* (September 2004); Defense Science Board, *Strategic Communication* (September 2004); National Commission on Terrorist Attacks Upon the United States, *The 9/11 Commission Report*, July 2004; Advisory Group on Public Diplomacy for the Arab and Muslim World, *Changing Minds, Winning Peace: A New Strategic Direction for US Public Diplomacy in the Arab and Muslim World* (October 2003); Council on Foreign Relations, *Finding America's Voice: A Strategy for Reinvigorating US Public Diplomacy* (June 2003); U.S. Advisory Commission on Public Diplomacy, *Building America's Public Diplomacy Through a Reformed Structure and Additional Resources* (September 2002); Defense Science Board, *Managed Information Dissemination* (October 2001).

3. General Accounting Office, *Broadcasting Board of Governors: Report to the Committee on Appropriations, House of Representatives GAO-04–627T* (Washington DC: 2003), p. 34.

4. See: Broadcasting Board of Governors website: <http://www.bbg.gov/bbg_aboutus.cfm>

5. Norman Pattiz, "Radio Sawa and AlHurra TV: Opening Channels of Mass Communication in the Middle East" in William A. Rugh (ed.), *Engaging the Arab and Islamic Worlds Through Public Diplomacy: A Report and Action Recommendations* (Washington: George Washington University Press, 2004), p. 70.

6. General Accounting Office, *Broadcasting Board of Governors: Report to the Committee on Appropriations, House of Representatives GAO-04–627T*, p. 9.

7. See. Voice of America website: <http://www.voanews.com/english/About/restructuring-in-the-1990s.cfm> visited: May 3, 2005.

8. For the text of the Foreign Affairs Reform and Restructuring Act, see: <http://usinfo.org/usia/usinfo.state.gov/usa/infousa/laws/majorlaw/hr1757.htm> visited: June 10, 2005.

9. Foreign Affairs Reform and Restructuring Act, Section 305-d.

10. Author's interview with Mr. Heil, Washington, DC, May 2, 2005.

11. Author's interview with Mr. Heil, Washington, DC, May 2, 2005.

12. Norman Pattiz does not speak Arabic and therefore cannot begin to assess the success or failure of his project. On top of that, in the two years that one journalist worked at Radio Sawa, he never met Mr. Pattiz. "He probably visits the station once a year," he said. Without Arabic or first-hand knowledge of what goes on at the stations he controls, how can Mr. Pattiz be taken seriously when he talks about Arab media?

13. Wendy Feliz Sefsaf, "US International Broadcasting Strategies in the Arab World: An Analysis of the Broadcasting Board of Governors' strategy from a Public Communication Standpoint," *Transnational Broadcasting Journal* (Fall 2004).

14. For a good study of media systems from a theoretical perspective, see Hallin and Mancini, *Comparing Media Systems*.

15. Allen Heil, *Voice of America: A History* (New York: Columbia University Press, 2003), p. 419.

16. Ibid., p. 419.

17. Author interview with Mohamed Shenawi, Washington, DC, April 26, 2005.

18. Pattiz, "Radio Sawa and Al-Hurra TV," p. 84.

19. Ibid.

20. See the official Al-Hurra website at: http://www.alhurra.com/

21. *Asharq Al-Awsat*, July 12, 2004.

22. Interview with Salwa Al-Saeeda, Kuwait City, May 14, 2005.

23. "Al-Hurra Satellite Television: Getting the Message Out (Slowly)" *Civilities: Constructing Informed Viewpoints*, May 20, 2004, <http://civilities.net/alHurra> visited: April 23, 2005.

24. Author interview with Allen Heil, Washington, DC, May 2, 2005.

25. Ibid.

26. Office of the Inspector General, "Review of the Broadcasting Board of Governors' Middle East Radio Network Launch and Broadcast Initiatives", Report Number IBO-A-04–12, p. 22.

27. Author interview with Munir Mawari, Washington, DC, June 15, 2005.

28. Interview with a Sawa producer who asked not to be identified, June 17, 2005.

29. Author interview with Munir Mawari, Washington, DC, June 15, 2005.

30. Author interview with Nasser Al-Husseini, former Al-Hurra news anchor, Washington, DC, May 1, 2005.

31. Ibid.

32. Author interview with Tariq Al-Zarouni, former Al-Hurra news anchor, Washington, DC, May 14, 2005.

33. Author interview with Munir Mawari, Washington, DC, March 29, 2005.

34. Munir Mawari, "Washington plans to counter Islamic militancy in Europe by extending Al-Hurra broadcasts to Europe," *Asharq Al-Awsat*, March 2, 2005.

35. Telephone interview with Magdi Khalil, August 15, 2005.

36. Ibid.

37. Author interview with Munir Mawari, Washington, DC, March 29, 2005.

38. Ibid.

39. Author interview with Munir Mawari, Washington, DC, March 30, 2005.

40. Pattiz, "Radio Sawa and Al-Hurra TV," p. 78.

41. Author interview with Sam Hilmy, former chief of VOA's Near East and South Asia Division and of its Arabic service, Washington, DC, February 3, 2005.

42. Email from James Hooper to MERN editors February 14, 2003, 5:06 pm.

43. See "A Report by the American Embassy in Cairo," *Asharq Al-Awsat*, June 6, 2004.

44. Claude Salhani during a briefing at the Middle East Institute, Washington DC, June 2, 2004.

45. Author interview with Sam Hilmy, Washington, DC, February 3, 2005.

46. Ibid.

47. Office of the Inspector General, "Review of the Broadcasting Board of Governors' Middle East Radio Network Launch and Broadcast Initiatives", Report Number IBO-A-04–12, p. 31.

48. Author interview with Mohamed Shenawi, Washington, DC, April 26, 2005.

49. Pattiz, "Radio Sawa and AlHurra TV," p. 80.

50. Author interview with Munir Mawari, Washington, DC, March 29, 2005.

51. Office of the Inspector General, "Review of the Broadcasting Board of Governors' Middle East Radio Network Launch and Broadcast Initiatives," Report Number IBO-A-04–12, p. 7.

52. Mouafac Harb's statement to the House Foreign Relations Committee.

53. Sefsaf, "US International Broadcasting Strategies in the Arab World."

54. This idea is supported by the writings of Ross Howard, *An Operational Framework for Media and Peacebuilding* (Vancouver: Institute for Media, Policy and Civil Society, 2002), and Sarah Melone, Georgios Terzis, and Ozsel Beleli, *Berghof Handbook for Conflict Transformation* (Berlin: Berghof Research Center for Constructive Conflict Management, 2003).

Chapter 6: Arab Media and Political Change in the Middle East

1. James R. Beniger, *The Control Revolution* (Cambridge, MA: Harvard University Press, 1986).

2. Robert W. Fogel, *Railroads and American Economic Growth* (Baltimore: The Johns Hopkins Press, 1964), p. 235.

3. Daniel C. Lynch, *After the Propaganda State: Media, Politics and "Thought Work" in Reformed China* (Sandford: Stanford University Press, 1999), p. 22.

4. Examples of these include Dale F. Eickelman and Jon W. Anderson (eds.), *New Media in the Muslim World: The Emerging Public Sphere* (Bloomington: Indiana University Press, 1999).

5. See Marshall McLuhan and Quintin Fiore, *The Medium is the Message* (New York: Simon and Schuster, 1967).

6. Arguments that link media and political change date back to the 1950s and the work of Daniel Lerner. They have continued in to the 1990s in the work of Samuel Huntington. For examples, See Daniel Lerner, *The Passing of Traditional Society* (Glencoe: The Free Press, 1958); see also, Samuel Huntington, *The Third Wave: Democratization in the Late Twentieth Century* (Norman: University of Oklahoma Press, 1991).

7. My arguments here are informed by David Harvey's *The Condition of Postmodernity* (Cambridge, MA: Blackwell, 1989) and Anthony Giddens's, *The Consequences of Modernity* (Stanford: Stanford University Press, 1990).

8. Giddens, *The Consequences of Modernity*.

9. Giddens, *The Consequences of Modernity*.

10. For more on this, see Brinkley Messick, *The Calligraphic State* (Berkeley: University of California Press, 1993) pp. 24–26.

11. William A. Rugh, *The Arab Press* (Syracuse: Syracuse University Press, 1989).

12. Boyd, *Broadcasting in the Arab World*.

13. For more on this see Fandy, *Saudi Arabia and the Politics of Dissent*, p. 137.

14. For more on the CDLR and its leader Muhammad Al-Mas'ari, see Fandy, *Saudi Arabia and the Politics of Dissent*, Chapter 4.

15. On the split, see ibid., pp. 140–143, and on Sa'd Al-Faqih and MIRA in general, all of Chapter 5.

16. "Following Washington, the UN, Britain Freezes Assets of the Saudi Islamic Movement for Reforms," *arabicnews.com*, December 25, 2005, <http://www.arabicnews.com/ansub/Daily/Day/041225/2004122504.html> visited: March 24, 2006.

17. Fandy, *Saudi Arabia and the Politics of Dissent*, p. 137.

18. For more on Voice of the Arabs, see Ahmed Shalaby, *Tarikh al-Idha'a al-Misriyya* (History of Egyptian Broadcasting) (Cairo: Al-Hay'a Al-Misriyya Al-'Amma li al-Kitab, 1995).

19. Interview with 'Abd al-Mun'im Sa'id, Washington DC, March 21, 2000.

20. See UNDP, *Human Development Report: 2004*.

21. Unless otherwise indicated, all figures were obtained from the Egyptian Ministry of Information website: "Monthly indicators: December 2005," <http://www.mcit.gov.eg/newindicator.asp> visited: March 24, 2006.

22. For a serious discussion of the Egyptian political parties, see Waheed 'Abd Al-Majid, *al-Azmah al-masriyya* (The Egyptian crisis) (Cairo: Dar al-Qar'i Al-'Arabi, 1993).

23. 'Abd al-Wahab Kahil, *ta'thir al-tilifiziun wa al-vidyu 'ala al-qariya al-misriyya* (The impact of television and video on the Egyptian village) (Nasir City, Egypt: Maktabat al-Madina, 1987).

24. For a more elaborate discussion, see Walter Armbrust, *Mass Culture and Modernism in Egypt* (New York: Cambridge University Press, 1996). Andrew Shryock discusses the interface between oral culture and the print medium in *Nationalism and the Genealogical Imagination* (Berkeley: University of California Press, 1997).

25. Pierre Bourdieu, *Language and Symbolic Power* (Cambridge, MA: Harvard University Press, 1991).

26. See Armbrust, *Mass Culture and Modernism in Egypt*.

27. For a discussion of Sheikh Kishk's sermons and his style, see Kepel, *Muslim Extremism in Egypt*. For sermons of preachers in Upper Egypt, see Patrick D. Gaffney, *The Prophet's Pulpit: Islamic Preaching in Contemporary Egypt* (Berkeley: University of California Press, 1994).

Index

About the Author

Dr. Fandy is Senior Fellow for Gulf Security and Director of the Middle East Program at the International Institute for Strategic Studies (IISS) in London. Previously Dr. Fandy was a Senior Fellow of Arab and Middle East Politics at the James A. Baker III Institute for Public Policy at Rice University in the U.S. Prior to that he was a Senior Fellow at the United States Institute of Peace in Washington DC, Professor of Middle East Politics at the Near East–South Asia Center for Strategic Studies (NESA) at the National Defense University, and Professor of Arab Politics at Georgetown University. His publications include Saudi Arabia and the Politics of Dissent; Kuwait as a New Concept of International Politics. Dr. Fandy's articles have appeared the *New York Times*, *Washington Post*, *Los Angeles Times*, *Christian Science Monitor*, and *Financial Times*. He is a columnist for the pan-Arab daily *Asharq Al-Awsat*. He has appeared on TV channels such as CNN, Fox News, BBC and PBS, and many Arabic TV channels.